Christmas
TV
Memories

Christmas TV Memories

NOSTALGIC HOLIDAY FAVORITES OF THE SMALL SCREEN

HERBIE J PILATO

FOREWORD BY MARLO THOMAS

APPLAUSE
THEATRE & CINEMA BOOKS

APPLAUSE
THEATRE & CINEMA BOOKS
Bloomsbury Publishing Group, Inc.
4501 Forbes Blvd., Ste. 200
Lanham, MD 20706
ApplauseBooks.com

Distributed by NATIONAL BOOK NETWORK

Library of Congress Cataloging-in-Publication Data

Names: Pilato, Herbie J, author. | Thomas, Marlo, writer of foreword.
Title: Christmas TV memories : nostalgic holiday favorites of the small
    screen / Herbie J Pilato ; foreword by Marlo Thomas.
Description: Essex, Connecticut : Applause, [2024] | Includes
    bibliographical references.
Identifiers: LCCN 2024014129 (print) | LCCN 2024014130 (ebook) | ISBN
    9781493079704 (paperback) | ISBN 9781493079711 (ebook)
Subjects: LCSH: Christmas television programs—United States—History and
    criticism.
Classification: LCC PN1992.8.C5 P55 2024 (print) | LCC PN1992.8.C5
    (ebook) | DDC 791.45/634—dc23/eng/20240618
LC record available at https://lccn.loc.gov/2024014129
LC ebook record available at https://lccn.loc.gov/2024014130

♾™ The paper used in this publication meets the minimum requirements of American National Standard for Information Sciences—Permanence of Paper for Printed Library Materials, ANSI/NISO Z39.48-1992.

CONTENTS

CONTENTS

PART 2
THE YULETIDE ANIMATRIX

PART 3
THE MERRY M.O.W.

FOREWORD

Move over Lucy and Ricky Ricardo, Ralph and Alice Kramden, and yes, even Ann Marie and Donald Hollinger. When they beamed into our homes every week, we could see these were couples meant for each other. But the greatest love story in the history of television would have to be Herbie J Pilato and television itself.

They first cast eyes on each other in the 1960s, with young Herbie stretched out on his living room floor in Rochester, New York, soaking up every image that glorious box projected into his home. Over the years, Herbie's boyhood crush grew into a TV-centric passion, as he embarked on a lifelong dream date—starting out as an NBC page at Burbank Studios, then racking up an impressive credit roll that includes commentator, on-screen personality, cultural historian, and founder of the Classic TV Preservation Society.

But it is his books—more than a dozen of them—that best prove the true affection Herbie holds for his favorite medium. His latest love letter, *Christmas TV Memories: Nostalgic Holiday Favorites of the Small Screen*, could very well be his most heartfelt.

In his introduction, Herbie calls *Christmas TV Memories* "a narrative family gathering"—a perfect description, really, because in the good old days of three channels, that's exactly what television was. So what a joy it is to wrap ourselves once again inside the warm nostalgia of TV's best-loved holiday programming. To that end, Herbie doesn't miss a Christmas beat, filling the merry pages of his book with colorful déjà-vus of every imaginable yuletide offering—from those indelible animated specials (*A Charlie Brown Christmas, How the Grinch Stole Christmas, Rudolph the Red-Nosed Reindeer*), to musical variety fare (starring such twinkling Christmas stars as Bob Hope and Nat King Cole, Bing and Frank, Judy and Liza), to those special Christmas episodes that went on location with the favorite TV shows of the era—from *Christmas on Waltons' Mountain* to *A Very Brady Christmas*.

And thank you, Herbie, for tossing in a few Christmas memories that go directly to my heart—including *It Happened One Christmas*, my 1977 remake of *It's a Wonderful Life*. What fun it was for me to step into the shoes of Jimmy Stewart's memorable role, and for Wayne Rogers to channel Donna Reed. And then there's the 1967 animated special *Cricket on the Hearth*, in which I had the thrill of working with my adorable father—Dad as a poor toymaker, and me as his loyal daughter. Reliving those memories was like paging through a favorite family scrapbook.

So, no matter when you're reading this marvelous collection—whether it's while those first December snows are falling or if you're hanging at the beach on Fourth of July weekend—dangle some mistletoe above this beautiful book. It is worthy of your biggest Christmas kiss!

Marlo Thomas

INTRODUCTION

I n the fall of 1985, I was working as an NBC page at the network's studio in Burbank, California. One of my various assignments included *The Bob Hope Christmas Show*, which that year aired on December 15. As a child of the 1960s, I was born and raised in Rochester, New York, during a time when television was a big part of family life. For baby boomers like myself, the TV set was a member of the family, and sitting in front of it became the place to be. Two decades later I was *there*, amid NBC's then-bombastic promotional slogan, *"Let's all be there!"* I was ushering and seating audience members of a Bob Hope Christmas TV special featuring such stars as Barbara Eden and Brooke Shields. As with the rest of the world, my family viewed Hope as a legend, along with Milton Berle, Nat King Cole, Bing Crosby, Dinah Shore, Danny Thomas, and so many others of their ilk, especially at Christmastime. Hope's Christmas specials, such as those stationed in Vietnam, in front of the troops, are some of my most poignant December memories of the mid-1960s through early 1970s.

Some ten years later, my contracted eighteen-month tenure with NBC was over by the time *The Bob Hope Christmas Show* aired on December 15, 1985. I was back in Rochester, home for the holidays, as it were, sitting in front of the TV-set-now-turned-monitor. As with years prior, I was watching a Bob Hope Christmas TV special with my family, this time, ever slightly, as a member of the production team that brought the special to life. A measure of disbelief once more came into play, as did the unforgettable words of my father, a World War II (WWII) veteran: "There's no one like Bob Hope." What he said that night resonates today as much as it did on December 15, 1985, or for that matter any year prior.

TV has always provided a *special* platform for those like Bob Hope and other celebrities, personalities, and public figures. Welcomed into our homes since the late 1940s (and before), they have transmitted a mix of entertainment, news, and information in one form or the other. Such is still the case today, exacerbated by the high-tech frequencies teamed with social media and other newfangled forms of technology and communication. We tend to perceive and retrieve our past life experiences, positive or not, with a kind of murky tunnel vision that documents only the happy moments. It's a retrospection periodically filtered through rose-colored glasses, especially during the holidays. Or as television historian and author Professor John R. Holmes, of Franciscan University of Steubenville, Ohio, observed: "When it comes to Christmas, memory is more like a kaleidoscope or a telescope than an HD camera. Sometimes we remember things bigger and brighter than they were."

Recalling events of the past differently from how we originally experienced them allows us to edit at will and hold on to our sweet and bitter moments as we see fit. In doing so, we compare the developing, fresh seconds of the present with a more dominant element of hope for a better future with each new passing day. Every decade, century, millennium, era, year, month, day, hour, minute, and second infinitum have their triumphs and tragedies, if not always of equal measure. Some experiences are more intense or uplifting than others, with varied impact. We seek escape to a different time and world, in many cases, the world of entertainment. Dating back to ancient Greece, through literature, art, performance, and performance art, we've embraced the classics of William Shakespeare, and Ibsen; been captivated by vaudeville, Broadway, silent film, *talkies*, television, and any of the scaffold of the modern multimedia mosaic. Of recent, entertainment has surpassed "popular culture" and become just "culture."

During any holiday season, from New Year's Day and back around to December, many cherish the mainstream TV special programming sector of our culture. Those being music-variety productions hosted by Bob Hope, animated classics (drawn with traditional methods like *A Charlie Brown Christmas* or the stop-action-photography of Animagic as with *Rudolph the Red-Nosed Reindeer*), TV-movies (*It Happened One Christmas*, starring Marlo Thomas), or episodic weekly series (every show from *The Adventures of Ozzie and Harriet* to *Frasier* and beyond has produced Christmas segments). All such programming is a treasure trove accessible today as broadcast reruns, via streaming, YouTube, DVD, Blu-ray, or any of the new developing digital destinations. With whatever comes next, many tend to take pause, mentally, and remote-controlled with a grand appreciation for the "Christmas special," in particular.

Just ask Melissa Byers. An entertainment historian and former English teacher with a theatrical background, Byers has also served as producer of digital content for Emmys.com, the prestigious, official website of the Television Academy. As she observed: "Christmas, more than any other holiday, is about memories, nostalgia, magic, and family. The specials or shows that resonate are often dependent on the time in our lives when we saw them. Different generations have different shows, particularly the children's shows, that mean a lot to them. My own favorites are *A Charlie Brown Christmas* and the *Mr. Magoo Christmas Carol*. Some in my generation and just after love the stop-action photography of *Rudolph the Red-Nosed Reindeer*. I have memories of being very little and watching the *Mr. Magoo Christmas Carol* with my best friend, lying on the living room floor, each of us pretending not to be scared when the ghost of Christmas Future came on the scene. And the Vince Guaraldi score for *Charlie Brown* is the first thing I reach for to get me in the spirit as the season approaches."

Byers is compelled to watch *A Charlie Brown Christmas* every year, "even if I see nothing else Christmas related," she said. The classic PBS special *A Child's Christmas in Wales*, based on the 1952 poem by Welsch poet Dylan Thomas, is also a favorite. "I adore it," added Byers, who discovered the special when the Thomas sonnet was part of her school curriculum. "I can say that it also resonated with my very twentieth-century students, even though they were too-too cool teenagers."

According to film and television historian/archivist Robert S. Ray, classic Christmas TV specials in any format were the "must see" programming of their day and remain so with a caveat. "Those who have grown up in the era of home video and streaming may have difficulty grasping the concept of 'event television,' where a large segment of the country would gather around their television sets at the same time to watch a highly anticipated special presentation. In 1955, Mary Martin in *Peter Pan* was one such event. In 1957, *Cinderella*, starring Julie Andrews, broke new records in the ratings. The annual showings of *The Wizard of Oz* continued the tradition for decades to come."

Into that tradition was indeed born the Christmas spectacle, the prominent force upon which this book makes and places its focus. *Christmas TV Memories: Nostalgic Holiday Favorites of the Small Screen* chronicles a select list of television specials mostly from the 1960s and 1970s, with a few pertinent nods to other eras. This book is not an encyclopedia of every single TV production with a Christmas theme, nor does it explore each and every music-variety special or animated or live-action Christmas TV-movie ever made (the enormity of that task would be endless, especially in view of the recent and continued expansion of the genre by such networks as the Hallmark Channel and Lifetime).

INTRODUCTION

Christmas TV Memories imbues a narrative family gathering of its own; a particular group of December-geared programs with a retroactive spark. A sentimental Christmas TV tome, this book offers a sweeping portrait of television's ultimate holiday past. Curated archival material is complemented by memories drawn from diverse entertainment professionals and media sources; hitherto unpublished accounts from those who performed and/or in some capacity worked on, were involved with, or somehow contributed to the special presentations.

Christmas TV Memories is divided into four main sections, each a particular category of specials. Part 1: *A Gifted Variety Pack*, focuses on comedy/music/variety specials. Part 2: *The Yuletide Animatrix*, concentrates on animated specials. Part 3: *The Merry M.O.W.* discusses the narrative scripted movie made for television. Part 4: *Copacetic Episodic Holidays* addresses individual episodes of sitcoms, dramas, and other weekly scripted shows.

Some chapters within the four main parts of the book will feature commentary with an overlap of the same subject or topic. For example, the African American Christmas TV experience is explored in part 1, chapter 6, *Black and White Christmas Music on TV*, and slightly in chapter 7, *It's a Wunnerful Christmas*, regarding Arthur Duncan (one of Lawrence Welk's most prominent dancers). In part 4, chapter 42, *Black and White Christmas Situations*, the African American Christmas TV experience is revisited with an in-depth discussion about specific sitcom episodes.

Another example of crossover topics within part 4 is chapter 46: *Christmas by Moonlighting, She Wrote with a Little Golden Barnaby on the Side*, a portion of which addresses the singular Christmas episode of *Murder, She Wrote* starring Angela Lansbury as mystery author/sleuth Jessica Fletcher. Because the actress also made a pre–*Murder, She Wrote* holiday appearance in the 1975 NBC animated (and awkwardly titled) special, *The First Christmas: The Story of the First Christmas Snow*, and a post–*Murder, She Wrote* mark as the star of the 1996 CBS TV-movie *Mrs. Santa Claus*, both of those productions will also be discussed in chapter 46.

Throughout its pages, *Christmas TV Memories* offers exclusive recollections from such legendary actors as the aforementioned Marlo Thomas (who recalls two Christmas episodes of *That Girl*, her beloved ABC sitcom that originally aired from 1966 to 1971), as well as the animated NBC 1967 special *Cricket on the Hearth*, on which she teamed with her father, Danny Thomas (another iconic multitalented entertainer).

Other actors sharing their holiday memories within these pages include Elinor Donahue (*Father Knows Best, The Andy Griffith Show, The Odd Couple*); Richard Thomas, Michael Learned, Eric Scott, Judy Norton Taylor, Mary

McDonough, Jon Walmsley, Kami Cotler, David Harper (all from *The Waltons*); Damon Evans (*The Jeffersons*), Tina Cole (*My Three Sons, The King Family Christmas Specials*), Tanya Welk (*The Lawrence Welk Show*), and Lisa Lucas (*The House Without a Christmas Tree*, CBS, 1972); voice-over artists such as Jerry Houser (who for twenty-three years did TV commercials/promotions for *Rudolph the Red-Nosed Reindeer* and various *Frosty the Snowman* specials) and Alexander Williams (who provided the voice-over for Tiny Tim in 1971's acclaimed syndicated half-hour animated rendition of *A Christmas Carol*); directors such as Randal Kleiser (*The Gathering*, ABC, 1979); studio executives including Craig Kausen (*How the Grinch Stole Christmas*); entertainment professionals-turned-clergy-turned-authors, such as Peter Ackerman (son of Elinor Donahue and CBS entertainment-turned Screen Gems TV executive producer Harry Ackerman), and talent agents Pierre Patrick (who's also an author) and Pilar Carrington (both from the Starburst Agency), among others.

New, exclusive quotes and insight are also shared by various esteemed entertainment historians, authors, and archivists such as the aforesaid Melissa Byers and Robert S. Ray; Randy Skretvedt (who, like Ray, was a facilitator of the distinguished Long Beach Film Forum in Long Beach, California); Telly Davidson, David Laurell, Johnny Ray Miller, David Van Deusen, Professor John Holmes, Ken Gehrig, and Pat McFadden; award-winning writer/producers such as Les Perkins (Les Is More Productions), Dan Wingate, and more.

Completing this manuscript has been nothing less than a daunting task. Unlike any book about classic Christmas feature films, writing a book about classic Christmas television programming is a whole other animal. There are maybe, just *maybe*, only thirty or so big-screen movies that have been explored in Christmas companion books.

With television, there are thousands of Christmas programs that have aired over the years, most of which are significant and are still seen and mean a great deal to a great number of people of all ages and generations. As such the reference to "nostalgia" will mean different eras to different people.

In today's all-accessible era, each decade of programming is available to everyone of any age, via YouTube and the nostalgia networks MeTV, Cozi TV, Hallmark Channel, and more. Everybody from every generation is more than aware of classic programs dating back to Frank Sinatra, Bing Crosby, and Bob Hope, just as much as they are to such stalwarts as Cher and Barry Manilow (who have recently performed in new Christmas TV specials) and such latest contemporary artists as Taylor Swift.

The enormous popularity of the near-immortal Brenda Lee's "Rockin' Around the Christmas Tree" hit song has proven just how popular the "classics" really are (the decades-old tune was the Number 1 Single at Christmas 2023!).

INTRODUCTION

Similarly, contemporary TV viewers, even more so than the original viewers of the 1950s, 1960s, and 1970s, can watch Christmas TV shows from any of those decades, any time they want, and ditto for the lovers of 1980s, 1990s, and 2000s Christmas TV specials and onward.

Consequently, with regard to this book, a few key focus questions arose: Who is this book for? Which generation? Which age group? Which generation will feel neglected if "their" decade is not covered in the book? Which programs should appear in the book from which era? Should the book cover the entire spectrum of Christmas television programming from the core 1950s, 1960s, and 1970s through the 1980s, 1990s, and beyond? If this book covered only the 1950s, 1960s, and 1970s, the somewhat "newer" generation of TV fans from the 1980s, 1990s, and 2000s and beyond will subsequently wonder:

What about the *Seinfeld* Christmas episodes of the 1990s? They are just as important as the *All in the Family* Christmas episodes of the 1970s. What about *The Simpsons* Christmas episodes of the 1990s and 2000s? They are just as important as *The Flintstones* Christmas episodes of the 1960s and 1970s. What about the *Friends* and *Frasier* episodes of the 1990s and 2000s? They are just as important as the *Happy Days* and *Laverne & Shirley* episodes of the 1970s and early 1980s. What about the *How I Met Your Mother* Christmas episodes? They are just as important as the *Father Knows Best* Christmas episodes of the 1950s and 1960s.

The inclusion of cultural diversity is equally pertinent, such as the contributions of the multitalented African American entertainer Nat King Cole; Diahann Carroll's benchmark "Black Christmas" episode of her groundbreaking *Julia* sitcom of the 1960s; subsequent trailblazing Christmas episodes of *The Jeffersons* and *Good Times* of the 1970s, the *Family Matters* Christmas episodes of the 1980s, the *Fresh Prince of Bel-Air* Christmas episodes from the 1990s, the Christmas episodes of *Everybody Hates Chris* from the 2000s, and more.

As a collection of television times gone by, *Christmas TV Memories* makes every merry attempt to hit all the right visual, vertical, and horizontal holiday chords across the board; to cover, if not every Christmas TV special ever created in every era, then to at least chronicle a representative of each type of Christmas TV special showcased through the decades.

In this way, *Christmas TV Memories* seeks to be the very stuff and fiber of which Christmas tube stockings are made of when it comes to, as its subtitle implies . . . the *Nostalgic Holiday Favorites of the Small Screen*.

PART 1

A GIFTED VARIETY PACK

O f all the varied Christmas TV special formats, the musical comedy variety program holds an inaugural, pertinent place and portion of the pie in the Christmas special spectrum, either as a singular hour, airing just once, as a series of specials hosted by the same performer over time, or as a one-hour episode of an established variety series.

In many ways, the TV variety-special format began with famed outdoor events such as America's Thanksgiving Day Parade in Detroit and Macy's Thanksgiving Day Parade, which marked its hundredth anniversary in 2024.

Still other unique and relatively reverent evening hours include the annual Kennedy Center Honors, which applauds a select, small, and distinguished group of entertainers and artists every year between Christmas and New Year's Eve. Juxtaposed to the latter, Guy Lombardo's famed New Year's Eve specials brought in the post-Christmastimes for the more senior, traditional set before *The Midnight Special* and *Dick Clark's New Year's Rockin' Eve* outings began to roll with a bit more spiked punch for the younger crowd, into which *American Idol*'s original host Ryan Seacrest continues to throw his baton today.

The evening TV talk show, led by *The Tonight Show*, also circulated its own brand of Christmas episodes hosted by Steve Allen, Jack Paar, and Johnny Carson, as did the morning and afternoon chat shows hosted by Merv Griffin, Mike Douglas, and Dinah Shore. Seacrest once again popped into the picture when he briefly stepped into the *Live with* duties for Regis Philbin opposite Kelly Ripa (who had replaced Philbin's original female cohort Kathy Lee Gifford, and who now shares the stage with her real-life husband Mark Consuelos). But still, it is the one-hour, prime-time specials of the Christmas variety that aired mostly between the 1950s and 1980s that hold the most bang for their holiday buck (or should that be "deer"?).

Who can forget how two music worlds collided with grace during host Bing Crosby's "Little Drummer Boy" duet with special guest star David Bowie from Crosby's famed Christmas special in 1977? Or when Perry Como, Julie Andrews, and John Denver paid periodic Christmas visits on-location to the Colorado Rockies and other December destinations? Or when Bing Crosby and Andy Williams taped their holiday specials more tradition-ally inside a studio, surrounded by their real-life family members who were incorporated into the show? Or how Lawrence Welk made sure to do the same with annual Christmas segments that showcased his "musical family" moments every December?

Additional Christmas musical/comedy variety specials or show episodes were hosted by Mac Davis, Captain & Tennille, Glen Campbell, and more; even Walt Disney's Sunday-night staple did special Christmas entries ("From All of Us to All of You").

According to producer, documentarian, and TV historian Dan Wingate, such grand celebratory gatherings raised the musical variety genre to a new level, "decorated for the holidays with Christmas trees bursting with presents, lots of snow coming down, and people bundled up in winter clothes." Such programming often began with "a bustling musical number showing prepara-tions for the big celebration, whether it was shopping, getting a tree, decorat-ing the house." It all matched the anticipation of the coming holiday and "set the stage for the arrival of family. Once that was settled, the main component would set in—nostalgia. No holiday special succeeds without this ingredi-ent—they can't be completely modern and evoke the feelings we associate with this time of year. Loved ones, near and dear to our hearts—with whom we have shared this experience since we were very young—are ever-present during the holidays."

Christmas songs and music, in general, are also, of course, key ingredi-ents, said Wingate. Many familiar tunes date "back to the youth of the oldest viewers—practically guaranteeing the evocation of childhood memories and feelings which are seldom experienced in the more challenging later years. These songs tie the traditional American Christmas celebrations together for all generations—and elevate these specials beyond the traditional vaudeville aspects of the then-ubiquitous musical variety format."

As a child born in 1967, entertainment historian Bob Barnett's memories of TV Christmas variety shows were "like stepping into a storybook filled with enchantment and merriment." For Barnett, such shows were more than just entertainment, but the source of "holiday dreams and the embodiment of the magic of Christmas." Each year, Barnett was "whisked away to a world of music, laughter, and togetherness." He was left with "a deep appreciation for the enchanting spirit of the season." Such memories, seen through the eyes of his childhood, continue to fill Barnett with "warmth and a sense of wonder, even now as an adult."

Fellow author and entertainment historian David Laurell was party to "the first generation to grow up immersed in the programs, personalities, characters, and culture of television." As he continued to observe: "Baby boomers—unlike their parents or offspring—lived through that pre-cable extremely-limited-choice era when everyone, of every age, watched or was familiar with the same shows. Throughout the 1960s and 1970s, variety shows and situation comedies attracted cross-generational viewing and, when it came to the holiday season, just about every family gathered around the tube for 'specials' hosted by a cavalcade of entertainers such as Perry Como, Bing Crosby, Bob Hope, and Andy Williams."

For Telly Davidson, author of *TV's Grooviest Variety Shows (of the '60 and '70s)*, the "great and groundbreaking Flip Wilson" played a pertinent role in variety show history, particularly when it came to Christmas. Wilson arrived on the TV scene toward the end of the genre's golden age with a show made of what the entertainer called "a fruit salad,"or as Davidson explained it, presenting "weekly guests and performers that were different enough to keep things tart and tasty, but compatible enough not to be dissonant and just vulgar-campy or cringe.

"The big, spectacular, MGM-musical-style numbers and laugh-out-loud comedy," Davidson continued, were pertinent components of the variety show format, as a weekly or single-special presentation. It was all about showcasing "an earnest sense of family—whether it was the 'we're all in this together' show business sense [as with *The Ed Sullivan Show*, which had a new lineup of top-name performers each week] or the sense that we were 'dropping in on' a holiday party amongst the regulars."

Davidson, also the author of *Culture War: How the '90s Made Us Who We Are Today (Whether We Like It or Not)*, pointed to Lawrence Welk and Carol Burnett as prime examples of variety family programming. Welk referred to his weekly show's cast as a "musical family." Burnett's long-running variety hour featured a regular band of performers that both she and the audience viewed as family, including Harvey Korman, Vicki Lawrence, Lyle Waggoner, and Tim Conway. "Even for a hip-for-its-time show like Rowan & Martin's *Laugh-In*," Davidson said, "viewers tuned in as much for the regular weekly cast and co-stars, as they did for the leading performer or the A-list guest stars.

"*Saturday Night Live* was 'made' by its cast members," he continued, "every bit as much as its weekly guest hosts. People wanted to see what their favorite TV 'friends' were up to each week. . . . It was all about the importance of the 'family atmosphere,' on-screen and off, which was encouraged, especially around Christmas."

CHAPTER 1

MACY'S MERRY MARCH THROUGH ROCKEFELLER CENTER

"Bring it."

—From the *Bring It On* movie cheer squad in the
2018 Macy's Thanksgiving Day Parade

Every holiday has its traditions, and though Thanksgiving Day settles in one month before Christmas, it becomes just as much a part of the December festivities as it is in November. Thanksgiving, too, is not just about an exuberant assortment of food, but being grateful for any of the few or numerous blessings that we each may have.

In that sense, the Macy's Thanksgiving Day Parade, particularly due to its introduction of Santa Claus at the end of the long line of decorative and entertaining floats, amid various other "celebrity" appearances and performances of all kinds, is the ideal way to officially ignite the holiday season. It's all about experiencing and sharing the parade with others, whether there in person or on television.

The musical TV extravaganza was ignited in 1924 by the Macy's Thanksgiving Day Parade in New York City, from where it has been televised since 1953. The parade began as a way to showcase Macy's flagship store, which was expanded in 1924 to become the "world's largest store" with one million square feet of retail space.

From 1942 to 1944, the Macy's parade went on hiatus due to WWII and the needed access to rubber and helium. In 2020, the pandemic forced the parade to downsize and be closed off to the public. But beyond those constrictive periods, the festivities were in full swing, with Macy's famed march becoming a countrywide sensation by the late 1940s after being showcased in the beloved 1947 motion picture *Miracle on 34th Street.*

Several legendary floats and balloons have been associated with the parade, including Macy's star balloons, Snoopy, Garfield, and SpongeBob SquarePants. In recent years, the floats have often promoted upcoming feature films, as it did on Thanksgiving Day, November 23, 2023, with the reimaged *Willy Wonka* movie. Performers that year included, among others, Bell Biv DeVoe, Chicago, Brandy, and Cher, the latter of whom had just released a chart-topping new Christmas album.

NBC's grandiose Rockefeller Center Christmas Tree prime-time specials, which began in 1931, today screen on platforms such as FuboTV, Peacock, and DIRECTV Stream.

According to journalist Joyann Jeffrey and Today.com, "The Rockefeller Center Christmas tree has stood tall in the heart of New York City ever since the first one was hoisted into place in the 1930s."

For the last thirty years, the monumental scrub has been located by Rockefeller Center supervising gardener Erik Pauze, who began working for the facility in the summer of 1988. In an interview with RockefellerCenter .com, Pauze once explained what makes an optimum tree choice: "What I look for is a tree you would want in your living room, but on a grander scale. It's got that nice, perfect shape all around. And most of all, it's gotta look good for those kids who turn the corner at 30 Rock; it needs to instantly put a huge smile on their faces. It needs to evoke that feeling of happiness."

In 2023, Pauze located the ideal tree in Vestral, New York, enroute from scouting a different selection. As he explained: "I had driven to the other tree and took a slow road back, and saw this one. I went back this spring and decided to knock. . . . The McGinley family told me that not too long before I knocked on the door, someone told them, 'That looks like a Rockefeller Center Christmas Tree.'"

That individual was correct. The McGinley's tree was placed and decorated in Rockefeller Center, and on November 29, 2023, the annual tree-lighting ceremony was held.

However, as Jeffrey noted on Today.com, it was quite a different process in 1931. That's when "workers at Rockefeller Center pooled their money together to buy a twenty-foot balsam fir, which they decorated with handmade garlands made by their families."

Two years later, the first tree-lighting ceremony was held in Rockefeller Center, and a new tradition was born. According to Thrillist.com, the tree that year was a fifty-foot pine, decorated with seven hundred lights.

During WWII, Rockefeller Center opted for a patriotic motif. In 1942, just three small trees were erected and garnished in red, white, and blue. Although due to blackout restrictions, the trees remained unilluminated, and they remained so until after the war.

In 1999, Rockefeller Center erected a record-setting tree from Killingworth, Connecticut, which towered one hundred feet. As Pauze explained, transporting such a tree was no simple task: "Moving the tree is an operation in and of itself that can take months to plan and execute—from wrapping each branch of the tree so it doesn't bend or snap to compressing the width down so it's fit for travel [to Rockefeller Center]."

In 2001, following the September 11 terrorist attacks, Rockefeller Center also opted to decorate its tree in patriotic colors. Three years later, the tree glistened with a 550-pound Swarovski star made of 25,000 crystals and 1 million facets. In 2018, another Swarovski star was created, this time designed by legendary architect Daniel Libeskind and glimmering with 3 million Swarovski crystals and 70 triangular spikes, and it was backlit by LEDs.

In 2023, Pauze stayed with an eighty-foot-tall Norway spruce from Vestal. "It's so tall . . . and it has the perfect shape," he said. "I knew when I saw it that it was going to work. I just had to trim the branches up to five or six feet. It's a nice shaped tree, and it looks beautiful. When you stand in the street and look at it against the blue sky, it really looks awesome."

That tree was ornamented with more than fifty thousand multicolored LED lights, topped with a Swarovski crystal star, and illuminated on the evening of November 29 for the official Rockefeller Center Christmas Tree-lighting ceremony. The tradition was retained with glorious grandeur.

CHAPTER 2
THE EARLY DAYS OF TV WINTER

Gracie Allen: "Well, you see, one Christmas my father caught a wild turkey and he fed him corn and chestnuts. But then we didn't have the heart to kill him so we let him get away."

George Burns: "Oh, I see."

Gracie Allen: "But the turkey liked the food so well that he came back each year. And that way, we always had . . ."

George Burns: ". . . A turkey for Christmas dinner?"

Gracie Allen: "Yes."

—*The Burns and Allen Show* (1950)

The ostentatious traditions of the Macy's Thanksgiving Day Parade and the Rockefeller Center Christmas Tree-lighting ceremony has been countered over the holiday years with the less flamboyant, but no less cherished or entertaining musical variety program. Entertainers such as Jack Benny, George Burns, his wife Gracie Allen, Milton Berle, Jackie Gleason, Bob Hope, and Red Skelton, among others, made their Christmas variety special mark on the small screen. Each served as building blocks in the early days of television, and subsequently, Christmas episodes or specials, with most, in some fashion, springboarding their careers from radio and vaudeville.

As one example, *Milton Berle's Salute to Christmas* aired on NBC, Tuesday, December 23, 1947, at 8:00 p.m. One year later, on the same night and at the same time, Berle, who at one point was crowned "Mr. Television," saw the premiere of his weekly Philip Morris–sponsored show, which ended in April 1948.

According to entertainment historian, author, and radio host Randy Skretvedt, George Burns and Gracie Allen were extremely popular favorites in vaudeville, radio, movies, and TV for thirty-five years. "In their vaudeville debut, Gracie was the straight woman and George had the punch lines, but that switched before their second performance."

After conquering vaudeville, Burns and Allen relocated to radio in 1932 and began making short films for Paramount. "By the late 1930s they were among the top stars in radio and feature films," Skretvedt noted. "Moving to TV in October 1950, their half-hour CBS situation comedy was highly rated for eight seasons, ending only when Gracie retired for health reasons in September 1958."

Five of Burns and Allen's 292 episodes were centered around Christmas, but one from the second season, December 20, 1951, is most memorable. As Skretvedt explained:

> Gracie's friend Mamie Kelly—played by Sarah Selby in a character who shows up in four episodes—is visiting for Christmas, but unfortunately, she's bringing her three rambunctious daughters, Jeri, Melinda, and Jill [played by eleven-year-old Jill Oppenheim, later better known as Jill St. John]. They run afoul of next-door neighbors Harry and Blanche Morton [Fred Clark and Bea Benaderet] by finding the handbag and shoes that Harry has stashed in the Burnses' hall closet as Blanche's hidden Christmas present. The kids also spoil George's surprise visit as Santa Claus by immediately recognizing him. Gracie predictably confuses everyone at various points with her misinterpretations.

The highlights of the show and most episodes are, as Skretvedt observed, "George's periodic monologues, no doubt a necessity for scenery changes in this live, all-in-one-take performance. These made the public realize that he was more than Gracie's straight man and paved the way for his successful solo career. Another highlight is the live commercial for Carnation condensed milk from announcer Harry Von Zell, who also proves to be a capable supporting comedian."

The Burnses' best friends in real life were Jack Benny and his wife, Mary Livingstone, formerly Sadye Marks. Like Burns, Benny—born in Waukegan, Illinois, in 1894—had been a vaudeville favorite from the early 1920s until his switch to radio in 1932. After that, Skretvedt explained, Benny gradually developed a character who was "cheap, vain, with jokes about his toupee, and age-sensitive at perpetually thirty-nine. This character should have been obnoxious, but he was beloved by audiences because Benny and his writers were always careful to make him the butt of the jokes, and also because Benny's genuine charm and warmth came over the airwaves so vividly."

Benny's TV series debuted on CBS on October 28, 1950—sixteen days after Burns and Allen's show began. It ran for fifteen seasons through April 16, 1965, with the last one—and all of Benny's subsequent specials until his demise in December 1974—on NBC. Christmas played a part in 5 of the 261 episodes, as well as on Benny's radio show in the mid-1940s. The plot best remembered involved Benny's gift-shopping for his announcer, Don Wilson. Benny's assistant, Rochester, would, as Skretvedt said, "try to find something for his boss on the meager salary Jack paid him; Jack would run afoul of department store floorwalker Frank Nelson ['Yeeeessssss???']; and perpetually clueless boy singer Dennis Day would try to find a gift for his overbearing mother."

The episode's thrust had Benny driving a sales clerk, played by Mel Blanc, from being meek and welcoming to near lunacy. "The gift Jack chose for Don was always seemingly benign," Skretvedt said. "One year it was shoelaces, another year it was cuff links, on yet another it was a gopher trap. . . . Mel would lovingly wrap Jack's gift, and repeatedly be defeated when Jack wanted him to unwrap the gift, change the present . . . or change the card Jack was including . . . and rewrap it. Each time Benny appeared, Mel was more forlorn and ultimately angrier until the final explosion."

However, the TV episode from December 15, 1957, is the ultimate Benny-Blanc Christmas encounter. "This time," Skretvedt explained, "Jack wants to purchase a wallet for Wilson and is tempted to choose the least expensive one for $1.98. That is, until Rochester reminds him that Wilson has been his announcer for more than two decades. At which point, Benny splurges for the $40 wallet but makes sure to include a card, which reads: 'Merry Christmas to Don, Oh, golly, oh, shucks; I hope that you like this, it cost forty bucks.'"

After Blanc takes the time to wrap the gift "with all sorts of tinsel and ribbon," Benny demands that he unwrap it so he can sign the card making sure Don knows it came from "Jack." After another rewrapping, Benny decides that it's "the spirit in which a gift is given, not the cost," Skretvedt observed. "So, he wants to replace the $40 wallet with the one for $1.98. Mel is crushed by this news and leaves his counter. A gunshot rings out, and Jack, shocked, says 'Gee, he was such a *young* fellow, too.' However, Jack is careful to retrieve his $40 from Mel's cash register before leaving."

As a sidenote, it was Mel Blanc who provided the voices of several animated cartoon characters, including Bugs Bunny, Porky Pig, Barney Rubble, and more. His on-camera performances were few, but equally masterful to vocal deliveries. As Skretvedt said, in the Benny episode, Blanc is "just as lethal to Benny as Tim Conway was to Harvey Korman" [on *The Carol Burnett Show*].

Telly Davidson also hailed Benny, who, along with his contemporaries Jimmy Durante and George Burns, was "probably the most gifted and influential comedian of his generation. While other turn-of-the-century-born comedians from the World War I generation relied on snappy one-liners [Bob Hope was known as "Rapid Robert"], Benny pioneered the comedian-as-storyteller and was as good a *re*-actor as he was an actor."

The same could be said for Red Skelton, who brought his own brand of variety first to NBC and then CBS and even HBO. Skelton's most famous production, which was selected for YouTube display by his estate, is most likely the 1968 show "narrated" by the entertainer's dear friend, the legendary Illinois US senator Everett Dirksen (who died only nine months after in September of 1969).

In 1981, Skelton unexpectedly returned to TV for a Christmas special on what Davidson called the "hip, hot, and happening HBO cable network." At the time, HBO was emerging with its slate of R-rated feature films, heavyweight sporting events, and uncensored comedy shows hosted by Richard Pryor, Redd Foxx, David Letterman, and George Carlin, all of whom were "the antithesis of Red Skelton's old vaudeville style and wholesome-family appeal," Davidson said. "But what a treat for his old fans!"

That HBO treat delivered *Freddie the Freeloader's Christmas Dinner* (a.k.a. *Red Skelton's Christmas Dinner*) with Vincent Price and early TV–comedy icon Imogene Coca, Tudi Wiggins (Mrs. Witherspoon), and Jack Duffy (as Santa). The exact premiere date was December 13, 1981, as part of the then relatively new cable network's *Standing Room Only* series. Directed by John Trent and written by Skelton, who also composed songs with Ian Bernard, this program was one of Skelton's final TV appearances and features one of his most famous characters.

The story goes like this:

Freddie prepares to scrape together money and enjoy a Christmas dinner with his equally poverty-stricken friend Professor Humperdoo (Price) at one of New York's fancy restaurants. When a lost dog appears in his apartment, he is accused of thievery by his wealthy owner. After a meeting with the bag lady Molly (Coca), he visits a hospital and entertains some children for Christmas. Freddie busts the professor out of the drunk tank and the two eventually reach the restaurant—and treat themselves to a feast.

The special includes drama, miming, and music, for which Skelton was noted. Songs sung by Skelton in this special include "Christmas Comes but Once a Year" and "I Believe."

Skelton's HBO show was not viewed by even a fraction of those who watched his original weekly variety show and, as Davidson noted, "it could seem like a 'lame,' maudlin play for laughs and sympathy by a group of aging stars." However, it was "genuinely funny, poignant, and featured some great pantomiming and surprisingly tasteful [in context] holiday music moments." It was also one of Skelton's last TV appearances, even though he lived fifteen more years.

For Dan Wingate, Skelton in summary was "another beloved figure from the pioneer days of television, Red's gentle humor and childlike expressions made him a natural fit—and his gift of pantomime often lent itself to memorable Christmas programs—many of which are presented on YouTube through his museum."

Meanwhile, Jackie Gleason was another classic TV icon who remained current with Christmas shows and specials on CBS through the decades, from the 1950s through the 1980s. Executive-produced by Jack Philbin, with music by Sammy Spear and his orchestra, announcer Johnny Olsen, and the June Taylor dancers, Gleason's programming had several titles over the years, including *The Jackie Gleason Show* from 1952 to 1961 and 1966 to 1970 and *Jackie Gleason and His American Scene Magazine* from 1962 to 1966. *The Honeymooners* spin-off replaced the variety series from 1955 to 1956.

One of Gleason's earliest holiday specials was *The Honeymooners* episode "'Twas the Night Before Christmas." In this adventure, which premiered December 24, 1955, Ralph sells his bowling ball to get a last-minute Christmas present for Alice. It was directed by Frank Satenstein and written by Gleason and Marvin Marx.

Following "'Twas" was the segment "The Poor Soul in Christmas-Land," which aired during *The Jackie Gleason Show* on Saturday, December 24, 1966, at 7:30 p.m.

In this adventure, Christmas approaches, and the Poor Soul falls asleep on a busy city street. A Fairy Princess, with the touch of her wand, whisks him away to a fantasy land where he meets numerous storybook characters, such as Goldilocks and the Three Bears, the Shoemaker and the Elves, Little Bo Peep and her sheep, St. George and the Dragon, Alice in Wonderland, Rumpelstiltskin, the Old Woman in the Shoe, Old King Cole, and the Phantom Regiment.

According to PaleyCenter.org, this special opens with a dance number by the June Taylor Dancers, as on-screen narrator Art Carney says the Poor

Soul "dreams his way into a land of pantomimed fairy tales." Highlights include: the Poor Soul has no one to spend Christmas Eve with until his fairy godmother appears and takes him to Christmas Land of Fairy Tales; the first storybook characters he meets are Goldilocks and the Three Bears, who involve the Poor Soul in their dance routine; the Poor Soul also helps Little Bo Peep find her sheep and gives a hand to some knights who are battling a fire-breathing dragon that is chasing a princess; he encounters Alice (Sheila MacRae) and some other characters from *Alice in Wonderland*, who are having a tea party; he watches the Old Woman in the Shoe and her large family dance; later he is entertained by some court jesters and meets Old King Cole; when he proudly opens a present, wooden soldiers march out of the box; the Poor Soul wakes up back on the street and realizes that this whole adventure was just a dream—or was it?; and to close the program, Gleason introduces the cast and choreographer June Taylor. (This is a black-and-white telecast of a color program with Jane Kean as Trixie Norton.)

Years later *The Honeymooners* reunited for several specials, including a new Christmas adventure, while Art Carney played Santa in a 1970 Christmas special edition of *The Ed Sullivan Show* and in the 1984 CBS TV-movie *The Night They Saved Christmas*. Directed by former child star Jackie Cooper (not to be confused with Jackie Coogan) and written by Jim Maloney, this film is much grander than its simple title implies. It also features *Charlie's Angels* icon Jaclyn Smith, Paul Le Mat (who starred opposite *Angels'* co-star Farrah Fawcett in 1985's groundbreaking TV-movie *The Burning Bed*), June Lockhart (*Lost in Space*), acclaimed songwriter Paul Williams, Scott Grimes, and others.

CHAPTER 3
HOPE AND CHARITY

"It's Christmastime in the city."

—"Silver Bells," Bob Hope's signature Christmas song

Many consider Bob Hope to be a true Christmas angel. Like Gleason, Skelton, Benny, Burns, Berle, and others, Hope began in vaudeville, found fame on radio, and moved toward moviemaking. His most popular big-screen productions, the *Road to . . .* films, co-starred Bing Crosby and Dorothy Lamour, while *The Lemon Drop Kid*, from 1951, features his first performance of "Silver Bells," which became his signature Christmas TV carol (performed variedly with Shirley Jones, Barbara Eden, and other well-known female stars).

Assuredly it was on TV where Hope made his most indelible mark, on NBC from 1950 to 1994. Just two of countless mentions include the *Bob Hope Christmas Special* from 1979, featuring Angie Dickinson, Bonnie Franklin (*One Day at a Time*), the Rose Bowl Queen, the All-America Football Team, Adam Rich (*Eight Is Enough*), and the *Bob Hope Christmas Special* from 1982, featuring Mac Davis, Loni Anderson, Phyllis Diller, the All-America Football Team, the Rose Bowl Queen, Olivia Newton-John (singing "Silver Bells"), and a "Special Memory with John Wayne" (who had by then passed away).

However, it was Hope's Christmas overseas specials broadcast during wartimes with American troops that proved the most inspiring programs to ever air, holiday or otherwise. Hope gave hope, comfort, and joy on war-torn grounds abroad and on American soil. Families in the States ached from the absence of sons and daughters, brothers and sisters, mothers and fathers, and cousins and friends who so courageously served their country.

Journalists Mike Case and Sandi Gohn documented it all so very well in their article for uso.org, "For 40 Years, Bob Hope USO [United Service Organizations] Christmas Shows Brightened the Holidays for Deployed Troops" (which was originally published in 2019 and revised in 2021).

"Bob Hope knew what it meant to be away from home during the holidays," they noted. "From World War II to Desert Shield, the legendary star spent scores of December days on the front lines entertaining service members all around the world."

Hope began entertaining service members in May 1941 when he recorded an episode of his NBC radio show, *The Pepsodent Show*, during a visit to a California naval base. Over the next eighteen months, he continued to host and record additional radio and USO performances at bases around America (including during the holidays), before traveling overseas for his first USO "camp show" tour in 1943.

During this and several WWII USO camp show journeys that followed, Hope hosted music/variety-like shows with some of Hollywood's biggest stars. During WWII, with only a few exceptions, all of his shows were presented before the military.

However, it wasn't until the mid-twentieth century, when the comedian/ actor/singer began hosting his infamous *Bob Hope Christmas Show*, that his iconic charitable status was solidified.

As Case and Gohn explained, although various sources document different dates as to when the first official *Bob Hope Christmas Show* aired on radio or television, the National Archives records state Hope hosted special recordings of *The Pepsodent Show* at Sawtelle Veterans' Hospital on December 24, 1946. Similarly, Navy records chronicle that on December 23, 1947, Hope hosted a special recording of *The Pepsodent Show* at the US Naval Hospital in Corona, California, for a military crowd.

In December 1948, Hope and his USO troupe (which included Irving Berlin at the time) recorded a *Bob Hope Show* radio segment in front of troops in Germany supporting the Berlin Airlift, per the request of the Pentagon. According to the Bob and Dolores Hope Foundation, it was this USO trip that inspired Hope to begin his tradition of entertaining the military community during the holiday season.

After 1948, Hope's radio show switched titles to *The Bob Hope Show*. Over the next few decades, his various specials on TV and radio would reflect various iterations of that title.

In December 1950, Hope somewhat apprehensively began making regular TV appearances. He taped his initial variety special for a New York studio audience after returning from a fall USO tour to Korea, where he also recorded episodes of his show.

In December 1951, in San Diego, Hope recorded his show in front of service members returning home from Korea on the USS *Boxer*.

By 1954, Hope began taking his show overseas to record its holiday episodes, which he continued to do for the next several decades. He traveled to Iceland, Greenland, Alaska, the Caribbean, the Mediterranean, and the Western Pacific.

In 1957, for example, his celebrity guests included Johnny Grant, Jayne Mansfield, Hedda Hopper, and others.

In 1964, Hope took the first of nine USO trips to Vietnam to record special holiday episodes of his show, and he never went alone. "In retrospect," Case and Gohn noted, "it was these performances that endeared Hope into the hearts and minds of patriotic citizens for years to come. With him on each of these annual treks, Hope brought along notable names of the time, including Ann-Margret, Lola Falana, Rosey Grier, Neil Armstrong, Sammy Davis Jr., as well as other lesser-known comedians, singers, and dance troupes, such as TV's "Golddiggers" (borrowed from *The Dean Martin Show*).

In December 1967, the Bob Hope Holiday Tour included Raquel Welch, Elaine Dunn, Miss World Madeleine Bel, and Barbara McNair.

As a sidenote, Jerry Colonna, Hope's longtime sideman since WWII, would often play Santa Claus.

For troops who were fortunate enough to see him perform in person, despite, as Case and Gohn explained, "having very different tastes and attitudes compared to the generation of service members before them," Hope's Vietnam-era shows were the highlight of their stations in Vietnam. As Case and Gohn noted, "Letters from the time or later reflections show that their USO *Bob Hope Christmas Show* experiences were similar: being selected to go to the show; being issued clean uniforms; the trip from the field to the base where the show was being held; the disbelief at seeing Bob Hope and other stars; the singing of 'Silent Night' at the end of the show."

Meanwhile, American TV audiences looked forward to viewing Bob's Christmas shows, "hoping to catch a glimpse of their soldier serving overseas," Case and Gohn said. The specials became so popular that the 1970 edition was one of the highest rated, while the last Bob Hope Christmas Vietnam special aired in 1972.

Bob recalled at the time, "I hope I can be excused a little sentimentality as I look back over twenty-two of these Christmas trips [and remember] the millions of service men and women who responded to our efforts with warmth, enthusiasm, and affection."

However, the Vietnam holiday special was not the last of Hope's USO tours or holiday-themed military programs.

In 1983, he spent Christmas with US troops in Beirut and in December 1988, performed on bases and ships in the Persian Gulf. Two years after that, Hope and his wife, Dolores, headlined their final USO tour, again to the Middle East, and hosted their final *Bob Hope Christmas Show* for service members deployed as part of Operation Desert Shield.

As Case and Gohn pointed out: "Many of the service members in the crowd during this last USO tour had a grandfather who had seen Hope perform in WWII or Korea, as well as a father who had seen Hope perform in Vietnam."

In 1990, Johnny Bench, Ann Jillian, and others joined Hope for a USO tour. In 1991, Hope told the *Baltimore Sun*: "It's the best audience. I mean, it's amazing how high the morale is. On account of that general saying we're not ready, my opening line was, 'Are you ready?' And they went wild. You know, they just jumped up at it."

Interestingly, Dolores Hope was the only woman allowed to perform for Americans in Saudi Arabia during the tour; the other women were only permitted to perform on aircraft carriers stationed offshore. Apparently, this worked in her favor, as Dolores delivered a show-stealing performance of "White Christmas."

Although Hope hosted his last USO tour in 1990 and his final holiday special, *Hopes for the Holidays*, which aired on NBC in 1994, the tradition he ignited of entertaining the troops during the holidays still continues at the USO. In the past decade, the USO has sent such celebrities as Marvel superhero stars Scarlett Johansson and Chris Evans, as well as Elizabeth Banks, Ray Allen, Wilmer Valderrama, Meghan Markle, Dianna Agron, and others to bring a little joy to the modern military.

According to Dan Wingate, Hope's Vietnam specials became "legendary":

He had a long, steady career in show biz—and once he came to television, he never left. Although most of his traditional Christmas offerings skewed heavily toward sketch comedy frolics with beautiful guest stars—his Christmas Specials during the time of the Vietnam War were unique in that they spent Christmas with the troops instead of pre-recording the shows, and they would air in early January of the next year. Bob's unwavering support over the years of those serving our country further endeared him to the nation and provided great comfort to the families back home watching and hoping for a glimpse of their loved ones in a faraway land. His last Christmas special aired in 1994.

Writer and entertainment historian Melissa Byers recalled "being so grateful to Bob Hope and his guests on those shows for being there for my friends who were serving in that awful war, and wishing I were one of those on the stage performing for them."

CHAPTER 4

WHEN BING SANG WITH FRANK, WHO LATER DANCED WITH DEAN

"I'm dreaming of a White Christmas . . ."

—From "White Christmas," Bing Crosby's signature Christmas song

When the direct Vietnam conflict ended in 1973, Bob Hope and others, like his good friend and frequent film co-star Bing Crosby, continued to make holiday TV specials in their homeland.

In music, on the big screen, and via television, Crosby's name became synonymous with Christmas mostly due to his historic recording of Irving Berlin's "White Christmas." The song first appeared in the 1942 feature film *Holiday Inn*, in which Crosby starred with Fred Astaire, Marjorie Reynolds, and Virginia Dale. In 1954, the movie was semi-rebooted as *White Christmas*, this time co-featuring Danny Kaye, Rosemary Clooney (aunt to George Clooney), and Vera-Ellen.

Crosby, a successful recording star prior to Frank Sinatra conquering that world, continued his Christmas fame with a string of TV specials showcasing his second real-life family. Those included his second wife, Kathryn, their young children Harry, Nathaniel, and Mary, who would later "shoot" to fame as the diabolical woman who shot Larry Hagman's dastardly J.R. on TV's *Dallas*. The Bing gang appeared in such specials as *The All-Star Christmas Show* (1968, with Anna Maria Alberghetti and June Allyson); *Bing Crosby's Christmas Show* (1970), *Bing Crosby and the Sounds of Christmas* (1971, with Robert Goulet, and The Robert Mitchell Boy Choir); *Bing Crosby's Sun Valley Christmas Show* (1973); *Christmas with the Bing Crosbys* (1974); *Merry Christmas Fred, from the Crosbys* (1975), *Bing Crosby's White Christmas* (1976), *Bing Crosby and the Christmas Years* (1978), and more.

For Telly Davidson, each of Crosby's Christmas specials remain "some of the most iconic and best-remembered holiday specials of all time, and for good reason. Bing was one of the biggest stars ever, having virtually invented or at least popularized 'mic singing,' where instead of shouting and booming for the rafters as one had to do in opera or on the vaudeville stage, he used a much more subtle, smooth, and inflected style suited for then-new recording and amplifying technology as he started out in the 1920s and 1930s.

"Dean Martin, Perry Como, Tony Bennett, Billy Eckstine, Nat King Cole, Sinatra—all the great Greatest Generation male singers patterned themselves on 'der Bingle'; to some degree," Davidson continued. "He was a top film draw for decades, his *Road* pictures alone with his best friend and fellow permanent superstar Bob Hope would've seen to that and could pack them in at Vegas or New York to the very end."

In the early 1960s, as Crosby's film career ended, he starred in a short-lived sitcom and hosted and executive-produced shows such as *The Hollywood Palace* on ABC. As Dan Wingate explained, by this time Crosby was "already an elder statesman of entertainment and Christmas with his eternal recording of the holiday perennial 'White Christmas' . . . and in 1962, having appeared in his first Christmas special the previous year, ABC telecast their very first color program—*The Bing Crosby Show with Mary Martin and the International Children's Choir.*"

With shows such as *Choir* and *The Hollywood Palace*, Crosby found what Davidson called "the perfect *second act* for his career." Similar in budget and relative tone to *The Lawrence Welk Show* on Saturday nights, *The Hollywood Palace* was the West Coast answer to Ed Sullivan. Or as Davidson noted, "a mind-blowingly campy 'video vaudeville' with a twist first used on the *Colgate Comedy Hour* and later perfected by *Saturday Night Live*."

Palace constructed a weekly round of A-list guest hosts and their talents and capabilities, while producers Bill Harbach and Nick Vanoff, who later helped create the Kennedy Center Honors, credited it all to Crosby happily serving as host on the first episode. "If I can get Crosby," said Vanoff, "I can get anyone."

Among those *anyones* were Judy Garland, Sammy Davis Jr., Bette Davis, Milton Berle, Groucho Marx, Sid Caesar, Rowan and Martin, Diahann Carroll, and *Bewitched* star Elizabeth Montgomery. The latter rarely performed in "live" variety shows, not even *The Carol Burnett Show*, which was hosted by her good friend and former co-star from the 1963 feature film *Who's Been Sleeping in My Bed?* which also starred Dean Martin, who also guest-hosted *Hollywood Palace*, as did his fellow-Italian crooner Frank Sinatra.

Although, as Davidson observed, "Nobody hosted the show more often or was more identified with it than Bing. He truly regarded it as 'his' show—and so did almost everyone else at the time—and hosted the first and last installments of almost every season, as well as the series finale in 1970. That's where his tinsel-and-glitter-laden, old-Hollywood, all-the-stops Christmas specials began, as a regular yearly feature at the *Palace*. As the 1960s moved along, the *Palace* also showed just how well this sixtyish, old-Hollywood fixture could do mixing with current, younger stars."

One episode from 1968 has Crosby in a duet of sorts with hippie-era icon Tiny Tim who, as Davidson explained, "*fanboy-ed* over perhaps Bing's favorite female co-star besides Dorothy Lamour, the legendary in her own right Kitty Carlisle, as they reminisced and *traded* bits of his old songs with each other."

The following fall premiere featured Bing performing a Beatles medley on a *mod* set, with Englebert Humperdinck and Dick Shawn among others, and singing duets of current hits with Bobbie Gentry. By that time, *The Hollywood Palace* was "already a goner," Davidson said, having been renewed for only seventeen episodes instead of the usual twenty-six to thirty-five.

However, just prior to the show's official cancelation, Crosby was invited to produce holiday stand-alone specials for NBC, which Davidson said, "had the biggest of budgets and pulled out all the stops—as well as kept the tradition of showing Bing with both old-time stars from his era and the one immediately after, and up-to-the-minute stars."

That included, most memorably, Crosby's final appearance in *Bing Crosby's Merrie Olde Christmas*, which was taped just before his death on October 14, 1977, and broadcast that December in his memory. Directed by Dwight Hemion and written by Buz Kohan, the special showcases Crosby and his family's Christmas visit to the estate of a distant relative in England. As fate would have it, Bob Hope had scheduled a Christmas *clips* special for that December, which he transformed into a tribute to his pal Crosby.

Bing Crosby's Merrie Olde Christmas features guest stars Twiggy, Ron Moody, Stanley Baxter, and the Trinity Boys Choir. However, it remains most notable for the special appearance by glitter-rock star David Bowie. According to the pop culture enthusiast Melissa Byers: "The blending of two completely different kinds of performers spoke to me of the magic of Christmas. The idea that *Mr. Christmas*, Bing Crosby, and *Ziggy Stardust* could find common ground in Christmas and music was revelatory." Or as Bob Barnett observed: "*Bing Crosby's Merrie Olde Christmas* transports us to a storybook world. It enthralls us by presenting an old-fashioned English Christmas with its charming cottages and snow-covered landscapes. Bing's voice, the cozy scenes, and the unexpected guest, David Bowie, leaves us feeling that any-thing is possible during the holiday season."

In 2014, Mary Crosby recalled the inter-dynamic pairing for *Billboard* magazine:

"The doors opened and David walked in with his wife. They were both wearing full-length mink coats, they [had] matching full makeup and their hair was bright red. They sat at the piano and David was a little nervous. Dad realized David was [an] amazing musician, and David realized Dad was an amazing musician. You could see them both collectively relax and then magic was made."

"As you might imagine," Telly Davidson said, Bowie's "*Ziggy Stardust* getup did *not* favorably impress the old-school legend," but the overall result was nothing less than impressive for the Crosby family and the view-ers at home. "What could have been a cringy disaster was a showstopper moment—the two singing," Davidson said.

The Crosby/Bowie duet with the former singing "The Little Drummer Boy" as the latter voices "Peace on Earth" has since become a standard on radio stations at Christmastime. Bowie appeared on the special as an attempt to mainstream his career and because his mother was a fan of Crosby. He was not particularly fond of "The Little Drummer Boy" tune, so his "Peace on Earth" song was composed specifically for him by Ian Fraser, Larry Gross-man, and Buz Kohan and later released by RCA in 1982.

In 1979, Gene Kelly and Kathryn Crosby hosted *A Bing Crosby Christmas: Just Like the Ones We Used to Know*, a retrospective of clips from Crosby's Christmas past dating all the way back to his radio days. This featured accumulated appearances by Fred Astaire, Carol Burnett, Roy Clark, Jackie Gleason, Michael Landon, Mary Martin, Melba Moore, Twiggy, and David Bowie.

While Crosby's small-screen holiday specials became what Dan Wingate referred to as "regular appointment TV viewing," also remembered is an early gem of a performance from 1957, when Crosby made a guest appearance with Frank Sinatra on a half-hour Christmas episode of the latter's short-lived variety series, *The Frank Sinatra Show*. The half-hour music/variety Christ-mas special simply does not get any better than that, as two of the world's leading male music icons performing classics like "Jingle Bells" and naturally, Crosby's "White Christmas," performed by Crosby and Sinatra. As Wingate went on to express, this special was "a very relaxed affair with Bing and Frank, and although it originally aired in black-and-white on ABC, unlike most of Frank's shows of the time, it was shot on color film—allowing for seasonal repeats and home video release well into the next century."

Sean Curnyn, of CinchReview.com, offered a thorough review of this special Sinatra/Crosby pairing, which as he noted was directed by Sinatra, sponsored by "the good people of Bulova and Chesterfield," and is "surely one of the classiest Christmas specials ever to go out over the airwaves: twenty-five minutes of unassuming Yuletide excellence."

The special aired the same year Sinatra recorded his renowned *Jolly Christmas* album. Besides the fact that "Ol' Blue Eyes" performs a few songs in the special in the same style as on *Jolly Christmas*, as Curnyn noted, "there is another kind of mirroring of the album" that he found charming and intriguing. "I've always felt that that record captures a sense of someone celebrating Christmas *alone*. Not necessarily lonely, but *solitary*, as if standing at a window benignly watching people scurrying below carrying their presents and their trees and heading off to parties and gatherings. The singer seems to be there watching, a little wistful, but ultimately cheerful all the same.

"The conceit of the show," Curnyn continued to explain, "is that we are seeing Frank Sinatra at his own home, a bachelor pad [which instead of a fireplace has some funny kind of Weber grill in the middle of the living room]. He is alone at Christmas. However, on this night at least he is expecting one special guest, for whom he and his unobtrusive but dependable hired hand Leon have prepared a fine festive repast. That guest is, of course, Bing Crosby, who shows up *sans famille*, as if he too is a bachelor."

Alongside "a little low-key ribbing between the two crooners," Curnyn said, "the whole show is about the music. At one point there is a kind of fantasy sequence where they head outside and join some carol singers in *Merry Old England*." [Which might be perceived as a precursor or foreshadow to Crosby's future and final special of the same name.]

However, as Curnyn also noted, "They come back inside to Frank's place, where Sinatra delivers a genuinely gorgeous, intimate, and reverent rendition of 'It Came Upon a Midnight Clear,' followed by Bing's lovely 'Away in a Manger.' Bing throws in a version of 'Rudolph the Red-Nosed Reindeer,' which builds to a hip and jazzy conclusion, and Frank does something similarly cool with 'Santa Claus Is Coming to Town.'

"With Nelson Riddle conducting and arranging as necessary," Curnyn said, "there cannot be a wrong note, and the whole thing is just a pleasure to watch and listen to; it's people who know how to do these things, pulling it all off with good taste and just the right spirit. Before you can even find yourself checking your Bulova watch, it's over, and then you just might want to light up another Chesterfield and watch the thing again."

Or as Melissa Byers noted, "Most households of my generation had Christmas albums by one or both of these legends, so to see them singing the soundtracks of our Christmases was thrilling."

Two decades later, Sinatra made a special guest appearance with his pal Dean Martin on a Christmas episode of the latter's popular 1965–1974 NBC variety show. This dynamic dual performance was made all the more spectacular when Frank and Dean were joined by their respective Sinatra and Martin family members. On Frank's side, that included Frank Jr. and his siblings Tina and Nancy. The Martin camp was made up of Deanna Martin, who's still performing today, and Dean Paul Martin (a.k.a. Dino from the short-lived Dino, Desi, & Billy band), who died tragically in a small-plane accident in 1987.

Martin even got into the "Christmas Special on Location" act when on December 18, 1977, he presented, *Dean Martin's Christmas in California*. The guest stars included Martin favorites Dom DeLuise and Jerry Reed, Shirley Jones, Linda Lavin, Crystal Gale, Mireille Mathieu, Dionne Warwick, and Jonathan Winters.

Bob Hope donated a grand portion of his time, money, and talent to delivering Christmas specials overseas during times of war, and Martin did his TV part for charity. Specifically, children's charities, donations for which he requested during the closing portion of his Christmas specials.

Dan Wingate concluded:

Dean's relaxed, unrehearsed style was part of the reason his variety series lasted so long—and fit perfectly into his Christmas offerings, as well. The 1967 special with Dean's family and guests Frank Sinatra, Nancy Sinatra and Frank Jr. is one of my favorite Christmas shows from the 1960s. Frank and Dean had so much fun singing "Marshmallow World" and Nancy got to sing with a chorus line of Santas for a special version of "These Boots Are Made for (Santa)"—and you could tell the kids had all grown up together. This was the apex of the genre—just before the counterculture tide swept in and made it uncool to spend time with the older generation.

CHAPTER 5

CHRISTMAS GARLAND, DAUGHTER LIZA, AND *DINAH!*

"Have Yourself a Merry Little Christmas . . ."

—Judy Garland's signature Christmas song

The Christmas TV star family celebrations also included female-lead-driven content like a holiday episode of *The Judy Garland Christmas Show*, a CBS variety series featuring the iconic former child star turned immortal legend.

Garland is best known for countless movie musicals, including *The Wizard of Oz*, the *Andy Hardy* film series with Mickey Rooney, classics with Gene Kelly and Fred Astaire, and 1944's *Meet Me in St. Louis*. Though not technically a Christmas movie, *St. Louis* includes Garland's famed rendition of "Have Yourself a Merry Little Christmas," as part of a family headed by Leon Ames with Margaret O'Brien playing her sister. That's also the same song that she sings to open the Christmas episode of her TV variety show.

In that segment, Garland welcomed her real-life family in the guise of children Lorna Luft and Joey Luft (from her third marriage to Sidney Luft) and Liza Minelli, whose father was director Vincent Minelli. Those also along for this TV sleigh ride were vocalist Jack Jones, who later became most identified for lending his voice to *The Love Boat* theme song, and Mel Tormé, the "velvet fog," who composed "The Christmas Song" (which elegantly branded Nat King Cole's own velvety voice).

Garland sang "The Christmas Song," "Merry Little Christmas," and "Santa Claus Is Coming to Town," among other holiday tunes in *The Judy Garland Christmas Show*, which she opted to tape due to America's despondency following John F. Kennedy's assassination.

According to a December 3, 2015, *New York Times* article, "The Ghosts of TV Christmas Specials Past," by Neil Genzlinger, the 1963 episode of Judy's challenged weekly series is "both sweet and bittersweet. Garland, already looking haggard, had less than six years left before an overdose killed her at forty-seven. But she made it a family show, which gave the public a good look at her children."

As Genzlinger continued to explain, "The setting is supposed to be Garland's home, and Ms. Minnelli, still a teenager, turns up with her 'beau' [as Garland calls him], Tracy Everitt, who is wearing a dark sweater [the show was taped in black and white] with two broad white bands that start at each shoulder and converge in a V at the waist. Every time he's on, your eye is drawn straight to his crotch."

Minnelli and Everitt perform a song-and-dance of "Steam Heat," which Genzlinger called "a startlingly suggestive tune that *Dancing with the Stars* would welcome."

At another point in the episode, "Six dancing Santas burst through the door not once but twice, a sort of holiday home invasion. In their second appearance, they force Garland into a kick line."

Like many of the classic Christmas special moments, including Bing Crosby's duet with David Bowie, *The Judy Garland Christmas Show* may be found on YouTube. It's also one of several classic Christmas specials that get (great entertainment television) broadcasts during the holiday season, beginning on Thanksgiving all the way through its thirty-hour marathon commencing on Christmas Eve.

Two years after this Garland Christmas family affair, daughter Liza Minelli, by then age nineteen, starred in probably one of the oddest Christmas TV specials ever produced, ABC's *The Dangerous Christmas of Red Riding Hood*. That special premiered "in color" on November 28, 1965, and was rerun one year later on December 25.

Emmy Award–winning writer/producer Les Perkins, of Less Is More Productions, classified *Dangerous*, which is also known as *Oh Wolf, Poor Wolf,* as "perhaps too modern for its time" and "a delightful, original, made-for-television musical special."

Starring alongside Minelli, who according to Perkins was "on the crest of superstardom," was stage veteran Cyril Ritchard, singer Vic Damone, and, for the teen audience, British rockers Eric Burdon and the Animals. Although *Danger* is, according to Perkins, "largely forgotten and the color master video-tape is nowhere to be found," it's also a clever reimagining of *Little Red Riding Hood* told from "the rather gay Wolf's point of view."

The Wolf is "alone, living caged in a zoo, claiming misunderstood good intentions," Perkins explained. "Pounding on a storybook, he tells his TV audience, 'This thing is a complete fairy tale! And, now that it's out in paperback I shall never live it down.' He then proceeds to set the record *straight*, in a highly campy performance by Cyril Ritchard, reminiscent of his Captain Hook in the earlier *Peter Pan* musical. Bemoaning his lot of being alone on Christmas Eve, the Wolf sings, '*Left out of all the merriment. My heart's not broke. But very bent.*' A marvelous double entendre because 'bent' was a slang term for 'gay,' no doubt missed by most 1965 viewers."

The Dangerous Christmas of Red Riding Hood did not do well in the ratings, but as Perkins observed, that may have been because "such sophistication, or broad satire, was *too* New York Broadway for middle America. Plus, the show was listed in *TV Guide* as a 'Children's Special.' Seen today, it is remarkably fresh and entertainingly adult. The tongue-in-cheek script was by Robert Emmett, and roughly ten songs were composed by Jule Styne and Bob Merrill, fresh off the success of their Broadway hit *Funny Girl*. They had just three years earlier composed the terrific score for *Mr. Magoo's Christmas Carol*, the first rerunning animated Christmas special. Unlike *Magoo*, *Dangerous Christmas* had a soundtrack album, on ABC-Paramount records, although the speed is a little slow and robs the music of its broadcast vitality. And, like *Magoo*, the great arrangements were by Walter Scharf."

Earlier in 1965, producer Richard Lewine delivered Barbra Streisand's Emmy-winning first TV special, also with writer Robert Emmett. At the time, Lewine said: "Liza was the original thought for this part. We never even went after anybody else. It's very hard to find a complete pro in a girl who can look like fifteen or sixteen and still really sing."

"By this time," Perkins noted, "Liza had been in two Broadway shows, nightclub acts, and multiple TV guest appearances. 'Oh, she was a cutie-pie!' comments the Wolf. Her comedic performance is both smart and enchantingly innocent, as expressed in one of her solos, 'I'm Naïve,' after a flirtation with woodsman Vic Damone, who has a marvelous ballad, '(You'll Need a Song) Along the Way.'"

As Perkins concluded, "Decades ago a black-and-white kinescope of a somewhat worn, syndicated [thus, eliminating the sponsor elements] poor-quality 16mm print started showing up on public domain VHS tapes and DVDs. All the sadder because the original videotape was an elegant production that sparkled in color, which was rare for ABC, in the year before all the networks went full color. Searches for the master tape have included sponsor General Electric, ABC-TV vaults, UCLA Film and Television Archives, and even Liza Minnelli herself. A color tape was rumored to exist with Jule Styne's widow but never confirmed. It's a shame that this fun, original musical is all but lost to time."

Meanwhile, Dinah Shore became another strong female voice of the TV musical-comedy variety, so to speak. With her affable Southern belle charm, Shore added a delightful style, flair, and timeless appeal to the holiday season.

Telly Davidson: "Even today, it would be hard to find someone who was more universally beloved both by fans and by some of the biggest names in Hollywood as Miss Dinah Shore. In fact, her epitaph, to which there was more truth than poetry, said, 'Loved by all who knew her, and millions more who never did.'

"Dinah was an MGM film star," Davidson continued, "a top-selling recording artist from World War II into the 1970s, and one of the 'quintessential' big-band 'girl singers' of the 1940s. She appeared in some of the first 'Christmas specials' on her prime-time NBC *Chevy Show* ('See the USA in Your Chevrolet!') in the 1950s and, in the process, became the first female solo star of a successful variety show."

After Shore's own weekly prime-time variety show ended in 1963, the entertainer made frequent guest appearances on other talk, game, and variety series until 1970. That's when she returned to daytime TV with a half-hour NBC daytime talk show called *Dinah's Place*, which as Davidson noted, "morphed into her iconic *Dinah & Friends* syndicated talk/variety show [which aired from 1974 to 1980]."

According to Davidson, Shore's syndicated series was "bicycled," a reference to programming that periodically aired out of taping order to "save dubbing and distribution costs in those early satellite days."

With her wheels still turning in 1969, Shore hosted a special that transmitted and closed with pizazz the generational and cultural gap between Lucille Ball and Diana Ross of the Supremes. Together, these three legends of various backgrounds performed a song titled "Like Hep [Not Hip]."

In 1976, Shore later made a guest appearance on *The Carol Burnett Show*, which included that program's most famous skit that satirized *Gone with the Wind*. It was Burnett who "credited Dinah for breaking the glass ceiling for women variety hostesses," Davidson said.

Shore would continue performing on TV, including holiday-themed episodes of her daytime talk show, *Dinah's Place*, as she did throughout December of 1979. As Davidson noted, "That was a real treat," in reference to one episode that featured "a 1970s TV 'Who's Who,' including Fernando Lamas, pop composer Paul Williams, football legend Don Meredith, singer/

composer Andrew Belling, and all-time comedy and theatre icon Charles Nelson Reilly."

Almost ten years later, Shore was still going like the Energizer Bunny. With a little twinkle-in-her-eye nod to Santa, she made another memorable guest-star TV appearance. In a 1988 segment on *Pee-Wee's Playhouse Christmas Special*, just five short years before she died in early 1994, Shore, still-youthful and lovely at age seventy, performed what Davidson called "a hilariously campy and intentionally repetitive version of 'The Twelve Days of Christmas.'"

Shore was surrounded by other cultural female icons such as Charo, Annette Funicello, Joan Rivers, Zsa Zsa Gabor, Oprah Winfrey, Grace Jones, and Whoopi Goldberg, as well as Magic Johnson. "Talk about mixing a metaphorical 'fruit salad!'" Davidson said. "It was just as cringe-comical and funny as you'd think it was, and proved once again that our Miss Dinah was nothing if not a good sport and up for almost anything."

CHAPTER 6
BLACK AND WHITE CHRISTMAS MUSIC ON TV

"Chestnuts roasting on an open fire . . ."

—The opening lyric and alternate title to "The Christmas
Song," Mel Tormé's classic made famous by Nat King Cole

While Judy Garland and Dinah Shore paved the way for women in television variety programming, African American performers such as Nat King Cole blazed their own trail for the multicultural media spectrum. Christmas would simply not be Christmas without the Christmas performances by the Golden Globe– and Grammy Award–winning entertainer. Cole's rendition of "The Christmas Song" ("Chestnuts Roasting on an Open Fire"), the optimum Christmas carol, is considered his signature song, with a joyful, warm message representative of the man who sang it. Cole, who died of lung cancer on February 15, 1965, enjoyed financial success but managed to retain a fine balance of priorities. As he once said, "I make no claim to being a business genius. You can make so much money in this business that it loses its value."

The Nat King Cole Show became the first TV musical/variety series to be hosted by an African American male, debuting November 5, 1956, on NBC. The series began as a fifteen-minute pop-oriented show, expanding to a half hour in July 1957. NBC made great strides to keep Cole's show afloat and under budget, as did several of Cole's colleagues, several of whom (Ella Fitzgerald, Harry Belafonte, Mel Tormé, Peggy Lee, Eartha Kitt) worked for scale (or free of charge).

Unfortunately, *The Nat King Cole Show* was canceled mainly because it lacked a national sponsorship. The program's final segment was broadcast on

December 17, 1957, after which the performer retorted: "Madison Avenue is afraid of the dark. . . . The only prejudice I have found anywhere in TV is in some advertising agencies, and there isn't so much prejudice as just fear."

For African American talent agent Pilar Carrington, Nat King Cole, "a beloved crooner of the 1950s and 1960s, broke the color barrier on the charts with not only his Christmas album but many other top charting hits. Although his stint on television was brief, his continued specials brought America around the hearth to celebrate the holiday season, amidst racist backlash from sponsors."

Recognized for his velvet vocal cords combined with an eloquent articulation, Cole composed his first big musical hit, "That Ain't Right," which he performed extensively on tour in 1943 with the King Cole Trio. That tune was followed by others, including "Straighten Up and Fly Right," inspired by one of his dad's sermons, and another hit for the trio, "Nature Boy." Additional tunes included "Mona Lisa," "Too Young," and "Unforgettable," the latter of which was rerecorded decades later as a "duet" (utilizing contemporary technology) by his daughter Natalie Cole—who succumbed to ongoing health issues at only age sixty-five on December 31, 2015.

Other chart-toppers from the father Cole include: "(I Love You) for Sentimental Reasons," "Ramblin' Rose" (which, in 1962, attained Billboard's #2 spot), "Those Lazy-Hazy-Crazy Days of Summer," and moderate hits "I Don't Want to Hurt Anymore" and "I Don't Want to See Tomorrow" (both charting in 1964).

In 1956, Cole was assaulted by White supremacists during a mixed-race performance in Alabama and reprimanded by fellow Blacks for his less-than-ancillary remarks about racial integration afterward. But he was not one to utilize his public persona as a political forum. "The Whites come to applaud a Negro performer just like the colored do," he said. "When you've got the respect for White and colored, you can ease a lot of things."

Cole's chain-smoking served as both a blessing and a curse. The constant inhales of cigarettes contributed to both his velvet voice and death from lung cancer. He married twice: Nadine Robinson, from 1937 to 1948; and Maria Cole, from 1948 to his demise.

According to Telly Davidson, Cole, along with others, such as Sammy Davis Jr., made an impact. Who among us, even to this day, hasn't heard and enjoyed Cole's definitive version of 'The Christmas Song.' He was quietly revolutionary in the best sense."

According to Dan Wingate, who's written and produced several classic TV show/star documentaries for DVD and Blu-ray release: "It's really too bad that we lost Nat King Cole when we did, for surely, he would have given us many beautiful renditions of his immortal recording of 'The Christmas Song' over the years on specials of his own, or others. Fortunately, he did perform a lovely live version on the very last installment of his historic NBC variety show, airing in December 1957—which was directed by Bob Henry, who would go on to helm many artists' holiday offerings over the years, including the Carpenters."

Actor Damon Evans, who replaced Michael Evans (no relation) as Lionel Jefferson on TV's 1970s daring African American sitcom *The Jeffersons*, had this to say about Cole:

"Singing performing artists like Johnny Mathis, Nancy Wilson, and most especially Nat King Cole always represented for me the epitome of class and taste. I can't think of another human being in this country, or elsewhere for that matter, who automatically associates Nat King Cole's rendition of 'A Christmas Song' whenever this holiday approaches. It's like singing the National Anthem at a football game.

"Other performers such as Darlene Love and Mariah Carey don't come close to erasing the nostalgia that Nat's voice engenders from others at Christmas," Evans noted. "The only other major competition that Nat would have, are most possibly Judy Garland and her rendition of 'Have Yourself a Merry Little Christmas' and/or Bing Crosby's 'White Christmas.'"

In the 1950s TV world of dance, specifically Black dancers, *The Lawrence Welk Show*'s future No. 1 tap dancer Arthur Duncan made his mark. In 1954, Duncan, then only age twenty-one, made his TV debut with Betty White on one of her two shows that aired that year. Her first series, a sitcom, *Life with Elizabeth* (which ran from 1953 to 1955), became so popular, White simultaneously also starred in her own variety show. Before the civil rights movement, the US Supreme Court ruled on the *Brown v. Board of Education* case, outlawing segregated schools, and there was Duncan on White's show in the midst of it all. Betty faced backlash for featuring a Black performer, but she told her critics, point-blank: "I'm sorry. Live with it." She then proceeded to give Duncan additional airtime, if only to have her show be canceled shortly thereafter.

Duncan, who reunited with White for a TV special in 2017, had nothing but kind words for the actress, who died on December 31, 2021, just days before what would have been her one hundredth birthday: "She was probably one of the nicest, grandest, and greatest people I've had the chance to meet in my life. Whenever she walked into a room, it lit up. She was very thoughtful and helpful. She launched me into show business."

Echoing Nat King Cole's experience on his variety show, Duncan said: "During my appearance on [Betty's] show, some viewers from different areas resented the inclusion of Black Americans and threatened to withdraw their support. I was unaware of these events at the time and only learned about them several years later after Betty wrote her book. She explained it this way: 'Needless to say, we used Arthur Duncan every opportunity we could.' She stood up for her beliefs, and that resolved the situation."

As Pilar Carrington explained: "Betty White was a huge proponent of Duncan's work and championed his success, as she had on her long-running TV show for other performers of color, despite the fact she received various threats from viewers.

"Duncan," Pilar concluded, "was a timeless and talented hoofer who displayed dignity, grace, and downright exceptionalism in his tap-dancing performance on *The Lawrence Welk Show*. That show ran for years but was notably geared toward middle and White America, with most of its cast performers, acts, and sketches featuring Caucasian actors and bands. Arthur Duncan's dance routines, which were included on all of the Welk Christmas episodes, may have lasted only a few minutes but made an indelible impression on everyone who saw it forever."

CHAPTER 7

IT'S A WUNNERFUL CHRISTMAS

"Wunnerful, Wunnerful."

—Lawrence Welk's signature phrase

From 1955 to 1982, on ABC and later in syndication, *The Lawrence Welk Show* undoubtably made an impression, with a notably diverse senior set of viewers. Meanwhile, too, viewers of every generation have enjoyed the show, which produced several Christmas-special episodes that are still rerun to this day on PBS.

As with Bing Crosby and Dean Martin, the Welk Christmas episodes featured family members of the show's cast, as well as some from the behind-the-scenes production team. Tanya Welk, one of the show's most popular performers, was married to the son of the show's star. She talked about working on the Christmas segments and what made them so endearing: "They were probably our best episodes ever. Everyone wanted to do them. All of us together were like a real family, and having our actual relatives gathered at the same time on TV, it was like a very special Christmas Eve that we were sharing with the viewers. Everyone came and showed up with their children. The scenery was so great, I can't even explain it. Even the camera guys would bring their kids."

Welk performed several Christmas songs on her former father-in-law's show, but her favorite was "The Best Gift," which was made popular by Barbra Streisand. Welk also presented one sequence during the song that featured her eldest child, then a toddler in a walker. "That episode has not been shown in reruns," she said. "But I just heard that they are going into the old archives and airing the episodes that have not been seen in years."

A few of those segments feature other Christmas songs Welk enjoyed performing, including "Do You Hear What I Hear?" and "'Twas the Night Before Christmas," and more. "We would sing those favorites every year," she said. "Everyone on our show had so much talent and were so diverse. Gail Farrell, for one, composed so much music and later worked on *Knots Landing*. The musicians we had were all triple-scale musicians. They did every movie and series in town."

Although *The Lawrence Welk Show* was geared toward the senior community, young children and teenagers watched, and not just because there was, on average, only one TV per household at the time. According to Tanya: "I think everybody enjoyed the show because it was so simple. We would perform songs that everyone at home could sing along to. We didn't have all the hoopla around you, or dubbed voices or anything like that. Everything was live, and we never stopped tape for anything . . . ever."

Tanya recalled one instance when dancer Sissy King was hoofing it with partner Bobby Burgess, a former Mouseketeer (who had several dance partners on *The Lawrence Welk Show*, including Barbara Boreland): "Sissy forgot her dance pads and she only had pantyhose on that you could see right through. We all came running and said, 'You forgot your pants!' Bobby picks her up and starts twirling her around. We almost lost it because Lawrence would never *stop tape*." [halt recording]

Lawrence did not even halt production when Tanya's water broke during her pregnancy with her second child. "Lawrence wanted me to continue," she remembered with a smile. "It was crazy. I was standing in a pile of water."

Tanya began appearing on the show for the New Year's Eve episode in 1967. "I did just the one episode, and then they called me back three months later, and I stayed with the show for the next ten years."

The Lawrence Welk Show officially ended in 1982, with its last few years on PBS. "It wasn't the same anymore," Tanya observed. "Everyone kind of left. And I wanted to stay home and have kids [she has five]." But the cast remains in touch to this day. "Everyone is so close, and many visit at my home all the time." Those being Ralna English, who frequently performed with her husband, Guy Lee Holvis Jr., and Kathy Lennon of the Lennon Sisters, who got their start on *The Lawrence Welk Show*. "We're all like sisters," Tanya said. In fact, Lennon, who lives in Branson, Missouri, where many former *Welk Show* stars abide, periodically spends Easter at Tanya's family home in California (close to Burbank).

As to other Christmas variety shows and specials that she may have enjoyed as a viewer, Tanya said: "I loved *The Andy Williams Christmas Show*. It was like our Christmas show." She, of course, enjoyed the Lennon Sisters and specials with the King Family. "There were so many of them," she said with regard to the number of those in the latter TV brood. But it was the Williams specials in particular that gave her "a warm and fuzzy feeling," as did the Bob Hope shows. "They were great, and he was my neighbor for a long time.

"Our neighborhood had everybody back in the day," including Henry Winkler, a.k.a. The Fonz from TV's *Happy Days*. "We were in Little League with Henry's kids," she said. "But [the celebrity neighbors] were so not like they are today. We were just regular people."

As to why she thinks *The Lawrence Welk Show*, in general, has lasted so long, Tanya said: "When we were on the road, people would come up to us and say, 'We feel like we know you. It is like you are part of our family.' I still get that. It was just so simple. If there is a successful show, it is always because the people on the show were truly good friends and truly loved what they were doing. And not all this fake stuff. I was stunned the first time I went on the road with the Welks. We sold out Madison Square Garden two times. It was like The Beatles. We filled arenas." But they would never do Christmas or New Year's shows live on the road. "We did those at home," she said. "And everyone got antsy and excited in doing them."

That's where viewers sensed the real-life joy that seeped through the screen and into their living rooms. "But Lawrence was a real stickler," Welk admitted. "You had to do his rules or you were out. It was kind of like he was our dad. I felt like I was going to school."

One popular regular sequence on the *Welk* series featured Lawrence dancing with the audience members. "Oh, my gosh, yeah," Tanya recalled. "He started that before Dick Clark did [on *American Bandstand*]. People would fight to get up there. They just felt like they were a part of the show. But they were never starstruck or anything. They treated us like we lived next door."

Welk, who died in 1992, was born and raised a Catholic, and as Tanya explained, "He went to church every morning before doing the show. We would come in on a Thursday and pre-record [the music] for the entire show that week. Then we would go in on Friday, a half a day, for costume fittings. The following Monday we would block the show, and on Tuesday, we'd tape it, and that would take about twelve hours. We were an extended family on the show, which allowed many of us the luxury to do other things, such as commercials, voice-overs, and live shows, etc."

All the while, Welk was adored by his musical family, and countless fans at home, as well as Hollywood's upper echelon, including Bob Hope, Jack Benny, Johnny Carson, and Lucille Ball. In fact, Welk made a guest appearance on Ball's third series, *Here's Lucy* (in the episode "Lucy and Lawrence Welk," from January 19, 1970). "Those seasoned performers just hung Lawrence on the Moon," Tanya said.

Although some others were not so appreciative, especially when the Welk show was at its peak. "Some people thought he was corny," Tanya noted. "But he was corny like a fox. He was brilliant. When we went live, he was such a showman. He was so much better going live, and improvising. But the sponsors made him read everything" [off a teleprompter].

In assessing the modern TV landscape, Tanya was unsure how any applicable new program could compare to *The Lawrence Welk Show*. "I don't know," she said. "All of today's shows like *American Idol*, and all the performers . . . they all look and sound the same to me. I love old shows. They were corny sitcoms, but they were simple. You didn't have to think. You were just entertained. There's not a lot of charm today or showmanship. Both of these elements are critical in a television show, especially when the show centers around Christmas."

CHAPTER 8
A *KING*-SIZE CHRISTMAS

"When there's love at home . . ."

—The King Family

A long the similarly lilting Lawrence Welk musical family lines of the
1960s and 1970s was the King Family. This talented band of relatives
became a popular mainstream entertainment presence on television
during that time, hosting seventeen specials and two TV series. A holiday
phenomenon if there ever was one, the King Family, consisting of sisters,
cousins, mothers, daughters, fathers, sons, and brothers, literally gave it their
all on TV, especially at Christmas.

The King Family, which closed every show with the song "Love at
Home," arrived on the scene toward the end of a performing-family era that,
according to Telly Davidson, harkened "back to vaudeville and the great theatrical acting families," such as the Barrymores and Redgraves. This type of
family grouping "renewed itself in popular music with the Andrews Sisters,
the McGuire Sisters, and their near-contemporaries the Lennon Sisters, and
pretty much finished out on TV with Donny and Marie Osmond and Barbara Mandrell and her sisters," Davidson said.

"The Kings were very prolific," he noted of the musical family (who
gathered for a reunion special in 2009). "I think a lot of viewers really identified with seeing a family jam-packed into celebrating the holidays. I don't
come from a very large family—I know some families that have dozens and
hundreds of members of the 'cousin's club' at every wedding or holiday or
funeral—but even a small family looks gigantic and disorderly packed into
a tract house for Thanksgiving or Christmas dinner, and the King Family

specials really brought that 'home,' in every sense of the word, with talent and fun."

Tina Cole, a.k.a. Tina King, became one of the prominent members of the King Family. She performed on all their musical variety shows and specials, while also portraying Katie Douglas on the long-running TV sitcom *My Three Sons*. In that show, film-icon Fred MacMurray played the widowed father of three boys. Cole portrayed the wife of son Robbie, who was played by Don Grady. As it turned out, Cole and Grady fell in love off-screen but never wed. They remained friends until he passed away in 2012.

Cole explained there was a time when she was on television every day of the week appearing in *My Three Sons*, *The King Family Show*, specials with the Four King Cousins, game shows, and talk shows.

Cole and her uplifting spirit, which to this day represents the ideal Christmas TV special personality, discussed how the King Family Christmas specials and weekly shows began:

> It was my mother, Yvonne's idea. The bishop of our church in North-ern California asked if the King Sisters would perform at a fundraiser to build a new chapel and she said they had done that before so what if they did a show with the King Sisters and their families. Everyone in our family was available. We did the benefit in Oakland, California, in front of a thousand people and received a standing ovation. We did another benefit for our church in Los Angeles. This time for three thousand people, many of whom were in show business, and got another standing ovation.

Shortly after, Brigham Young University called and asked if the Kings could perform at a benefit to help fund the construction of the new Cougar Stadium and, as Cole explained: "Eleven thousand people gave us a standing ovation." After that show, a man approached Cole's mother and said, "This needs to be on television. Here is the number of the head of ABC program-ming. Please call and talk to him."

Cole's mother made the call and sold the show to ABC, which led to the 1964 premiere of *The Family Is King*, a one-hour special. That special was picked up for a series, which ran from 1965 to 1966, with a 1969 revival. As an introduction to the mainstream TV viewer, the King Family made several appearances at *The Hollywood Palace* where, as Cole explained, "Christmas musical king, Bing Crosby, announced the upcoming King Family series. We were the first real family on television."

The TV audience embraced *The King Family Show* immediately. "People absolutely loved it," Cole said. "We received over 53,000 letters of fan mail. People told us they wanted to be in our family. They felt comforted when they watched us."

Besides the two Christmas episodes of *The King Family* series, three additional Christmas specials were produced. As Cole continued to explain: "One of the highlights of our second Christmas special was the story about Alfred Burt, who was a singer in my uncle Alvino's band. Every year between 1942 and 1954, he sent a Christmas card to his friends that contained an original Christmas carol written by him and a friend. Every year at our Christmas parties, he would introduce and conduct these carols until, in his early thirties, he developed cancer of the throat. My mother said, 'We have to record these carols or they will be lost.'

"Over thirty of the best singers in town agreed to come to our church," Cole continued, "where my father, Buddy Cole, brought his recording equipment to record the carols. Al conducted from his wheelchair. My mother then sent the recordings to my uncle Jim Conkling, a record executive who became Capitol Record's first vice president, then president of Columbia Records, and the founder and first president of Warner Bros. Records."

Conkling had produced Nat King Cole's famed Christmas album, helped to found the Grammy Awards, and became the music academy's first national chairman. It was also he who agreed to produce *The Christmas Mood*, the album of Alfred Burt's carols, which was released in 1954. "Sadly," Tina relayed, "Al passed before it was released. In a sense, the King Family was responsible for introducing these truly American Christmas carols to the mainstream music audience. We sang most of his songs on our shows. Our Christmases would not be complete without singing Alfred Burt's carols."

A highlight of the King Family TV legacy is a moment from the 1967 Christmas show, which features a surprise on-camera reunion of King sister Alyce King with her son Ric, who was serving in the US Army during the Vietnam War. Unbeknownst to her, Ric had been given a special leave to appear on the show and surprised his mother. This classic reunion captured the longing of families across the country whose relatives were in the military and remains to this day one of the most memorable *King Family* moments in television history. Cole recalled, "The sequence itself was authentic. It hit home with the audience."

The 1960s, and early 1970s, like every decade, are comprised of definitive moments that lend to the kind of comfort that Christmas TV specials can and do bring. TV audiences, and people in general, are frequently seeking in reality what many are still unable to find today. Or as Cole observed, "I think people have become anonymous in this world right now. The breakup of the family is probably the most serious problem we have."

In the modern world, people are living longer, and many adult children are serving as caregivers to their elderly parents. "Caring for them should not be a burden, but an honor," Cole added. "Our parents raised us, and in return, we now have the opportunity to offer, what I refer to as a 'grateful inconvenience.' That's the way I look at it."

The King Family–type programming is the kind of television that simply does not exist today. "So many people are not connected anymore like we were and are to this very day," said Cole. As to the King Family Christmas celebrations off-screen, Cole concluded: "We have had a Christmas caroling party every year since the 1940s. Many of them have been recorded—not for television, but for our own posterity."

CHAPTER 9
A MITZI CHRISTMAS

"We need a little Christmas . . ."

—Mitzi Gaynor

On December 20, 1967, NBC aired an ideal example of what a classic TV Christmas musical variety special should be: *Kraft Music Hall: The Mitzi Gaynor Christmas Show*. Probably best known for her portrayal of Nellie in the 1959 big-screen adaption of Rodgers and Hammerstein's *South Pacific*, the multitalented Gaynor parades her way through a number of seasonal wardrobe changes as she sings and dances to several classic holiday carols in her 1967 NBC holiday special.

According to TV historian Dan Wingate, *The Mitzi Gaynor Christmas Show* is from the post–Perry Como episodes of *The Music Hall* series, which "brought a fresh new zing to the male-dominated holiday specials with the irrepressible Mitzi Gaynor doing a Christmas jig in the snow in her fur-lined miniskirt and go-go boots. The special was so well-received that it was repeated the following year and led to a whole new career path for Miss Gaynor in a series of specials well into the 1970s."

A few of the glowing moments from the special include a segment with Ed McMahon, Johnny Carson's longtime, hearty-laughing *Tonight Show* sidekick, giving his all as Santa Claus (and singing "Have a Merry Little Christmas"). The skit also features Cyril Ritchard and Tony Tanner as an upbeat Ebenezer Scrooge and Cratchit, respectively, performing, "Where Would You Be Without Me?" and Gayner hoofing it down an old-fashioned, Christmas-decorated street-scene (with fake snow and all).

In 2015, journalist Neil Genzlinger offered his observations about the special, with retrospect, in the *New York Times*: "Ms. Gaynor infuses it with an energy that contrasts noticeably with specials headlined by bigger stars who seem to sleepwalk through them." With regard to the special's lengthy opening medley, Genzlinger noted how Gaynor dons "Christmas-ball earrings that look as if they could knock her out should her dance steps get too enthusiastic." Though Genzlinger was less impressed by Gaynor's performance as Raggedy Ann with four Raggedy Andys dancers. They performed, according to Genzlinger, "a garish medley that, inexplicably, is built around 'I Dig Rock and Roll Music,' a Peter, Paul and Mary hit that had nothing to do with Christmas."

For Telly Davidson, Gaynor's *Kraft Music Hall Christmas* is "the 'ultimate' TV Christmas special of the early years of such shows. . . . It had all—1960s-style glam and makeup galore, chorus lines of dancing Santas and elves and bouncy musical numbers." He favored the "The First North Pole Toy Solider Division!" sequence and the Dancing Raggedy Andys, both of which he said, "can't be beat for holiday camp and cheer."

Davidson said the opening Scrooge/Cratchit sequence "kicked off the special with what Ed Sullivan always called a 'grabber.' In this case, a high-energy, bouncy rendition of 'We Need a Little Christmas!' And while the energy slowed down when appropriate, it sure didn't stop until the hour was up. It was even inclusive for its time, with a big number where Mitzi and Santa celebrated Hanukkah as well as Christmas.

"The *Mitzi Gaynor Christmas Special* might look like pure fluff and escapism on the surface," Davidson continued, "but her duet with [McMahon's] Santa Claus really brought things home. When Santa commented that it didn't matter so much if grown-ups didn't believe in him anymore, so long as the children still did, his only 'Christmas wish' that year was if only the adults of the world could practice the Christmas spirit all year long.'

"While that might sound like boilerplate or throwaway," Davidson said, "remember, this was December of 1967—the height of the civil rights movement, just before the assassinations of Martin Luther King and Robert F. Kennedy, and when the protests against Vietnam were just igniting. We were on the bridge between a more innocent time, especially in TV and films and Broadway, to a much harder-edged one, which reflected the larger society. This show, while feel-good and upbeat, gently and tastefully drove home that point of unity and universal humanity—one that's still obviously called for and needed today."

Davidson continued to assess: "Mitzi Gaynor was one of the last of the great movie-musical stars of the late 1940s and early to mid-1950s, a contemporary of Debbie Reynolds and later Julie Andrews, and her *Kraft Music Hall* Christmas special really marked her transition to TV as those kinds of movies began to drop off. Partially because of the huge, top-rated success of this special, Mitzi's savvy agent/publicist husband, manager, and life partner, Jack Bean [who was to Gaynor what Grant Tinker was to Mary Tyler Moore and William Asher was to *Bewitched* star Elizabeth Montgomery] was able to book a contract with NBC for several prime-time specials, the first the following fall in October of 1968."

Those productions, Davidson clarified, aired alongside the "perfectly compatible *Laugh-In* and on the same night as CBS's *The Carol Burnett Show*, which was then just establishing itself on Monday nights before it later transitioned to its legendary Saturday-night time slot in 1972—they even used much the same format, with Bob Mackie costumes and Golden Age movie spoofs."

Gaynor's subsequent "razzle-dazzle" NBC special from 1968 did so well, Davidson said, the network "gave her another one before she transitioned to CBS, where she continued making specials on a regular basis until 1978. She could easily have launched a prime-time network variety hour, but my conjecture is she likely wanted the freedom of being able to do Vegas, Broadway, travel the country and overseas, and cruise ships—which she did to great success for decades—instead of tied down to twenty-four TV episodes a year. I think she also didn't want to be overexposed and wanted to keep her specials *special*."

At the time, there were several movie-musical and theater singers/dancers in Gaynor's league, including Debbie Reynolds, Juliet Prowse, Bobby Van, Chita Rivera, Gwen Verdon, Leslie Caron, Ruta Lee, Rita Moreno, Cyd Charisse, Grover Dale, and Howard Keel, each of whom Davidson said, "really had to find numerous ways to keep going as filmed musicals and old-fashioned Broadway shows declined. 1970s game and talk shows were mainstays for almost all of them." Added to that were variety specials and Las Vegas appearances, with "Gwen, Debbie, Juliet, and Howard, in particular, capable of straight-ahead acting."

As her ex-husband Bob Fosse's most trusted collaborator, Vernon (who was by Fosse's side when he suffered his final heart attack) would make TV guest appearances on shows like *Magnum*, *The Equalizer*, and *Touched by an Angel*. Keel gained an entirely new generation of fans on *Dallas*, where for ten years he played the second "husband" to his fellow senior Hollywood and Broadway legend Barbara Bel Geddes. Others, such as Moreno, became an Emmy, Grammy, Oscar, and Tony award winner, or EGOT.

For Davidson, "it's a little sad to think how much more such Hollywood legends could have accomplished had there continued to be an audience for big-budget film musicals, a la MGM in the 1930s, 1940s, and 1950s, and Broadway through the late 1960s." However, even when these performers were "doing work that wasn't really at the height of their talents, they really helped put the *class* in 'Classic TV' whenever they showed up, especially at Christmastime."

CHAPTER 10

CHRISTMAS LOCATION

"I had thirteen weeks off and I would pack up the family and drive to some mountain retreat where we could be together and fish all day. I loved it. I needed it."

—Perry Como

With or without big names taking the lead or making guest appearances, the live Christmas musical-comedy-variety special assuredly evolved over the years from traditional in-studio fake-snow specials, which many viewers (like this author) prefer to periodically aired, more realistic on-location specials. Certainly, none could compare to the *Bob Hope Christmas* shows for the troops abroad, but non-studio specials hosted by John Denver, Julie Andrews, and Perry Como made their impression. That proved especially intriguing, juxtaposed to one of Como's Christmas songs, "There's No Place Like Home for the Holidays." According to Dan Wingate, it was the "familiarity breeds contempt" scenario that "probably had a hand in changes to the more 'traditional' holiday specials of the 1950s and 1960s . . . along with a complete cultural revolution.

"Television technology itself had evolved and become more portable—allowing for more remote production," Wingate explained. "Into the 1970s, the three kings of the holiday specials—Bing [Crosby], Perry [Como], and Andy [Williams]—were still showing up right on schedule every year, Julie Andrews did a few lavishly produced Christmas offerings—her personality and gentle English reserve being perfectly suited to the genre. John Denver was probably the most successful heir to the throne—he was sort of the younger Perry Como in terms of the musical range he could get away with and still have a younger following—he also had a gosh-darn likable sincerity that made him a natural for the format in the way that grandmas loved him as much as the younger audience."

There were still the exceptions, "the 'oversweetening' or 'laugh track' aspect is the primary differentiating element between the two eras," Wingate said. "There was also a lot more network interference in these shows by the 1970s—you had to have these guest stars to cross-promote and you had to do these many comedy skits, etc."

One of Como's *Kraft Music Hall* holiday shows, which were similar to Bing Crosby's *Hollywood Palace* Christmas episodes, featured a rare performance by Ritchie Valens. Valens was seventeen years old when he was killed on Tuesday, February 3, 1959, in the crash of a chartered plane during the infamous *Winter Dance Party Tour* in the Midwest. Those who perished along with Valens were fellow performers Buddy Holly, age twenty-two, and Giles Perry Richardson, a.k.a. "The Big Bopper," age twenty-eight. The pilot of the Beechcraft Bonanza, Roger Peterson, age twenty-one, was also killed. The Como Christmas *Kraft* episode with Valens aired on December 20, 1958.

Like Betty White did on her early variety show, Como, who was born in Canonsburg, Pennsylvania, was one of the first television performers to lend early support and exposure to African American performers, namely, Nat King Cole, as well as The Ravens musical group. On Christmas Eve, 1948, Como's show premiered on NBC in a fifteen-minute format, which then expanded to thirty minutes. The series switched back to fifteen minutes upon moving to CBS in October 1950, only to return to NBC by September 1955, when magnified to a full hour until its weekly run ended in June 1963. Two years before that, Kraft Foods, under their *Kraft Music Hall* emblem, assumed sponsorship from original advertiser Chesterfield cigarettes.

As with *Hallmark Hall of Fame*–sponsored programming, Como's Chesterfield-turned-Kraft Foods shows retained a consistent weekly popularity with viewers, amid holiday specials (broadcast through 1966), including those with Christmas themes. Through it all, it was Como's indelible charm that ignited and retained the consistent high ratings of shows no matter the network or the sponsor.

According to Dan Wingate, Como's appeal rested with his "early crooner image combined with an often-chided, but always admired easy, gentle charm that perfectly grounded the most electric of guests on his many variety programs over the years. He was genuinely beloved by the public and his shows were not only among the very best variety television ever produced, but the people who worked on his shows also went on to produce many of the most fondly remembered holiday specials in the ensuing decades, including Nick

Vanoff and Bill Harbach, Dwight Hemion and Gary Smith, Clark Jones, choral director Ray Charles, and Peter Matz, among others.

"He was also an unapologetically religious man in a time when TV didn't necessarily want you to be overt about that," Wingate said. "And his Christmas programs often featured elaborate re-creations of the 'Christmas Story,' and always concluded with 'Ave Maria' or 'The Lord's Prayer,' sung solo or with a choir in a simple setting in front of a stained-glass window. He continued to appear in holiday offerings well into the 1980s—and often traveled outside America to explore how Christmas is celebrated in other lands. He was among the last of this type of musical variety special—and maintained a sincere reverence for the true spirit of the season that made his Christmas programs as welcome in our homes as a visit with a longtime friend."

One of Como's first Christmas specials was a 1969 episode of *The Hollywood Palace*, in which he appeared with Diahann Carroll, just prior to that show's cancelation. According to Telly Davidson: "It was Perry's first time hosting the *Palace*, despite the fact that almost all of that show's key production staff [including showrunners Nick Vanoff and Bill Harbach and musical directors Joe Lipman and 'the other' Ray Charles] were a straight carryover from *The Perry Como Show* that had ended in 1963 just before *The Hollywood Palace* began.

"Usually," Davidson continued, "Bing Crosby did the annual 'Christmas at the Palace' episode, but that year, in anticipation of *Palace*'s cancelation in early 1970, Bing had signed with NBC for an annual series of Christmas specials that he kept doing until the year he died in 1977." And that included Crosby's *Merrie Olde Christmas* special, which was shot on location in England.

"Evidently, Perry liked that Bing Crosby special, in particular," Davidson said, "because he went on to make numerous similar specials and appearances, and helped pioneer the theme of the 'on-location, shot-outdoors' holiday special. These and all of his specials were some of the last of the great Christmas specials which were a perfect fit for his easygoing, subtle, warm, and charming style that had been serving up the hits since the 1930s."

By the 1970s and 1980s, Como's Christmas specials were shot at distinctive global destinations with themes highlighting the given culture of each location. In 1978, he taped *Perry Como's Early American Christmas* at Colonial Williamsburg, Virginia, because, as Davidson said, "it easily combines patriotism and the Christmas spirit." Como's guests for that Christmas show included actor John Wayne (who appeared in Bob Hope's 1976 Christmas special); actress/singer Diana Canova (then popular on TV's *Soap* sitcom); violinist Eugene Fodor; beauty pageant winner Kylene Barker; the College of

William & Mary choir; and the fife and drum corps, dancers, craftsmen, and costumed people of Colonial Williamsburg. [As a sidenote, a statue of Como was erected in Canonsburg, Pennsylvania, in September 2017.]

Como's final Christmas special, *Perry Como's Irish Christmas* (a.k.a. *Perry Como's Christmas Concert*), which was shot in Ireland, debuted on PBS, December 4, 1994. Filmed nearly one year earlier, the *Irish/Christmas Concert* featured film-legend Maureen O'Hara as a special guest star. In the process, as Davidson observed, Como offered "almost fifty years of outstanding holiday TV entertainment."

Andy Williams hosted his weekly musical variety show on NBC from 1962 to 1971. When it came to special Christmas shows, Williams, like Como, once followed Bing Crosby's on-location English lead, in "New-English." In 1982, Williams, who died in 2012, hosted *Andy Williams' Early New England Christmas*, which was shot at the Shelburne Museum, in Shelburne, Vermont.

Assuredly, Williams is in a Christmas-special class all his own. As Dan Wingate explained, all of Williams' programs featured family acts that began young and developed a wholesome style that was especially suited to holiday programing. "Andy's Christmas shows during his variety series days were perennial 'go to' programs for slickly produced holiday fare—often featuring his parents and siblings and their families—along with a guest star or two—and they continued into the early 1970s after his weekly series had ended. In addition to the Osmond family's early exposure on Andy's shows in the 1960s, musical director George Wyle would later perform the same duties on *Donny & Marie*'s program [ABC, 1975–1979]—often using arrangements originally performed on Andy's show, giving it a similar festive atmosphere."

Williams' weekly show became so well-known for its annual Christmas episode that he churned them out through the 1970s, and a few more times in the 1980s and 1990s, with two retrospectives in 2001. "Each special was a ratings winner, resplendent with elaborate sets, costumes, and even special effects," Wingate added. "Whereas a typical episode of *The Andy Williams Show* included special celebrity guest stars, his Christmas specials focused on his family. Guests included The Williams Brothers, Andy's real-life older brothers—Bob, Don, and Dick—with whom he began singing professionally when they were still children. Andy will also be sure to showcase his parents, his wife Claudine Longet, and eventually their three young children, Noelle, Christian, and Bobby."

The family atmosphere was periodically enhanced on the Christmas specials with early appearances by the Osmond brothers—Alan, Wayne, Merrill, and Jay. With four-part harmonies that echoed the lyrical sounds of The

Williams Brothers, the Osmond boys were eventually joined by their younger sibling Donny for five-part harmonies.

Other "location" Christmases were also hosted by other multitalented entertainers such as John Denver and Julie Andrews. With regard to the latter, Robert S. Ray observed: "In *Julie Andrews: The Sound of Christmas*, from 1987, the cherished star of *The Sound of Music* returns to Salzburg, Austria, the birthplace of Wolfgang Amadeus Mozart, where so much of the film version of Rodgers and Hammerstein's immortal classic was filmed. She is joined by John Denver, Plácido Domingo, and the King singers as she tours the city and its surrounding scenic hills and valleys.

"Though at times it is rather corny," Ray continued, "with its forced, scripted banter between Julie and her guests, it's nonetheless exhilarating to spend an hour with Julie as she revisits many of the locations featured in *The Sound of Music*. She duets with Plácido inside the Cathedral at Mondsee, where Maria and the Captain were married. We see the familiar sites— Nonnberg Abbey, the Horse Fountain, Residenzplatz Square, and the Mirabell Gardens—all blanketed in a Winter Wonderland of snow. The grounds surrounding the eighteenth-century rococo Schloss Leopoldskron were used for the Von Trapp terrace in the film, with the Untersberg towering in the distance across the lake. Inside the palace, we see the glorious Venetian Room, which was so meticulously duplicated by Hollywood magic on a Fox soundstage to serve as the Trapp Villa's ballroom. Here, the real ballroom is the setting for a lovely medley of songs by Stephen Sondheim, Lerner and Loewe, and other tunes appropriate for the Yuletide setting.

"By the late 1980s," Ray concluded, "Julie's voice had a deeper, richer tone which gave it a warmer quality even as time may have lessened its higher register. She's one of those singers, like Bing Crosby, Rosemary Clooney, Andy Williams, Perry Como, and Karen Carpenter, who seems to personify what Christmas is all about. And this special can't help but put one in that Christmas Spirit."

The same could be said for John Denver's on-location Christmas specials from 1975, 1979, and 1988. Those, too, reflected the musical variety Christmas special's evolution over the years from the traditional in-studio productions to the periodic ventures into more realistic on-location specials.

According to Telly Davidson:

I think the "big switch" happened largely because of the decline of the standard prime-time variety show format. In 1971, you couldn't shake a stick at how many variety shows were in prime time, and most of them were absolutely ruling the ratings—*Laugh-In*, Dean Martin, Flip

Wilson, Lawrence Welk, and Carol Burnett. Ed Sullivan and Andy Williams were wrapping up, while Sonny and Cher were getting started, and so on. By 1979 or 1980, almost all of them were gone, and the ones that remained were a very different breed of cat—hip, urban late-night or weekend shows like SNL, SCTV, *Midnight Special, Solid Gold,* and the start of Letterman, or kid-oriented shows like *Muppet Show* and *Sha Na Na* (and classic early evening game shows with a musical/variety element like *Gong Show, Dance Fever,* and *Name That Tune*).

I think the conviction was that the studio-type shows were old hat, outmoded, and tired-blooded, that you needed more than just an A-list star to bring in the ratings and justify those big budgets! So, you got these shows with the on-location gimmicks—Dean Martin's *Christmas at Sea World,* Perry Como's *Christmas in the Holy Land,* the wonderful *Dolly-wood* [Parton-like] shows, and so on—which were very visual and breathtaking to look at and did give viewers some beautiful imagery and sights to go with the sounds and the laughs. But a lot of the 'charm' of the big, festive, studio-variety specials started to go by the wayside, and things got more overproduced to the point where these kinds of specials risked becoming almost as much of a cliché as the old, 1960s-style ones.

CHAPTER 11
A CHRISTMAS WITH CAROL, SONNY & CHER

"The tradition of exchanging gifts at Christmas is a very beautiful one."

—Carol Burnett, closing her Christmas show in 1969

The variety show format of any era, be it the 1960s or 1970s, each have their fans, sometimes with an overlap of a year or so. For example, *The Carol Burnett Show* aired across two decades, from 1967 to 1978. Although Christmas was not the show's *specialty* (sorry), a few good episodes featured Burnett and company (Harvey Korman, Vicki Lawrence, Tim Conway, Lyle Waggoner) during the holiday season.

In its premiere season, for the episode airing December 4, 1967, Burnett's guests included Jonathan Winters and Barbara Eden. One satirical skit involved mimicking F. Lee Bailey's interview talk show of the day, with Harvey Korman as F. Lee Korman, interviewing Winters as Santa Claus. Just a few weeks later, on Christmas Day, December 25, Burnett's guests include Sid Caesar, but as author Wesley Hyatt remarks in his book, *The Carol Burnett Show Companion: So Glad We Had This Time*: "Overall this [episode] alternately embraces and avoids its Christmas airing date, making it a rather disjoined affair throughout. The highs outnumber the lows in the end, however."

On December 16, 1968, Carol welcomed Marilyn Horne and Eileen Farrell and received a surprise visit from Bob Hope, who thanks Carol for having appeared on his first special that season. She returns the compliment by thanking him for popping in just prior to his upcoming NBC Christmas TV visit to Vietnam, which he promotes that night on her CBS show. Such cross-network mentions, relatively frequent then, would not be tolerated today.

On December 15, 1969, Burnett gives a loyal Christmas welcome to Garry Moore and Durward Kirby, with whom she appeared on *The Garry Moore Show* (CBS, 1958–1967), on which she got her mainstream weekly start as a regular. This would be the last time viewers would see all three performers together on-screen. Moore would go on to serve as game-show host on *To Tell the Truth* from 1969 to 1976 (on which Burnett would appear), and though Kirby would make one other guest spot with Carol the following Christmas season, he essentially retired after that.

On December 14, 1970, Carol brings back Kirby and frequent guest star Steve Lawrence, along with Julie Budd. This episode is one of the show's most Christmas-geared entries, as it opens with dancers dressed as Santa performing to the tunes "Elegance" (from *Hello, Dolly!*) and "Winter Wonderland." Other seasonal tunes include Budd's take on "The Christmas Song." The show's finale features *A Christmas Carol* send-off with Burnett and Budd dressed and singing as Scrooge amid dancers.

On December 15, 1971, Dionne Warwick and Ken Berry appear in an episode, in which Carol sings "The Dolly Song," a comic tune she first performed in 1969 on the NBC special *Bing Crosby and Carol Burnett—Together for the First Time*. In that show, she very politely requests a toy from Santa Claus but then goes for the jingle-jugular by the end of the song (which she performs again in her show episode airing December 25, 1976).

Bypassing Christmas-oriented episodes for 1972 and 1973, the December 21, 1974, episode features a seasonal skit with "Mama's Family" [then just referred to as "Family"] with guest star Alan Alda (a frequent film and stage co-star for Burnett). Here, Alda plays Larry, brother to Burnett's Eunice, who spends his first Christmas with the family since he was a kid.

On December 25, 1976, the show features only its regular cast of Vicki Lawrence, Harvey Korman, and Tim Conway (who has been elevated from frequent guest-star status), while Lyle Waggoner has by now moved on to playing Steve Trevor opposite Lynda Carter in *Wonder Woman*. The cast sings a few Christmas carols, with Burnett reprising "The Dolly Song."

By December 18, 1977, the show's last Christmas episode in its final season, Harvey Korman has now left the series for a failed attempt at sitcom status. Dick Van Dyke had been brought in to replace Korman, but his second-banana status did not gel opposite Burnett. In any case, guest stars Ken Berry and Helen Reddy pick up the holiday slack nicely with various songs, skits, and segments, one of which mentions the Ideal Toy Company's distribution of $10,000 worth of toys that will be donated to underprivileged children. A standout segment centers on the Christmas misadventures of Burnett's Mrs. Wiggins secretary and Tim Conway's Mr. Tudball.

Beyond Burnett holiday broadcasts of her weekly variety show, that genre was presented at Christmas with programs hosted by the married-then-divorced Sonny Bono and Cher and siblings Donny and Marie Osmond. Another sister-brother act, the Carpenters, headed by Karen and Richard, were well-established in the Christmas music album arena, and they transferred their sounds of the season into more than one terrific TV holiday special.

Bob Barnett got the conversation going with Sonny and Cher, who, as he recalled, "were like the wacky and entertaining elves of Christmas. I couldn't get enough of their playful banter and funky fashion. Their show was filled with catchy tunes, silly jokes, and the feeling that the holidays were meant to be fun and full of laughter."

According to Dan Wingate, "Sonny and Cher were the hippest act to have a variety show in the 1970s—and since they were produced by the same folks that had just finished Andy Williams' later comedy-variety format—Allan Blye and Chris Bearde, with Art Fisher directing—their holiday offerings leaned more heavily on the comedy side—with at least one or two guest stars currently on the CBS lineup. They were also notable for showing the memorable Fine Arts Films animated short *One Tin Soldier* and, of course, *Christmas Cher* all decked out in Bob Mackie splendor."

For Telly Davidson, *Sonny & Cher*'s most memorable Christmas moments transpired with their 1972 episode, featuring film noir and radio legend William Conrad, then at the height of his TV fame with the *Cannon* detective series, which followed the originally titled *Sonny & Cher Comedy Hour* on Wednesday nights. "In many ways it was just a typical *Sonny & Cher* show," Davidson said, "with the usual skits and musical numbers (although many of them set in winter wonderlands and with Christmas carols), complete with then avant-garde chroma key and 'Scanimation' special effects, and all the usual *Sonny & Cher* razzmatazz."

However, the special's closing segment made an impression on Davidson. That's when Conrad recited the moving poem "One Solitary Life," which was followed by Sonny and Cher in a living room set by a hearth with their daughter, Chastity. "It really showed a warm, affectionate, human side to one of the slickest and 'hippest,' by early 1970s TV standards, variety shows of its time."

There are several terrific *Sonny & Cher* Christmas episodes, including one from 1972, another from December 19, 1973, and another from December 6, 1976, the latter featuring guest stars Bob Keeshan (a.k.a. Captain Kangaroo), Bernadette Peters, Shields and Yarnell, and Sonny and Cher's daughter, Chastity, and Cher's son with Greg Allman, Elijah Blue Allman.

As is detailed on CherScholar.com, a "Laverne" highlight has bartender Ted Zeigler asking Laverne and Alvie, who are watching the *Sonny & Cher* Christmas show on TV, what they think Cher got Sonny for Christmas this year. Laverne says, "Last year she gave him the shaft."

The December 19, 1973, episode, directed by Art Fisher and written by Paul Wayne, George Burditt, and Coslough Johnson (brother of Arte Johnson), featured guest star William Conrad, then star of the 1970s hit TV detective series *Cannon*. It opened with a rendition of "Jingle Bells" followed by skits about a snow-seeking Indian and a bear and a dinner-seeking hobo. The last thirty minutes showcase additional Christmas carols and a skit about Sonny's Pizza.

In that pizza piece, Cher's Rosie sings "and may all your Christmases be white" and jokes with Ted Zeigler about Christmas songs while they fold napkins. Sonny wants everyone to work Christmas Eve and Christmas Day, which prompts Cher to say he's worse than Scrooge. But Sonny defends himself by saying every year he feeds a homeless man (Keeshan). Later, Sonny won't let Rosa leave early to take her niece (Chastity) to a Christmas pageant. Bernadette Peters arrives, saying she's lost her fifteen-piece marching band during a performance of "The Twelve Days of Christmas." Then Chastity arrives dressed as an angel.

In another "Laverne" skit, Alvin and Laverne are at his house. Sonny references O. Henry, which prompts Cher to crack an *Oh Henry!* candy bar joke. When Sonny explains the O. Henry story, Cher replies, "Well, at least they had a place to live!"

Another skit shows Sonny under a Christmas tree playing with Chastity's toys, including marionettes played by Shields and Yarnell. Chastity is like, "When do I get a turn?"

An additional sketch features lonely souls on Christmas Eve in the same posh restaurant with Keeshan as angelesque host. Also included is a crusty Ted Zeigler, a no-nonsense Cher, Sonny as a singing alcoholic, and an actress played by Bernadette Peters, whose mother thinks she's doing well.

Some of the Christmas carols performed in this episode include "White Christmas" by Bernadette Peters, "Frosty the Snowman" by Cher and Captain Kangaroo, "I Saw Mommy Kissing Santa Claus"—Chastity with Sonny, "Here Comes Santa Claus" and "Santa Claus Is Comin' to Town," both performed by everyone.

In the end, Sonny and Cher sing their signature "I Got You Babe" closing number and wish everyone a Merry Christmas. Chastity yawns and, with a slight nod to Tiny Tim and a Christmas Carol, says, "God bless everyone," which prompts Cher to tickle her as the credits roll.

CHAPTER 12
SIBLINGS GREETINGS

"Merry Christmas, Darling"

—Carpenters

In the world of the Carpenters, they did not have a weekly variety show and were not a married couple, but a sibling act like Donny and Marie.

The Carpenters are one of those magical groups of musical history that crisscross many platforms. As a sister-and-brother act, they flawlessly combined their talents into a history-making act that appeals to all generations. Karen Carpenter's remarkable lead vocals and precision rhythms and her brother Richard Carpenter's elegant keyboard and supporting sounds when matched are unmatched.

With the growing popularity of musical duos (and sometimes trios, when it came to Tony Orlando & Dawn), it was inevitable the Carpenters would find their way to television, specifically Christmas television, due to the massive popularity of their holiday music albums. Assuredly, the Carpenters were the ideal follow-up sister-brother TV act, if in periodic specials, after Donny and Marie Osmond's weekly foray onto the small screen.

In 1978, ABC initially aired *The Carpenters: A Christmas Portrait*, which was directed by Bob Henry and written by Rod Warren. Here, the dynamic Carpenter duo interact with special guests Gene Kelly, Georgia Engel (from *The Mary Tyler Moore Show*), and yet another talented brother/sister team: Kristy McNichol and Jimmy McNichol. *The Carpenters: A Christmas Portrait* is adapted from the group's first holiday album of the same name, which was their ninth studio album in total, formally released on October 13, 1978.

The album includes a revised rendition of their signature Christmas song, "Merry Christmas, Darling," and one of two renditions of "Santa Claus Is Comin' to Town," in addition to other unutilized tunes produced during recording sessions, some of which were later released on the Carpenters' album *An Old-Fashioned Christmas.*

According to Dan Wingate, the Carpenters' Christmas specials showcase in general "another sibling act perfectly suited to the holidays—both Karen and Richard's prodigious musical talents elevated their two late 1970s offerings above the typical ABC network tinkering of the time—and Karen's one-of-a-kind vocal intelligence conveys not only the innocent joy and anticipation of the coming days, but also that particular sadness one can feel when someone is missing from the celebration. The soundtracks that were also produced at the time are among the all-time best-selling Christmas recordings—and continue to top annual holiday-gathering playlists to this day.

"Richard Carpenter once talked about how hard they had to fight the network to finally get the Carpenters' last special to focus only on music and not force them to do comedy—and it was likely at least partly due to the success of their two Christmas specials—which were both helmed by seasoned variety veteran Bob Henry.

"The holiday specials of the earlier era benefited from the 'live' aspect of a television studio—even when they were pre-recording for later showing, as would become common in the 1960s. There's an energy in the specials recorded in front of an audience that elevated the performances and flooded the soundtrack with a warmth and goodwill that you just don't hear in later productions where there was no audience present and their reactions were added or 'sweetened' on the soundtrack," Wingate concluded.

For Telly Davidson, the Carpenter's Christmas specials were and remain particularly special. Like the Carpenters themselves, Davidson was born and raised in the Downey/Whittier/North Orange County of California. Consequently, that created a measure of affinity for Davidson in connecting the Carpenters and their music. "I could never forget Miss Karen or that groovy brother of hers," he said. "When the Carpenters first hit the big time in 1969 and 1970, they were one of the more TV-friendly top music acts because they were so mainstream—a lot of the edgier, more 'counterculture' performers were starting to refuse to do most TV even when it was offered them, at least up until *The Midnight Special* and of course *SNL*, as being quote-unquote lame and 'beneath' them."

A few years before, Ed Sullivan booked hard rock acts on his weekly variety show, which ended in 1971, because, as Davidson told it, such bands were "more popular and he wanted to keep his ratings current than because he enjoyed them himself at his advancing age. Most of the bigger-venue variety and talk shows like Johnny Carson and Merv Griffin only had youthful acts on very occasionally."

In their early years, circa 1969–1971, the Carpenters appeared on Sullivan's show, as well as *The Andy Williams Show*, and just prior to the latter, they received their "biggest breaks," Davidson noted, on *Your All-American College Show*, which was a syndicated talent show hosted by TV legends Dennis James and Arthur Godfrey. Often aired Saturday nights at 10:30 p.m., following *The Hollywood Palace* in several cities, *Your All-American College Show* was "a top draw for local non-network stations in the major markets from 1968 to 1970," Davidson said.

In 1971, the Carpenters hosted their own summer replacement series, *Make Your Own Kind of Music*, which, as Davidson further assessed, was "as cheesy as can be but boasted some great musical performances, and you've seen clips of it in almost any Carpenters retrospective. After Herb Alpert retired the Tijuana Brass around 1969 or 1970, and Burt Bacharach was no longer at his 1960s height, the Carpenters, and maybe Cat Stevens and Quincy Jones, were A&M Records' absolute number one act for the 1970s, and they were kept internationally on tour on an almost 24–7 basis, which a lot of people speculate led to Karen's difficulties."

By 1976, however, the Carpenters were ready to slow down, and their chart success, while still strong, was no longer a top draw. At which case, their manager signed them with ABC to host a special, with an option for more if it succeeded. That initial special, according to Davidson, "just blew the lid off ratings-wise and resulted in several more specials," with the final special, *Music, Music, Music*, airing in the spring of 1980. But the "crown jewels" of their TV specials, Davidson said, were their 1977 Christmas entry and its 1978 sequel, *A Christmas Portrait*.

Davidson explained: "The 1977 show was recently replayed on public television, and I have to say, it really still holds up. Yes, it has its dated qualities—what self-respecting 1970s holiday special doesn't?—but to see the big dance numbers, the sincere talent, and top-flight production values, and that quality of being a glamorous superstar but one who was also as approachable and down-to-earth as a next-door neighbor that Miss Karen had, made it one of the very best of its kind and one that deserves to be enjoyed today."

As noted earlier, Karen's recording of "Merry Christmas, Darling" had by then already clocked in as a holiday radio staple, but the 1978 TV *Portrait* special had, from Davidson's perspective, "the best visualization/sketch to go with it, with the studio 'snow' and cabin and costumes."

However, Davidson added, "a slightly uncomfortable in retrospect moment" transpired in the 1978 special. That's when Karen, who suffered and later died from complications from eating disorders, was shown cooking and "giving the gift of food" to friends and family. "At the time her anorexia was not out in the open, and she still maintained a fairly attractive presence, as opposed to some of her near-skeletal last photos and appearances. Ironically, it was said that she herself was a gourmet cook and enjoyed cooking—for other people, like friends and family."

The Carpenters' specials expanded that grouping in a much larger capacity by way of allowing viewers accessibility to the duo's touring band members. As Davidson explained: "Hardcore Carpenters fans will recognize the late guitar god Tony Peluso, who did the iconic fuzz-guitar solo on 'Goodbye to Love,' multi-instrumentalists Bob Messenger, Dan Woodhams, and Doug Strawn, who later did the voice of Donald Duck and worked for Disney for many years, and fellow Disney vet and 'Mouseketeer' drummer Cubby O'Brien."

With that said, the Carpenters' shows were some of the best non-location, and more traditionally studio-produced, holiday programs of their era. "They avoided the trap of looking low-budget or dull or overtly artificial despite the old-school, studio/tape confines," Davidson said.

The Carpenters frequently combined the talents of such legends as Gene Kelly and Ella Fitzgerald with what Davidson described as "definitive 1970s performers," such as Suzanne Somers, the McNichol teen idol siblings, Georgia Engel, John Denver, and John Davidson. The 1978 special in particular was the definitive example of this, Telly said, with Georgia Engel, the McNichols, and Gene Kelly "stopping by" the Carpenters' snowy studio "winter cabin" for Christmas. "For 1970s addicts and for fans of holiday specials alike, they were an absolute home run."

Around this time, Donny and Marie Osmond, with the help of who Telly Davidson described as "pioneering puppeteer" sibling producers Sid and Marty Kroft (best known for such classic 1970s Saturday-morning fare as *H.R. Pufnstuf*) then pitched a winning ball into that particular game of TV Christmas throngs. As Davidson explained, the ABC Friday-night, multitalented, toothy Osmond brother-sister act were some of "the last *name* stars to carry a successful weekly old-school variety show in prime time." Soon following were ABC's short-lived and notably bizarre *Brady Bunch Variety Hour* and NBC's *Barbara Mandrell and the Mandrell Sisters*, both also produced by Kroft, the latter of which Davidson described as "the last big network hour." After that arrived the syndicated *Solid Gold* series hosted by Dionne Warwick and then Marilyn McCoo, the half-hour *Tracey Ullman Show*, and periodic off-color, *SNL*-esque *In Living Color*, both airing "in the early days when Fox wrapped the era up completely," Davidson said.

The initial Christmas special hosted by Donny & Marie, as was their official show title, was, as Davidson noted, "appropriately filmed largely in their Utah home environs, with the snowy ski country of Salt Lake City and thereabouts lending itself so well to a 'winter wonderland.' A Christmas special was a no-brainer for the Osmonds. Not only are they devoutly Christian (Mormon) themselves, but coming from the winter resort of Salt Lake, when they returned for their specials, they were kind of in their 'natural habitat.' You'd be hard-pressed to find more unpretentious or approachable young stars of that era than Donny and Marie, and their specials really drove home the family atmosphere."

"The Osmond family was nothing if not king-size," Davidson said, if maybe with a slight, subconscious nod to the King Family, "and were deliberately goofy and had a great sense of humor about themselves."

For its initial three years, *Donny & Marie* taped at the KTLA Channel 5 Golden West Videotape Center (now Sunset-Bronson Studios). As Davidson explained, Golden West was operated by KTLA's then-owner Gene Autry's wife, Ina Mae, who was "largely the business brains of the two, until she passed in 1980 at the height of Golden West's video era. Not long after Autry purchased Channel 5 in the 1960s, Ina Mae saw to it that the KTLA studios got chroma-key and Scanimate computer effects and other network-level upgrades and a full studio audience rating from the insurance.

"Ina Mae might've seemed like a homespun, country-cookie housewife," Davidson said, "and was certainly as conservative as her husband." So much so, Mae tossed out Chuck *The Gong Show* Barris's slate of shows "after the first year or so in syndication because she thought they were too tasteless and exploitative," Davidson said [although KTLA carried the syndicated *Newlywed Game* and *Dating Game* due to high ratings].

Mae "insisted they have a 'Recommended for Mature Audiences' chyron before each local KTLA telecast," Davidson said. "But she was actually a very bright showbiz woman who foresaw the rise in first-run syndication and the need for non-network facilities, back when big studios like Fox and Columbia and MGM were selling off their backlots."

Golden West was home to what Davidson called a "Who's Who of polyester-prime-time TV," including *WKRP in Cincinnati, What's Happening, Sha Na Na, Name That Tune, Liar's Club, Make Me Laugh, Face the Music, Dinah's Place*, and *The Brady Bunch Variety Hour*, and much later, *Judge Judy*'s lengthy run of shows. Golden's sister studios were the former Screen Gems/Columbia stages where among other early TV jewels, *Bewitched* and *I Dream of Jeannie* were filmed; the former Desilu backlot on Cahuenga Boulevard became Sunset-Gower Studios and Television Center/Ren-Mar in the late 1970s, and between the two produced *Barbara Mandrell and the Mandrell Sisters*, the infamous *Pink Lady and Jeff* variety show, the Chuck Barris stable of game shows from that era, and more recent upscale productions such as *The Golden Girls*, *Monk*, and *Six Feet Under*.

As Davidson explained, "The KTLA staff really went to the mat for Sid & Marty." Even more so, when it came to *Donny & Marie*, which utilized two stages; one positioned for the studio audience for regular music and sketch comedy segments and an alternate location with a built-in ice rink. Meanwhile, *The Brady Bunch Variety Hour* utilized a fully-filtered and swimming-equipped pool constructed for aqua-dancers. As it turned out, the Kroft brothers "would never have paid ABC or CBS's high rent for their stages, if they could get away with it," Davidson said, "as they were responsible for the full production costs on their programs."

However, circa 1977 or 1978, the entire Osmond troupe (which includes several other brothers for Marie) had steep investments in what became the Osmond Studios, which remained in operation until it was sold in 1989. The Osmonds moved their show "lock, stock, and barrel to their Utah hometown for its last year or two," Davidson said. Subsequently, that's where the Osmonds presented the vast majority of their stand-alone Christmas and other specials. "And one can't help but wonder if they would have tried opening their own stages were it not for the excitement and investment in those early holiday winter and spring specials taped on location back in Utah."

Davidson then referred to "a tacky and vulgar, if admittedly shock-funny postscript to the *Donny & Marie*'s Christmas specials that aired as a segment on *SNL* in 1982. Here, Eddie Murphy's "foul-mouthed, stereotypical, Vegas-styled, cigar-waving has-been" take on the harmless and naive early-TV animated icon Gumby hosted a bitter-cold holiday special that featured Donny and Marie, as played by Gary Kroeger and a pre-*Seinfeld* Julia Louis-Dreyfus.

"The most memorable big moment came," explained Davidson, "when Donny and Marie started making out with each other under the mistletoe, as 'more than' brother and sister! While they probably weren't exactly thrilled by the skit," the real-life siblings "had nothing if not a sense of humor about themselves and their squeaky-clean Mormon image," Davidson noted. "And whatever else, it certainly showed just how perma-famous the Osmonds had become by then—and to their many fans, still are."

In an interview with *Entertainment Tonight* in December 2023, Donny reflected on the siblings' *Star Wars* special, which featured a pertinent detail that, in hindsight, is both startling and humorous. Apparently, in 1977,

Donny and his sister Marie unknowingly delivered a relatively major *Star Wars* reveal.

At the time, the Osmond siblings had their own variety series, *The Donny & Marie Show*. The initial *Star Wars* movie premiered in May 1977, igniting a pop culture craze. Consequently, the following September, *The Donny & Marie Show* produced a *Star Wars* special with Donny as Luke Skywalker, Marie as Princess Leia, and Kris Kristofferson as Han Solo, with other Osmond family members as dancing stormtroopers. Each performed *Star Wars*–inspired songs prior to boarding a spaceship before it took off.

Donny discussed the experience in a new documentary about another surreal *Star Wars* relic from the 1970s: the much-maligned *Star Wars Holiday Special*.

A Disturbance in the Force, which was released on digital platforms, DVD, and Blu-ray on December 5, 2023, chronicles the hilarious secrets behind the *Star Wars Holiday Special* and additional ways the franchise was exploited on TV in the 1970s.

"I'm thinking," Donny said, "'How in the world is George Lucas allowing this to happen?'"

Donny offered that reflection to *Entertainment Tonight* about the *Donny & Marie* special. "Because it's just so far from the movie. But it sure was funny at the time. And it's funny to look back on right now."

Donny joked that the production "broke a lot of [*Star Wars*] rules," going so far as to include a shot of Chewbacca with his arm around Darth Vader (which, as true *Star Wars* fans know, would never happen). "I guess on *Donny & Marie*, everyone was friends!" Donny mused.

The Osmond *Star Wars* special featured one shockingly interesting detail. Donny and Marie's portrayal of Luke and Leia was an unintended hint at one of *Star Wars*' biggest secrets: that Luke and Leia were actually siblings themselves—some fans would not become aware of that until 1983's *Return of the Jedi*.

CHAPTER 13
STAR WARS, NOTHING BUT STAR WARS

"*Star Wars*, nothing but *Star Wars*"

—Bill Murray, *Saturday Night Live*

The year after *Donny & Marie*'s *Star Wars* satire, Geroge Lucas premiered the two-hour *Star Wars Holiday Special*. In addition to the franchise's now-legendary cast of Mark Hamill (Luke Skywalker), Carrie Fisher (Princess Leia), Harrison Ford (Han Solo), Peter Mayhew (Chewbacca), Kenny Baker (R2-D2), Anthony Daniels (C-3PO), among others, the special featured odd cameos from quite non–*Star Wars* celebrities including Bea Arthur, Art Carney, Harvey Korman, and Jefferson Starship.

CBS aired the *Star Wars Holiday Special* during the week of Thanksgiving 1978, when it was viewed by thirteen million people. It never re-aired, but to this day it remains a cult collectors' favorite.

For those unfamiliar with the production, *The Star Wars Holiday Special* followed the story of Chewbacca and Han Solo making their way to the Wookiee planet of Kashyyyk to spend "Life Day" with Chewie's family. Oddly, but not, the *Holiday Special* holds a place of significance in *Star Wars* lore, as one of its cartoon segments serves as the official on-screen introduction of Boba Fett.

The Star Wars Holiday Special has gone down in history as probably the strangest Christmas special ever broadcast, or just the strangest TV special, period. As journalist Neil Genzlinger observed for the *New York Times* in 2015, this *Holiday Special* featured "a plotted tale" and was not really a variety show at all. But given the fact that it served as a pure promotional device—for both ABC's ratings and the initial *Star Wars* feature film, which had just been released, it's understandable why it was ever created and broadcast in the first place. The special "may have been the most bizarre television broadcast of 1978," Genzlinger noted, but he also categorized it as "possibly the most boring. Can Chewbacca get home for the Wookiee holiday called Life Day? Can a two-hour special in which the central characters communicate only in grunts and moans be entertaining?"

In the special, Genzlinger went on to explain: "Princess Leia famously called Chewbacca a walking carpet, but think of the Wookiees instead as wearing the shaggiest seasonal sweaters in history. . . . Chewbacca's father, Itchy, puts on a virtual-reality helmet that generates fantasies, and he experiences Diahann Carroll as Mermeia, every syllable she speaks or sings dripping pure sex. It could be a segment from [HBO's *Sex On* documentary series] about sex and pornography in the digital age. . . . Chewbacca's wife, Malla, is watching a cooking show about preparing a dish called bantha surprise. The TV chef is using bantha loin. 'But of course, if your family has a hearty appetite,' the chef says, 'I would suggest then that old popular holiday favorite, the bantha rump.'"

In the annals of the *Star Wars* fandom, the *Holiday Special* was based on a story by George Lucas, whose involvement was limited, and who was ultimately unhappy with the final product. Despite its celebrity guest infamy and the Boba Fett introduction, the special is notable for being the first film-length *Star Wars* story to appear following the release of the original movie.

Filming began in August 1978 under David Acomba, a friend of Lippincott and fellow USC schoolmate of Lucas's. The special was shot mostly on videotape on a budget of more than one million dollars. Acomba shot footage for three of the special's sequences—including the cantina sequence and the scene with Jefferson Starship. The cantina sequence took an entire day to film—from 6:00 a.m. one day to 6:00 a.m. the next. The costumed actors withstood heat, claustrophobia, and (for some) low oxygen intake.

When Bea Arthur's son Daniel Saks visited the set, he saw "a nurse running around feeding oxygen into the various aliens to make sure they didn't pass out." Rick Baker, who had worked on the original *Star Wars*, again served as creature supervisor for the scene. Although many of the cantina creatures were reused from *Star Wars*, Lion Man and Baboon Man were created for the special. These two wore complicated makeup that took two and a half hours to apply.

For Harvey Korman's scenes, he reportedly kept the cast and crew entertained and brought levity to the set. Acomba suggested a then-unknown comedian named Robin Willams for a role, but the Welches preferred to use established stars. Cher was the original choice to play Mermeia, but the part ultimately went to Diahann Carroll.

Kevin J. Anderson once summarized the special like this: "Well, I know that George Lucas doesn't like it at all—when I was working on *The Illustrated Star Wars Universe*, he told me that he would be happy if every copy could be tracked down and burned."

Decades later, the *Holiday Special* served as a surprisingly notable influence on *The Mandalorian*, the live-action *Star Wars* series, which premiered on Disney+ November 12, 2019.

The Mandalorian was executive-produced by director Jon Favreau. As he told *Entertainment Tonight* in 2019: "I love *The Holiday Special*—certain sequences more than others. I love the introduction of Boba Fett and that rifle that he had. That animated piece still holds up. It's pretty cool. I draw inspiration from that."

Another inspiring character for Favreau lies in Cara Dune, played by Gina Carano, who that year at the Saturn Awards presented him with the Visionary Award. Backstage at the event, Favreau expressed interest in producing a new iteration of *The Star Wars Holiday Special*. As he continued to tell *Entertainment Tonight*: "I would love to do a *Holiday Special*" [today]. Looking directly into the camera, he added, "If you want to see a *Holiday Special*, let Disney+ know."

Irreverent TV variety productions like *The Star Wars Holiday Special* were preceded by odd but in retrospect genius programming of those like Ernie Kovacs, who was no doubt ahead of his time. In 1988, however, Saturday-morning TV personality Pee-wee Herman, a.k.a. Paul Reubens, brought his own brand of odd to an award-winning Saturday-morning showcase that inspired a prime-time holiday presentation: *Pee-wee's Playhouse Christmas Special*.

A parody of TV and humanity, Pee-wee presents his usual unusually entertaining antics and a terrific lineup of guests, including the always entertaining Charo (in blazing red, no less, displaying lots of *cuchi-cuchi* and leg). There was also an appearance by The Del Rubio Triplets, three of a certain-age-women strumming guitars and wearing Christmas-colored short-shorts, or possibly miniskirts, singing "Winter Wonderland." There's also the off-color moment where Pee-wee spritzes women with perfume with a scent he refers to as "Eau de Pee-wee."

But the true weekly variety show king of irreverent television programming is the NBC weekend late-night entry, *Saturday Night Live*, which has had its share of Christmas episodes from its premiere in 1975. Case in point, post *Star Wars*, when Bill Murray sang, "*Star Wars* . . . nothing but *Star Wars*," as a bar singer. While, too, in 1978, NBC aired a Mac Davis special with a sci-fi-like theme, *Christmas Odyssey 2010*. That was a nod to the film

2001: A Space Odyssey, released in 1968 and based on Arthur C. Clark's remarkable novel, while almost eerily pre-dating the sequel, *2010: The Year We Make Contact*, released in 1984, if based on Clark's sequel publication, *2010: Odyssey Two*.

In totality, whether Christmas music/variety specials are produced the traditional way, housed within a studio, or on location, and take a wildly different path with even a science-fiction bent, as entertainment journalist Melissa Byers decided, "it's a moot point. All formats serve their purpose, as long as they contain certain key elements. I don't think I have a preference. For most Christmas shows, I am drawn either to the music or to the story. I've been in and around theater so long, I tend to look past the tech to the heart of the piece."

For Telly Davidson, the musical variety Christmas special metamorphosis was a gradual process and sign of the times. "Old-fashioned studio variety shows went the way of the dinosaur and were eventually thought of as old-hat. With the rise of MTV videos and uncensored comedians like Richard Pryor, George Carlin, and Lenny Bruce, the focus shifted to spectacle and glamorous and exciting locations. Those were visually attractive and sometimes even breathtaking to look at. As Merv Griffin frequently observed about his famed talk show, and his equally iconic *Jeopardy* and *Wheel of Fortune* game shows, at the end of the day, 'the play's the thing.'"

Or as Davidson concluded, "If it doesn't offer up music and comedy and the occasional tearjerker or touching story, all the travelogue scenery and boffo video effects in the world can't save it."

PART 2
THE YULETIDE ANIMATRIX

N ot to belabor the *Star Wars* influence in all pop culture, but as we begin to explore favorite animated Christmas TV specials, it seems fitting to note that George Lucas remains fond of a 1977 American-Canadian Christmas special, called, *A Cosmic Christmas*.

A Cosmic Christmas premiered on CBC Television in Canada and in syndication in America on December 4, 1977. It was the first special in the 1977–1980 series of television specials produced by Nelvana Ltd. and was also the first animated production from the studio. It was also submitted for the Best Animated Short Academy Award. The plot centered around three aliens (from an unknown planet) who bear a strong resemblance to the biblical Magi, and who visit Earth to know the true meaning of Christmas.

With that said, a plethora of animated Christmas TV specials have aired in the decades before and after *A Cosmic Christmas*, none the least of which were brought to the screen by the renowned Rankin/Bass band of Animagic productions. Those include, in chronological order, *Rudolph the Red-Nosed Reindeer* (NBC, December 6, 1964), *The Little Drummer Boy* (CTV, December 19, 1968, NBC, December 23, 1968), *Frosty the Snowman* (CBS, December 7, 1969), *Santa Claus Is Comin' to Town* (ABC, December 14, 1970), *'Twas the Night Before Christmas* (December 8, 1974), *The Year Without a Santa Claus* (ABC, December 10, 1974), *The First Christmas: The Story of the First Christmas Snow* (NBC, December 19, 1975), *Frosty's Winter Wonderland* (ABC, December 2, 1976), *Rudolph's Shiny New Year* (ABC, December 10, 1976), *The Little Drummer Boy: Book II* (NBC, December 13, 1976), *Nestor, the Long-Eared Christmas Donkey* (ABC, December 3, 1977), *Rudolph and Frosty's Christmas in July* (ABC, November 25, 1979), *Jack Frost*

(NBC, December 13, 1979), *Pinocchio's Christmas* (ABC, December 3, 1980), and *The Leprechauns' Christmas Gold* (NBC, December 23, 1981). Beyond the Rankin/Bass ranks are additionally cherished specials such as *A Charlie Brown Christmas* (CBS, December 9, 1965) and *The Grinch Who Stole Christmas* (CBS, December 18, 1966). In 1973, CBS aired *A Very Merry Cricket*, about Chester the Cricket, who brings the true Yuletide spirit to New York's Times Square.

In 1977, CBS aired a mainstream, animated version of Clement Clarke Moore's famed holiday tale, this time calling it *The Night Before Christmas*. One year later, the same network ran *Raggedy Ann and Andy in the Great Santa Claus Caper*, produced by Chuck Jones.

In 1979, *Casper's Christmas Wish* came to life right alongside *A Family Circus Christmas*, based on America's lovable comic strip family. In 1981, *Casper's First Christmas* unites everyone's "friendly ghost" with Yogi Bear, Huckleberry Hound, and Hairy Scary, among others. Also that year, on December 14, NBC aired *A Chipmunk Christmas* with characters from the *Alvin and the Chipmunks* band, which was produced by Bagdasarian Productions in association with Chuck Jones Enterprises. This special screened nine years after the demise of *Alvin and the Chipmunks* creator Ross Bagdasarian Sr. (also known as David Seville); marking the first time that Alvin, Simon, and David Seville were voiced by Ross Bagdasarian Jr. and the first time that Theodore was voiced by Janice Karman.

In 1982, a plethora of animated fare aired: *Christmas Comes to Pac-Land* (from the Pac-Man franchise) with Santa, *Ziggy's Gift* (with music and lyrics by Harry Nilsson), *Bugs Bunny's Looney Christmas Tales*, *A Disney Christmas Gift*, and *Yogi Bear's All-Star Comedy Christmas Caper*. The latter featured the animated-likes of Boo-Boo Bear, the Flintstones, Huckelberry Hound, Quick Draw McGraw, and other Hanna-Barbera favorites.

In 1983, *The Smurfs Christmas Special* premiered, while *A Jetson Christmas Carol* premiered two years later.

On December 6, 1986, ABC presented Jim Henson's *The Christmas Toy*, while 1987 brought us *A Claymation Christmas Celebration*.

Countless other animated Christmas specials aired in subsequent decades; even Casper coming back for *Casper's Haunted Christmas* in 2000 (with music provided by Randy Travis).

However, it was in 1950 that the animated specials brigade began with back-to-back specials and a unique feature: Mable and Les Beaton's marionettes. *The Spirit of Christmas*, presented by Bell Telephone, was a half-hour program divided into two segments. The first half dramatized Moore's *A Visit from St. Nicholas*, a.k.a. *'Twas The Night Before Christmas*; the second half told the story of the Nativity. [The jacket of the DVD edition calls it "The Philadelphia Holiday Classic," which refers to the historic American region where it was initially broadcast.]

The Spirit of Christmas aired multiple times at Christmastime during the 1950s and 1960s, without commercial interruptions except for opening and closing remarks by "your telephone company" (Bell Telephone). It was not seen for decades until recently on a local PBS station.

A Philadelphia TV viewer, who described himself as John L., documented his memory of *The Spirit of Christmas* on TVParty.com: "It was broadcast annually and sponsored by Bell Telephone. As my father worked for Bell Tel, I proudly watched it every time it was on. The local PBS station, WHYY, tracked it down years ago and broadcasts it several times each holiday season."

Even the commercials that aired during Christmas specials remain tender memories to some viewers. As fellow Christmas TV–lover Susan Rosko also documented on TVParty.com: "Along with Norelco shaver Santa Claus, who can forget the 'Give him British Sterling' ads with the Renaissance music and the woman riding the beautiful white horse, Kraft sponsored shows where all their commercials were recipes ('to make that clam dip special, use Philly-brand cream cheese . . .'), and the Coke 'Like to teach the world to sing' jingle."

Clearly, several television watchers will forever treasure their own trove and stable of Christmas TV specials, particularly the animated sector; a category that ultimately commenced in the most mainstream and memorable manner with *Mr. Magoo's Christmas Carol*.

CHAPTER 14
MR. MAGOO'S FIRST CHRISTMAS

"A Christmas far more glorious than grand."

"Was there ever such a Christmas?"

—Magoo, in *Mr. Magoo's Christmas Carol*

A *Christmas Carol* by Charles Dickens is a literary legend, a classic holiday tale that has been told and adapted countless times for the stage, film, and television, in animated and live-action form.

One such animated adaptation is *Mr. Magoo's Christmas Carol*, which was produced in just nine months by the United Producers of America (UPA) and originally aired on NBC December 18, 1962. A unique entry in the Dickens' *Carol* category, and in the big-picture Holiday general-spectrum scheme of things, *Magoo's Christmas Carol* is the first, full-blown animated Christmas special of television.

For any TV show, movie, or stage production to work, no matter the premise, whether it's stark reality, fantasy, or science fiction, it has to present a certain logic within what many times is an illogical world. Juxtaposed, and irrespective of the viewer's reality, the beholding production must still maintain a measure of sensible logic within the fabricated, sometimes non-sensical illogic at hand. Right out of the gate, *Mr. Magoo's Christmas Carol* messes with that concept, but to its and our delightful advantage. With its own brand of charm, *Magoo's* utilizes a "movie-within-a-movie" premise or, better said, a "stage play within a stage play premise," and the results are nothing less than, yes, magical.

According to award-winning producer/editor Les Perkins, *Mr. Magoo's Christmas Carol* "was the culmination of the then popular Mr. Magoo character. But how to cast him into a literary classic? That's why they came up with the opening and closing Broadway segments to establish that Magoo is an actor playing a stage role, not being Mr. Magoo himself. This success led to subsequent series and specials."

Jim Backus, perhaps best known in the classic TV world as Thurston Howell III from *Gilligan's Island*, offers his earmark vocals of the visually impaired Magoo. Distinguished vocal support is provided by Morey Amsterdam (*The Dick Van Dyke Show*), Joan Gardner, Jack Cassidy (father to David Cassidy of *The Partridge Family*), and Paul Frees (who will soon be heard in a number of now-famed Rankin/Bass Christmas TV specials), among others. Directed by Abe Levitow, *Mr. Magoo's Christmas Carol* features musical selections by Jule Styne with lyrics by Bob Merrill, while Walter Scharf arranged and conducted the orchestral score.

The core setting is this: Mr. Magoo is enroute to a Broadway theater, where he is portraying Ebenezer Scrooge in a musical production based on *A Christmas Carol*. Due to Magoo's visual challenges, he arrives thirty minutes tardy and mistakenly injures the director, and the production goes cheerfully amiss from there.

This *Christmas Carol* play-within-an-animated-TV-show is unique such that the initial spirit to visit Scrooge is the Spirit of Christmas Present, followed by the Spirits of Christmas Past and Yet to Come, whereas in all other versions, Scrooge is visited by the Ghost of Christmas Past first, then Present, and then Yet to Come. Although this alteration is never addressed, some TV historians have estimated that it had to do with the program's length and commercial time.

For some, the quality of UPA's animation may not compare to Walt Disney or even Hanna-Barbera, but *Mr. Magoo's Christmas Carol* leaves its colorful mark nonetheless. Though that almost was accomplished without Jim Backus as its star. At one point early on in production, the show's producers initially considered Robert Goulet for the lyrical lead, questioning whether Backus could muster and manage the vocal gymnastics necessary for the part.

Clearly, he did, and so much more. Film and television historian and archivist Robert S. Ray observed: "In the 1962 Christmas season, the success of *Mr. Magoo's Christmas Carol* ushered in the idea that the Christmas season was ripe for the creation of annual Christmas specials for the whole family. The holiday treats could be enjoyed year after year in seemingly endless repeats.

"This first of the animated Christmas specials was a *Big Deal* indeed," Ray continued. "With songs by Broadway stalwarts Jule Styne and Bob Merrill, who would both later go on to write *Funny Girl* for Broadway [and Barbra Streisand], and starring the ever-popular UPA cartoon star, Mr. Magoo, *Mr. Magoo's Christmas Carol* premiered to universal acclaim by critics and audiences alike. We baby boomers who were there to watch its first airing will never forget how special it felt. Those special feelings would be later replicated with *Rudolph the Red-Nosed Reindeer*, *A Charlie Brown Christmas*, and other later perennials, but Mr. Magoo was the first and will always remain dear to many as a result."

Mr. Magoo's Christmas Carol aired annually throughout most of the 1960s, Ray explained, "but for some reason NBC dropped it in the closing years of that decade and it drifted into semi-obscurity until it reappeared on home video many years later. As a result, it doesn't have the following that some of the later ones do, and it's a shame, because *Magoo* can stand proudly with anything released by Rankin/Bass and the others. It's a great way to introduce Dickens to young children and can be enjoyed and cherished by family members of all ages."

Les Perkins explained about the *Magoo* special: "NBC did try to revive it several years ago, unsuccessfully, but it was edited down since modern broadcast has nearly double the commercial time than in 1962. It has been beautifully restored on Blu-ray, through the passion of animation director Darrell Van Citters."

For Perkins, *Magoo's Christmas Carol* is a favorite adaptation of the Dickens classic. "Many people love the Albert Finney *Scrooge* or the 1951 British Alastair Sim films better. But to me all other versions seem padded. It was a short story to begin with and the UPA show clips along effortlessly, wasting no time, yet hitting all the essential story points, with excellent vocal performances and a terrific music score."

The stylized, limited animation of *Magoo* "doesn't bother me," Perkins said. "The credits read 'freely adapted from Dickens . . . adapted by Barbara Chain,' but it's actually very authentic to Dickens, with lines of dialogue almost as he wrote them. The biggest change is reversing the appearances of the Ghosts of Christmas Past and Present, which can be considered an improvement. But Chain even gets in the robbers, which most other versions drop. It's a tight condensation of Dickens with never a dull or wasted moment.

"Where the TV show excels," Perkins concluded, "is the soundtrack. It works perfectly like an elaborate radio show. In fact, I made a tape recording of the original broadcast in 1962 and played it often, which is how I became so familiar with the audio apart from the visuals. Every time I watch another version, there is dialogue where I hear Jim Backus's line readings in my head as being better than virtually every other Scrooge actor, and some of the other characters as well. Backus nailed it!"

CHAPTER 15

RUDOLPH'S SHINY NOSE,
NEW YEAR, AND CHRISTMAS IN JULY

"A toy is never truly happy unless it is loved by a child."

—King Moonracer in *Rudolph the Red-Nosed Reindeer*

Unlike *Mr. Magoo's Christmas Carol*, *Rudolph the Red-Nosed Reindeer* has aired annually, except once (in 1999 when a poorly made decision outraged viewers). In 1964, the same year the ninety-minute sci-fi feature film–oddity *Santa Claus Conquered the Martians* premiered on the big screen, the sixty-minute stop-motion Animagic of *Rudolph the Red-Nosed Reindeer* debuted on NBC.

Musician, author, and entertainment historian David Laurell explained: "Animagic was a technique that Bass and Rankin's company, Videocraft, used in which three-dimensional figures were animated via the process of single-frame photography."

However it was created, the special transported small-screen viewers to what media analyst and marketeer Bob Barnett called "a world of adventure and misfit toys." As a child, Barnett "related to Rudolph's being different. His journey to find his place in the world was both entertaining and comforting. The show created an enchanting magical Christmas atmosphere that was hard to resist."

Rudolph, most likely more than any other children's special, animated, live-action, Christmas, or otherwise (with *A Charlie Brown Christmas* a close second), is filtered with insightful and caring life lessons of humanity. Directed by Larry Roemer, with cinematography by Kizo Nagashima, and written by Robert May and Romeo Muller, the special tells a "true love" story with pervading messages about maturity, responsibility, pride, prejudice, ambition, and acceptance. It goes to great lengths to decipher things like "deer pressure" from "elf-improvement." There is a need to dispel the fear surrounding a visit to the dentist; to learn that no toy is happy unless it is truly loved by a child? It's all in there, as are some of the most tender and telling Christmas songs ever composed ("There's Always Tomorrow"; "Silver and Gold") and one of the happiest ("Holly Jolly Christmas"). What else could anyone want in a Christmas TV special?

Usually broadcast in late November or early December, the perennial classic signals the commencement of the holiday season, reminding viewers to slow down and shine on until the morning—and beyond. Featuring the stellar vocal talents of Burl Ives, as Sam the Snowman—who we first meet in the North Pole in the midst of a field of Christmas trees ("Yep—this is where we grow 'em!"), Paul Frees, and Billy Mae Richards as the leading reindeer, among others, *Rudolph* glows from one moment to the next.

For example, shortly after Rudolph arrives on the Island of Misfit Toys, with his friends, Yukon Cornelius (the arctic prospector, voiced by Larry Mann) and Herbie/Hermie (the elf who wants to be a dentist, voiced by Paul Solis), he buckles up and ventures full-speed ahead to fulfill his destiny. He does so by breaking off a piece of land-ice and using it as a drift device to carry him on his way through the icy sea. [Sidenote: the elf is referred to as "Herbie/Hermie," as his name changed from the first half of the show to the second, due to a production mishap. But for the sake of clarity, from here on in he will be referred to as "Hermie."]

As Rudolph drifts across the frigid waters, he wistfully bids farewell to his dear friends, saying, "Goodbye, Cornelius. I hope you find lots of tinsel. Goodbye, Hermie. Whatever a dentist is . . . I hope someday you will be . . . the greatest."

This scene is one of the most poignant moments in the special, and it speaks volumes about Rudolph's kind heart, leaving the viewer with food for thought . . . especially what he says to Hermie. Without understanding in the least anything about Hermie's intended profession, Rudolph wants only the highest good for his friend; for Hermie to excel with his aspirations.

According to Robert S. Ray:

> The enormous success of *Mr. Magoo's Christmas Carol* no doubt helped give the green light to the first of the Rankin-Bass Christmas peren-nials, *Rudolph the Red-Nosed Reindeer*. Based on the popular song by Johnny Marks and augmented by additional tunes by Johnny Marks, it starred Burl Ives in a flashback-filled retelling of the song's story. Like *Mr. Magoo's Christmas Carol* before it, this was "Event Television"

and as the first of the Rankin/Bass Christmas offerings, this was perhaps the best of them. All the ideas and concepts were fresh and new. Nothing seemed formulaic, as this was the one that invented the later formulas. The fact that the show included commercials featuring members of the puppet cast seen nowhere else made it even more special. This is the first Christmas special that never went away in the ensuing decades. In fact, it currently airs multiple times throughout the Christmas season, whereas in 1964, it only aired once and then was gone until next year.

David Laurell can further attest to that. As a child, he loved all of the Rankin/Bass productions, along with the various television variety shows and specials, especially Christmas presentations. "Those shows provided me with all kinds of ideas that I incorporated into my performances," said Laurell, who's also a former mayor of Burbank, California. Laurell's "special favorite" Christmas TV production was *Rudolph the Red-Nosed Reindeer*, partially due to the Animagic characters.

"With a script adapted by award-winning screenwriter Romeo Muller, the special was destined to become a timeless holiday classic," Laurell continued. That transpired when Rankin approached his neighbor, Johnny Marks, to write the songs for the production. Hesitant at first, Marks was, as Laurell explained, "finally persuaded into working on the *Rudolph* special, and dove in with inspired gusto."

Along with the "Rudolph the Red-Nosed Reindeer" tune, Marks composed other popular holiday tunes, including "I Heard the Bells on Christmas Day" and "Rockin' Around the Christmas Tree." (As noted in this book's introduction, the song, the original version of which was made popular by Brenda Lee, shot back to the top of charts in 2023, this time, in the No. 1 spot.)

For the *Rudolph* TV special's soundtrack, Marks delivered what Laurell called "another sack of tunes that have gone on to become Yuletide classics." Topping that list is "Have a Holly Jolly Christmas," which became a hit for balladeer Burl Ives. Other of Marks' compositions created for the *Rudolph* special include "We're a Couple of Misfits," "Silver and Gold," "We Are Santa's Elves," "The Most Wonderful Time of the Year," and the beloved ballad "There's Always Tomorrow."

Laurell's mother had received a promotional copy of the *Rudolph* soundtrack when she purchased a GE appliance; a then-designed LP that he "played *ad nauseum*, which resulted in every member of the family knowing the words to every song."

Laurell's talented younger brother, Jim, also appreciated the *Rudolph* special and memorized all of the show's lyrics. Consequently, whether it was Mother's Day, Easter, or Halloween, the Laurell brothers performed a duet of Christmas songs from the *Rudolph* special. Their two favorite tunes were "Silver and Gold" and "There's Always Tomorrow." The latter is performed by the doe Clarise [voiced by Janet Orenstein], Rudolph's romantic interest, in an attempt to cheer him up after his shimmering nose won't allow him to "join in any reindeer games."

That's an important moment from the special; one that countless viewers through the decades have held dear. As Laurell explained: "When Rudolph moans that it hadn't been a very lucky day for him, Clarise tells him that any doe would be lucky to be with him and that no matter how bad things may be at the moment, there's always another day for dreams to come true. She then breaks into the lovely lullaby."

In the early part of 1968, Laurell's father began experiencing health issues that, by late spring, had resulted in hospitalization and surgery. In short, his father was dying. That summer, the Laurell brothers were, as David put it, "shipped off to 'vacation' with relatives." By that summer's end, they returned home to find their father painfully weak. By October, doom and gloom had overshadowed the Laurell home and caused David's grades to plummet and his depression to surge. "I knew something had to be done to lift all of our spirits," he recalled, "and I decided I was the one to do it—with a show!"

Laurell began the production with a comedic musical number that was followed by the usual fare of illusory conjurations, puppetry, and sketches:

My brother and I ended the show by singing "There's Always Tomorrow." The vivid reminder of the emotional impact we caused by singing "There's Always Tomorrow," coupled with the fact that my father passed away just a few days before Christmas of that year, has forever made the *Rudolph* television special one that makes me think of him. Every year, when I see the special's annual airing promoted, I can't help but to think back on a time when I truly believed that there was always another day to do something—to right a wrong, to tell someone how much they mean to you, or to do something you have always dreamed of doing.

I have always believed that dreams can come true. I still do. But, when my father died, I realized that we must do everything we can to make our dreams become realities, not in the tomorrows that may never come, but in the one day we are assured of—today.

After *Rudolph's* initial screening on NBC in 1964, the special began annual broadcasts on CBS, during which its closing credits were revised. Influenced by TV watchers who pined for a happy ending, the visuals of wrapped gifts being dropped from Santa's sleigh were replaced by a scene in which Santa stops to pick up the Misfit Toys and delivers them to the homes of children below via umbrellas (with the exception of the misfit toy bird that swims but does not fly, who is dropped to its destination).

Rudolph's tale was told before, beginning in 1939, when Robert L. May was commissioned to create the new character for the Chicago-based Montgomery Ward department store, which, to save money, sought to market its own coloring book. Then in 1948, a short film about Rudolph was released by Max Fleischer. On June 27, 1949, Gene Autry recorded his now-famed children's song (which was released by Columbia Records in September 1949). In 1958, Little Golden Books published an illustrated storybook, adapted by Barbara Shook Hazen and illustrated by Richard Scarry. That publication was similar in story to Fleischer's 1948 film, and no longer in print, but a revised Little Golden Books adaptation of the storybook was reissued in 1972.

The original NBC TV production, produced for *The General Electric Fantasy Hour*, was followed by two sequels: *Rudolph's Shiny New Year* in 1976 and *Rudolph and Frosty's Christmas in July*, which was a feature-length movie. That latter entry found *Rudolph* amidst the Rankin/Bass world of *Frosty the Snowman*, which premiered on CBS in 1969, while Rudolph also made his cameo appearances in two more Animagic TV specials from the Rankin/Bass camp: *Santa Claus Is Comin' to Town* (ABC, 1970) and *Nestor, the Long-Eared Christmas Donkey* (ABC, 1977), and in the Easter television special *The First Easter Rabbit* (ABC, 1976) with cel animation by Toru Hara's Topcraft.

Decades later, the 1979 novelty, music pop-chart song "Grandma Got Run Over by a Reindeer," by Randy Brooks, was recorded by married bluegrass musicians Elmo and Patsy. In 2000, the song was adapted as an animated TV special.

In 1999, *Olive, the Other Reindeer,* based on the book by J. Otto Siebold and Vivian Walsh, was adapted into an animated TV special with a female twist. Here, Drew Barrymore lends her voice as Olive, who takes it upon herself to essentially approach Santa for a job. Upon learning that Blitzen the reindeer has been injured, Olive steps up to the plate, her sleigh, and as did Rudolph on NBC decades before her, she flies with Mr. Claus on Christmas eve.

But none of those compared to the charm of the original *Rudolph the Red-Nosed Reindeer* special, for which Jerry Houser did the commercial voice-overs for the show and other CBS animated specials in later decades.

I did their whole bank of shows. It was a cool gig. I did that for a long time. I'm really grateful for that. I did *Frosty the Snowman*, *Frosty Returns*, and others. Whatever animated specials they had I did.

I also did the commercial voice-overs for a bunch of their sitcoms and shows. Joe Cipriano was their main voice-over. But I did *Kids Say the Darndest Things . . . Candid Camera . . .* and all of those kinds of shows that my voice would lend itself to.

I'm not sure how to define my voice, but it is something that resonates with shows like *Rudolph*. I don't know. I didn't want to be too self-conscious about it. Because there were elements of me in the voice . . . which I see in all the acting I did.

I have taught voice-over classes over the years, and I would tell my students to focus on what makes "you unique . . . is you. Anybody can read these lines . . . but only you can do them like you. And that's what's special. And if they like it, they like it, and if they don't, they don't. But we all have that extra something that we *bring to the party*."

And I think that was the case with me which is why my voice worked for promoting Rudolph. I guess there is certain energy and friendliness . . . warmth . . . to my voice. But I feel like I can't really take any credit for it. I mean, the way you sound is the way you sound.

CHAPTER 16

A CHARLIE BROWN CHRISTMAS LIKE NO OTHER

"I can tell you what Christmas is all about, Charlie Brown. Lights, please."

—Linus

Bob Barnett remembered "sitting in front of our old television set with its rabbit-ear antennas, waiting for the annual broadcast of *A Charlie Brown Christmas*. The moment that tiny tree drooped under the weight of a single ornament I couldn't help but feel for Charlie Brown. The music, especially the song 'Linus and Lucy,' always brought a smile to my face. And Linus's speech about the true meaning of Christmas? It made my heart swell with the warmth of the season."

With good reason, as that speech includes this passage from the Bible, "for unto you is born this day in the city of David, a Savior which is Christ the Lord."

A monumental moment in the history of animated Christmas specials, Linus quoting the Bible is indeed historic, in every sense of the word.

Directed by Bill Melendez and written by Charles Schulz, *A Charlie Brown Christmas* clearly had a TV effect in the hearts and minds of viewers like Barnett. In the process, young voice-over talent Peter Robbins made his indelible mark as Charlie Brown in the poignant holiday classic that spawned a series of similar specials for every holiday.

Debuting on CBS in 1965, *A Charlie Brown Christmas* tells of its title character's search for the true meaning of Christmas and the perfect tree. While directing a school play, he finds both, though not before our young low-achiever is confronted by a number of obstacles. None the least of these conflicts is presented by his own dog Snoopy's obsession with winning first prize for a local decorations competition, or by his mean-spirited peers, who mock his choice of a tiny sickly tree.

Through it all, Charlie continues to struggle for peace of mind in his December time, when he is forced to visit with his pseudo-psychologist friend (and foe) Lucy, who offers him a 5¢ therapy session. Following a desperate plea during which he loudly laments, "Isn't there anyone who can tell me what Christmas is all about?!" Charlie Brown finally hears the real deal—from Lucy's younger brother Linus, of all people: "I can tell you," Linus reveals. And in one of the most uniquely animated moments in the history of the genre, Linus goes on to quote the biblical story of the first Christmas.

In a matter of moments, Charlie Brown's misguided pals realize their inconsideration and, with the help and reconfiguration of Snoopy's prize-winning decorations, breathe life into a once-listless tree—further uncovering and "illuminating" the true meaning of Christmas. "Hark! The Herald Angels Sing" these young TV animated angels then all sing.

According to Robert S. Ray:

Charles Schulz and his comic strip *Peanuts* gang of precocious youngsters entered the Christmas TV sweepstakes with *A Charlie Brown Christmas*. At a half hour as opposed to sixty minutes, it seemed more intimate and was profoundly touching in its humor and its bold attempt to bring the focus on the season back to the holy birth that the holiday commemorates. CBS network executives were no doubt nervous because the story criticized the trivialization of Christmas, with its emphasis on decorations, Christmas parties, Jingle Bells and Santa Claus at the expense of the sacred aspects of the day. Charles Schulz and his team of animators and writers, with a big assist from Linus and his remarkable speech, all alone on that empty stage, expertly explains with poignancy just exactly indeed "what Christmas is all about." And the fact that he has been doing it continually for nearly sixty years since tells us that it's a story that needs to be told again and again.

As an aside, the words to "Hark! The Herald Angels Sing" were written in 1739 by Charles Wesley, brother of the founder of the Methodist Church. The melody was composed in 1840 by Felix Mendelssohn as part of his "Canata Frestgesang." Fifteen years later, Dr. W. H. Cummings, the organist of Waltham Abbey in England, combined the words and music, and the new song was presented for the first time on Christmas Day.

Peanuts historian Pat McFadden offered this thorough summation of *A Charlie Brown Christmas*:

It was an instant hit in 1965 when it premiered on CBS, but that astonished the team that created it. Given only six months to take it from concept to completion, Lee Mendelson, producer, and Bill Melendez, animator, thought that they had delivered a sub-par project that would kill any chances of future *Peanuts* films. Their confidence wasn't helped by executives at CBS or Coca-Cola, the special's sponsor, who weren't pleased with the end result. But with less than two weeks before the announced air date of December 9th, CBS had no choice but to present it.

Even Charles "Sparky" Schulz, creator of *Peanuts* and writer of the screenplay for the special, was unsatisfied with it from an artistic standpoint. A perfectionist who drew and lettered his famous comic strip every day with no assistants, Sparky was unhappy with the way the characters were drawn and animated in the film, and still said so even decades after it had become an established classic. (He wasn't at odds with Bill Melendez, who would be Sparky's only animator until he died; he was simply correct that more time was needed to get it looking right.) Bill Melendez was embarrassed that, with such a short time to build an animation team from the ground up, inconsistency among different artists rushing through different shots resulted in Charlie Brown's head varying in size from scene to scene. Even the little tree championed by Charlie Brown for the school play, which one would think might be the easiest object to render, kept shape-shifting, adding or losing limbs, regrowing needles that had fallen off.

But none of this mattered, or was even noticed, by a television audience excited to see their favorite comic strip characters come to life. Some of the elements that the network was initially against—using real kids for the characters' voices instead of professional adult voice-over artists, eschewing the standard laugh track expected for television animation—were not only embraced with ease by the audience, they also set the standard for future animated television specials. Of course, in 1965, there weren't many rules to break. In one way, it was the first of its kind. Unlike preceding specials like *Mr. Magoo's Christmas Carol* and *Rudolph, the Red-Nosed Reindeer*, *Peanuts* wasn't rooted in literature or fantasy, but in the contemporary world, from a child's point of view. As fun as Christmas can be, it can also be a time of confusion and anxiety, for children as well as adults. *A Charlie Brown Christmas* teaches humility in the face of ego, calm in a season of stress, and the reminder that Christmas is simply about giving, with Christianity as an example, but not a rule. These elements of the holiday season don't change between generations, and *A Charlie Brown Christmas* is always hilariously and charmingly relevant.

After the great success of their first outing, the *Peanuts* animation crew continued to produce wonderful specials for decades. The topics were many, but they never forgot their holiday origin, and thus tried to have Charlie Brown and the gang join us for other yearly celebrations and traditions. To varying degrees of success, Easter, Valentine's Day, New Year's Eve, even Arbor Day were covered, but none could compete with "the big three": Halloween, Thanksgiving, and Christmas. These have been the most repeated and praised, and thus, especially for kids and kids at heart, the autumn-to-winter holiday season simply must be accompanied by our favorite faulted friends.

In 1966, Sparky, Bill and Lee took us from a story where Linus has all the answers, to one where he clings to his faith in an unproven, spectacular Secular Squash. *It's the Great Pumpkin, Charlie Brown*, the third *Peanuts* special, was their second holiday home run. It's technically better than *A Charlie Brown Christmas*, and many think it's the best of the *Peanuts* specials overall. The main voice cast returned, and it features fresh beautiful new jazz themes from Vince Guaraldi, now fully orchestrated. In 1973, *A Charlie Brown Thanksgiving* premiered, and it too has become a beloved part of the holiday it celebrates. By that year the voice cast had completely turned over to new kids, although Chris Shea (Linus) was replaced by his brother Stephen (not actor brother Eric, as sometimes assumed). Of "the big three," it is the only one to feature the classic muted trombone adult "voices."

There have even been other *Peanuts* specials about Christmas: *It's Christmastime Again, Charlie Brown* (1992), *Charlie Brown's Christmas Tales* (2002), and *I Want a Dog for Christmas, Charlie Brown* (2003). By the time these were made, the *Peanuts* animation formula had started shifting away from new narratives based on strips, to simply animating the strips themselves, using the exact dialogue and blocking, and freeing up Sparky, since in effect his task as writer was finished before a frame was drawn. This gave these new specials a slower pacing; a punch line every fifteen or twenty seconds that waited for the laugh, as though an adult was reading the strip to a child not old enough to do so alone. This method is great for the younger set but less appealing for adults.

Still, they're not without humor and charm, and even nods to the original Christmas classic. In *Charlie Brown's Christmas Tales*, Snoopy is a sidewalk Salvation Army Santa with an accordion, playing "Oh, Susanna." When Lucy passes and complains that the music isn't Christmassy enough, Santa switches to "Christmastime Is Here," the original song from the original Christmas special. A funnier in-joke occurs in *It's Christmas Time Again, Charlie Brown* (from 1992). Sally asks Linus to tell her the story of the first Christmas, and Linus begins to read, from the Bible, the same passage that he so famously recited in *A Charlie Brown Christmas*. But Sally won't even let him finish a verse, interrupting each attempt with non sequiturs about gifts she hopes to get from Santa, until Linus just sighs and gives up.

Of all these *Peanuts* specials, what makes *A Charlie Brown Christmas* the champ? For one thing it had a head start. Coming first, it's been repeated the most times. In fact, from 1965 until 2021, the special was rerun each year on broadcast television (both *Great Pumpkin* and *Thanksgiving* had years in which they were not broadcast). Today, sadly, "the big three" are only available for purchase on home media or via a paid streaming channel.

Ultimately, though, *A Charlie Brown Christmas* may be the most beloved because it represents a season, not just a day. *A Charlie Brown Christmas* is the messiah of holiday television specials. Other specials give us great stories, but *A Charlie Brown Christmas* gives us a long-lasting feeling. Its story is modern folklore. The snowy *Peanuts* neighborhood is one we all think (or wish) that we've lived in. The voices sound like our friends, or our children. The music is perfect for any holiday occasion. Everyone knows at least one line. It holds up well today, even among big-budget computer-animated Christmas fare. Our love for Sparky's characters and wit makes this modest little film feel epic, just as Charlie Brown's tiny failing tree grows so magically when the gang supplies it with love.

CHAPTER 17
WHEN *THE GRINCH STOLE CHRISTMAS*

"Maybe Christmas, he thought, doesn't come from a store.
Maybe Christmas, perhaps, means a little bit more."

—The Grinch

n 1966, the *Yule Log* TV program, which still airs today, debuted on
WPIX, catering to a New York City viewership who, for the most part,
had no easy access to a fireplace to sit in front of or hang stockings upon
at Christmastime.

That same year, animator Chuck Jones brought Dr. Seuss's *How the
Grinch Stole Christmas!* to television. As Robert S. Ray explained, this special
half hour continued "the annual holiday television parade of specials. Film
buffs like myself were excited by the presence of horror icon Boris Karloff as
the narrator. This one was special too because of its unique Seussian story and
dialogue, with no emphasis on either Santa or the sacred, but a unique tale
of the heart and its literal growth during the season of goodwill. Indeed, that
uniqueness has kept it standing apart from the others over the years."

Premiering December 18, 1966, on CBS, *How the Grinch Stole Christmas!* was directed by Jones and Ben Washam, with a teleplay by Irv Spector
and additional story work by Bob Ogle, based on the beloved 1957 book by
Seuss (a.k.a. Theodore Seuss Geisel, who passed away in 1991). Director
Ron Howard and actor Jim Carrey made a valiant attempt to bring Whoville
to the live-action big screen decades later, but that film does not compare to
the original small-screen rendition—especially due to the vocal brilliance of
Karloff.

Before untraditional animated holiday media fare such as Tim Burton's full-length theatrical film *The Nightmare Before Christmas* was released in 1993, there was television's mere half-hour *How the Grinch Stole Christmas!* an edgy, yet ultimately warmhearted musical that debuted on CBS December 18, 1966, and which has aired every year since.

Seuss had also subsequently penned lyrics to show tunes by Eugene Poddany and Albert Hague, primarily a Broadway-based composer who, after 1980 and until his death in 2001, was also a busy film and TV actor.

Fellow thespian Karloff, a master of horror, vocalized the grumpy *Grinch* lead and doubled as narrator. June Foray, best-known as the voice of Rocky the Squirrel from TV's *Rocky & Bullwinkle* cartoon (and who died in 2017 at age ninety-nine), spoke tiny words as little Cindy Lou Who from the depravedly designed small town of Whoville; Dallas "Dal" McKennon delivered sounds for Max, the sleigh dog that literally helps carry out the Grinch's evil plan to destroy the Whos' Christmas; while Thurl Ravencroft sang the show's theme, "You're a Mean One, Mr. Grinch," and also performed in the chorus for two other songs on the show.

However, the core creative force behind the animated scenes of *The Grinch* was none other than the Academy Award–winning Chuck Jones, who died on February 22, 2002. As one of the directors of Warner Bros.' animated division, the innovative Jones had for years brought to living color the adventures of Bugs Bunny, Daffy Duck, Road Runner, and Wile E. Coyote, among countless other characters from the studio's famed Looney Toons vault.

Jones exited Warner Bros. in 1963 and began animating for Metro-Goldwyn-Mayer (MGM), where he illustrated the popular *Tom and Jerry* shorts and such features as *The Dot and the Line* (1965), based on Norton Juster's short book. Jones won an Oscar for *Dot* as well as the following two films, both produced by Eddie Selzer and released in 1949: *Much for So Little* won in the Short-Subject Documentary division and *For Scent-imental Reasons*, a Pepé Le Pew cartoon, finished first in the Short-Subject Animated Film category.

Seventeen years later, Jones captured the hearts of TV viewers the world over by animating *The Grinch*, which has managed to cut out a unique niche of its own.

Craig Kausen is the president of Chuck Jones Companies, the chairman of the board for the Chuck Jones Center of Creativity nonprofit organization (based in Costa Mesa, California), and grandson to Jones. He explained the events leading up to his heralded grandfather's guiding grasp on *The Grinch*: "Chuck was the most voracious reader that I've ever known. He read everything from the time he was three years old. All kinds of literature found its way into his work, whether directly, as with *The Grinch*, or through the influence of a parody of some sort. Wile E. Coyote was developed in his mind when he was just seven while reading *Roughing It* by Mark Twain. So, it's no surprise that Chuck continuously sought out great stories to bring to light in his mind and then on film."

Once at MGM, Jones reunited with four men who Kausen described as "the great animators from the WB days." Jones also defined those creatives as "actors with pencils": Ken Harris, Lloyd Vaughn, Dick Thompson, and Ben Washam, who co-directed *The Grinch*. "When one of Chuck's team stepped up and took a bigger leadership role he would credit them with co-directing," Kausen said. "But Ben was really an animator because that is really what he did throughout his entire career. He definitely animated on *The Grinch* even though he was credited as co-director. In fact, he was one of the longest-running animators on Chuck's team. He even animated on Chuck's first film, *The Night Watchman*, which was released in 1938."

A few years before his only full-length feature film, *The Phantom Toll-booth*, released in 1970, and following his *Tom & Jerry* shorts, which were written by another of his trusted colleagues from his years at Warner Bros., Michael "Mike" Maltese, Jones began to explore the idea of doing a thirty-minute television special.

By then, Maltese was unavailable, but Phil Roman, who in the 1980s would establish Film Roman studios (which is still going strong today), art director and production designer Maurice Noble, and background painter Phil Deguard, also from Warner Bros., began to work with Jones on what would become *The Grinch* TV special.

But first there was a visit to the doctor, as in Seuss, a.k.a. Ted Geisel. Although they had known each other for decades, Seuss was a tough customer, cynical, and quite protective of the creative license for his work, evidenced even on the license plate of his car, which read: GRINCH.

Seuss was fifty-three years old when his *Grinch* tome was first published in 1957 and, as Kausen tells it, the following lyrical line in the book and subsequent TV special is a direct reference to that age-not-so-old-fact, which also tied into his real-life nature: "For fifty-three years I've put up with it now, I must stop Christmas from coming, but how?" With that one sentence, Kausen said, "Ted was ultimately expressing himself as the Grinch."

Besides *The Grinch*, Jones and Seuss had worked together on such animated features as the *Private Snafu* series of films from the WWII period of 1943–1945, which were designated as "for-soldiers-only" presentations produced largely by the Leon Schlesinger/WB cartoon staff.

After *The Grinch*, Jones drew similar *Grinch*-like small-screen specials based on other of Seuss's books such as *Horton Hears a Who* (CBS, March

19, 1970) and *The Cat in the Hat* (March 10, 1971), the latter of which, along with *The Grinch*, were eventually adapted as live movies for theatrical release (in 2003 and 2000, respectively). "But back in 1965," Kausen said, "it initially took some convincing before Ted agreed to have Chuck adapt *The Grinch* for TV."

Fortunately, after three different lengthy pitch sessions, with various storyboards and the general idea of how to flesh out the story, Seuss relented, trusting Jones's quality of work and vision.

At that point, Jones approached MGM and Roger Mayer (who passed away in 2016) with a projected budget of $370,000 for twenty-three minutes of animation. As Kausen recalled, Mayer looked at Jones and said: "'There is no way that this is going to happen.' Animators like Hanna-Barbera were making weekly half-hour television shows like *The Flintstones* in the low five figures. So, to do something like *The Grinch* for ten times that was just simply way out of the ballpark of anything that anyone had ever done before. And you just couldn't green-light a project and get sponsors, automatically. You had to have sponsors already on board. But Chuck didn't want to compromise his vision for cost."

Consequently, Jones approached the regular suspects like cereal companies and family television supporters, all to no avail. But he wouldn't give up. He created somewhere between four hundred and five hundred colored storyboards that were hand-painted and which, as Kausen said, "really communicated what *The Grinch* was all about. Then he traveled along the West Coast, even went to New York, and made twenty-five pitches there, and received twenty-five rejections."

Finally, Jones journeyed to Chicago, where he made a presentation to the Association of Community Banks, who agreed to a sponsorship, the irony of which did not go unnoticed. Kausen explained: "Commercial banks were now funding an animated TV special that was communicating to the masses the importance of a noncommercial Christmas."

Jones and Seuss then began to collaborate on everything from basic pastels to developing dialogue. Although there was no particular hue given to the Grinch in Seuss's book, the color green was selected for the character by animator Maurice Noble, of Disney's *Fantasia* fame, and whom Kausen called "a master of color and fine art.

"Maurice understood colors so brilliantly," Kausen continued. "He also understood what happens to color on television rather than on the big screen. He knew he needed to add more yellow into the green color to give it the appropriate green he wanted for TV, and Chuck trusted him, while in turn Seuss trusted Chuck."

Although Seuss was not interested in creating new lines that deviated from his original work, Jones was adamant about needing to expand the story for a twenty-three-minute version of the film and character development, which was ultimately implemented with Cindy Lou Who and Max, both of which were given more to do in the TV special than originally drawn out in the book. "It all came together so wonderfully," said Kausen, "all the components in all cylinders."

Entertainment historian Randy Skretvedt is the host of the popular retro radio show *Forward into the Past* (heard on KSPC 88.7 FM in Claremont, California) and the author of several media tie-in books, including his latest, the heralded, *The Magic of Laurel & Hardy*, about the famed silent-screen comedy team. Skretvedt said Karloff "had a magnificent speaking voice and an excellent singing one. It's ironic that he uttered only growls in two of the three movies in which he portrayed the Frankenstein monster, his most famous role [which was ignited by the 1931 big-screen gem of the same name]."

When *The Grinch*'s audio track is listened to carefully, the octaves in Karloff's voice can be heard to vary slightly from narrator to Grinch. Initially, the actor utilized the narrator's vocals throughout the entire half-hour run. After recording was completed, the higher sounds in his performance were then mechanically removed for the more gravely Grinch deliveries heard in the final cut.

While Kausen could not confirm rumors that Seuss had originally disputed Karloff's casting for fear that he would make the Grinch, as a character and a TV show, too frightening, he said Jones was "adamant" about having Karloff lend his iconic voice to the project.

Ravenscroft, best known as the voice of Tony the Tiger in several Frosted Flakes TV commercials, was then selected because of his baritone timbers, if receiving no screen credit for his performance. Seuss subsequently attempted to rectify this by informing all major journalists in America of the truth.

Rightfully so, said Skretvedt, as Ravenscroft's bass singing on "Mean" is "a highlight." Skretvedt went on to define *The Grinch* as one of Seuss's "most original and detailed stories, with a rich variety of characters populating his whimsical rhymed narrative," all created within "a whole world of Whoville that introduced us to many colorful residents."

With its unique music and story, Skretvedt called *The Grinch* "an unusual Christmas special," because unlike fellow TV Christmas classics, such as *Rudolph the Red-Nosed Reindeer* (NBC, 1964), *A Charlie Brown Christmas* (CBS, 1965), and *Frosty the Snowman* (CBS, 1969), its lead character is "anything but warm, cuddly, and sympathetic."

Even *A Christmas Carol*, the Charles Dickens tale oft told in animated and live form, on the small and large screens, is mainly about the redemption of its lead character; in this case, Scrooge. "But the Grinch," said Skretvedt, "gets [to] the Christmas spirit only at the show's end."

Film and television archivist Rob Ray served on the board of directors for the Classic TV Preservation Society nonprofit organization that was based in Los Angeles. He offered his take on what makes *The Grinch* stand separate from *Rudolph*, *Frosty*, *Charlie Brown*, and others:

First and foremost, there is the unique artistry of Chuck Jones. He brought his inimitable design to Dr. Seuss's original illustrations, creating something done exclusively in his own style, while fully capturing the feel of Dr. Seuss, and separating *The Grinch* from other beloved Christmas specials of the era. *Frosty* is typical TV-style limited animation, but more than serviceable for its condensed budget. *Charlie Brown* has an approach and appeal all its own, accented with religious overtones that can't be compared to other mainstream specials beyond *The Little Drummer Boy* (NBC, 1968), which was drawn specifically from a biblical story.

Rudolph and *Drummer Boy*, along with other Christmas favorites *Santa Claus Is Comin' to Town* (ABC, 1970) and *The Year Without a Santa Claus* (ABC, 1974), were from the Arthur Rankin Jr./Jules Bass wheelhouse, mostly known for their stop-motion style of animation (save their *Frosty* franchise), and each filled with what Ray called "a truckload of hummable tunes" and "more akin to a children's musical."

Conversely, Skretvedt said Jones was "the perfect choice" to bring *The Grinch* to life in flowing animation, as his earlier work for Warner Bros., such as the 1957 Bugs Bunny feature short, *What's Opera, Doc?* "had a richness and a delicate quality unlike that brought upon by other cartoon directors."

Or as Craig Kausen concluded, Dr. Seuss's *How the Grinch Stole Christmas!* "encapsulates the essence of Christmas, which at its core, has to do with the deeper bond between people. It's about the humanity that finally broke through the callous heart of the Grinch, how he learned to utilize the strength of 'ten-Grinches plus two' to change who he was for the betterment of himself and his place in Whoville, in the world and beyond."

CHAPTER 18
CRICKET ON THE HEARTH IN THOMASVILLE

"So light of spirit; so rough upon the surface, but so gentle at the core."

—Charles Dickens, *Cricket on the Hearth*

In what is assuredly one of the most uniquely monumental father-daughter pairings in the history of television entertainment, Danny Thomas and Marlo Thomas partnered with Rankin/Bass and executive producer Aaron Spelling for the one-hour animated TV production *Cricket on the Hearth*. A traditionally drawn adaptation by Japanese-studio Eiken (then known as Television Corporation of Japan), this is by far one of Charles Dickens' more obscure Christmas tales.

Premiering on NBC in 1967, *Cricket on the Hearth* was presented as the twelfth episode of *The Danny Thomas Show*, which featured opening and closing live interstitials by Danny Thomas. As Marlo Thomas soared to success in ABC's second hit season of *That Girl*, and Spelling unknowingly awaited what would be his and that same network's tremendous success with *The Mod Squad* the following fall, *Cricket* followed NBC's *Rudolph the Red-Nosed Reindeer* as the second of Rankin/Bass's eighteen Christmas TV productions.

As with *Rudolph*, and later *Frosty the Snowman*, and *Santa Claus Is Comin' to Town*, and others, *Cricket in the Hearth* is narrated by a celebrity voice, this time, Roddy McDowall as Cricket Crockett (a guardian angel of sorts who, in the book, does not have a name). Mr. Crockett lives in the hearth of a family home owned by the Plummers (named Peerybingles in the book). In retrospect in the future, he explains his involvement with the Plummers, including toy master Caleb (Danny) and his daughter Bertha (Marlo).

Entertainment historian/motivational speaker Bob Barnett recalled: "As a child, I was absolutely captivated by Marlo Thomas's voice. Her portrayal of Bertha was so graceful and kind, and I remember being enchanted by her character's innocence and charm. She brought a sense of wonder and magic to the story. My parents would often tell me how much they admired Danny Thomas as an actor and a person. I remember my dad saying, 'Danny Thomas is a class act,' and I couldn't help but agree. He made things special."

The *Cricket in the Hearth* special is "without a doubt one of my favorites," continued Barnett, the author of *From Boundaries to Boundless Love: Embracing Unconditional Love in Everyday Life.* "Dickens' novel was brought to life in such a captivating way. Its twinkling eyes and wise demeanor made it feel like a true guardian angel, and I couldn't help but believe in its magical abilities."

For Barnett, "*Cricket on the Hearth* has a way of bringing both laughter and tears. There are moments of humor and moments of heartache and, in watching it, we experience these emotions as a family. The shared laughter and occasional sniffles only make the experience all the more special." After first watching the show as a child, Barnett recalled how his family would "often sit in the dimmed living room, still basking in the afterglow of the story. My parents would talk about the importance of kindness and the magic of the holiday season. It was a time for reflection and bonding."

Early on in the hour, *Cricket on the Hearth* presents a serious tone. Upon learning her fiancé Edward (voiced by Ed Ames from TV's *Daniel Boone*) has been lost at sea and is presumably dead, Bertha, in shock, loses her sight (with a form of hysterical blindness), Caleb loses any desire to be useful, and the family loses their home. To keep a proverbial roof over his and Bertha's head and food on their table, Caleb is forced to serve in torment under the selfish watch of Mr. Tackleton. In the process, the latter becomes infatuated with Bertha, as does a mysterious elderly fellow who resembles Bertha's lost love.

A grim near-modern fairy tale in the least, *Cricket on the Hearth* is not your father's average uplifting animated Christmas special and is comparatively different from Dickens' original novella. In the book, several characters see through Edward's not-so-convincing disguise, whereas in the special, his cover is even less convincing. The main characters do not recognize him until Caleb's toys come to life and reveal his identity due to the magic of Christmas Eve (despite their vow of no human communication). Aside from Mr. Crockett, all of the talking toys and animals are created for the TV special and are not in the book. Despite the special's core premise that crickets bring good luck, Crockett's presence in the Plummer home does nothing to prevent that cascade of misfortune that strikes the family . . . including losing the hearth that is his home.

Besides *Cricket on the Hearth*, Marlo Thomas performed with her father in two episodes of *That Girl*. In his first episode, "My Sister's Keeper," which aired February 6, 1969, the father Thomas has a cameo role as just that, a father, as in "priest." Marlo's Ann Marie bumps into him ("Excuse me, Father." "That's alright my child.") near the end of the episode, during a Catholic church rectory visit to listen to a singing nun. The sister is played by Marlo's real-life sister, Terre Thomas, while their brother, Tony Thomas, also appears in the episode.

The second *That Girl* episode in which Danny Thomas appears is titled "Those Friars," which, as its title might imply otherwise, has nothing to do with men of the cloth, but rather the men of the Friars Club in New York. Originally airing January 8, 1971, "Those Friars" features Danny Thomas more prominently as himself, singing and dancing with Marlo's Ann Marie. Adding more flavor to the mix is guest star Milton Berle (playing himself).

Five years later, the TV tables are turned when Marlo Thomas makes a guest appearance in her father's short-lived, but classic sitcom, *The Practice*, which originally ran on NBC from 1976 to 1977. In the episode "Judy Sinclair," which aired October 17, 1976, Marlo plays the title character, a divorcée who refuses to be separated from her mentally disabled child to undergo hospital tests.

On whichever TV platform the talented Thomas family act was performed, Marlo reveled in the experience. "It was great fun," she said. "I just adored working with my father. We loved working and playing opposite each other." Concerning her ABC sitcom *That Girl*, Marlo never received any brass objections from that network to the *relatively* historic moment when she appeared with her father on the *Cricket* portion of his opposing NBC network show. Conversely, the senior Thomas did not receive any complaints from NBC about having an ABC star on his show. Any potential issues failed to materialize mostly because, as Marlo mused, "It helps to have a father like Danny Thomas."

Following its premiere during an episode of *The Danny Thomas Show*, *Cricket on the Hearth* screened just once, and it later resurfaced on PBS in the 2000s and in 2019 on Freeform's 25 Days of Christmas marathon. The special, owned by NBCUniversal, which holds the rights to the pre-1973 Rankin/Bass library, has been reissued on several media platforms.

CHAPTER 19
THE LITTLE DRUMMER BOY'S DILEMMA

"Blessed are the pure in heart, for they shall see God."

—Narrator, *The Little Drummer Boy*

n 1968, NBC aired *The Little Drummer Boy*, originally subtitled *Gift of Love*, another holiday production from the Rankin/Bass wheelhouse. Two years after CBS got heavy with *A Charlie Brown Christmas*, the then-nicknamed Peacock Network countered with its own relatively deep and spiritual take on an animated Christmas TV special. Based on the classic tune, this poignant special featured the vocal character prowess of José Ferrer, Paul Frees, and June Foray, with narration by Greer Garson and featuring Teddy Eccles as Aaron, the leading Little Drummer Boy character.

In July 2023, renowned writer Rick Goldschmidt interviewed Eccles for *Remind Magazine* regarding several of the actor's benchmark TV and film appearances, including and in addition to *The Little Drummer Boy* (which Goldschmidt discusses in the twentieth anniversary edition of his book, *The Enchanted World of Rankin/Bass: A Portfolio*).

Over the years, Eccles has lent his voice and acting talents to various TV productions. His premiere performance was as Christopher Robin in Bil Baird's marionette puppet rendition of "Winnie the Pooh" for *Shirley Temple's Storybook* series in 1960. As Goldschmidt noted, Eccles "recited some amazing lines of dialogue for a [then] five-year-old!"

Some of Eccles's live-action TV appearances include *The Munsters, The Beverly Hillbillies, Mr. Ed*, and the Christmas episode of *The Lucy Show*, titled, "Lucy the Choirmaster." His body of work also includes Sid & Marty Krofft's live-action series *Dr. Shrinker* and lending his voice as Dorno to

Hanna-Barbera's *The Herculoids* and as Tooly in Hanna-Barbera's *The Three Musketeers*, which was part of *The Banana Splits Adventure Hour*.

As Eccles told Goldschmidt, for the Hanna-Barbera productions, he recorded with the other actors during sessions in recording booths. "For *The Little Drummer Boy*," Eccles said, "I recorded at a microphone in the middle of a studio and Arthur Rankin Jr. read the other actors' lines to me for about two hours. Then Arthur gave me a tape of a song he wanted me to rehearse and come back to the studio to sing. I began to panic a bit. I was not a good singer."

For *The Lucy Show* Christmas episode, he "sang so poorly" Ball instructed him to merely mouth the lyrics to "The Twelve Days of Christmas."

Eccles was then cast in the 1968 movie classic *In Cold Blood*. Subsequently, his agent informed *Drummer* producer Rankin that Eccles had to begin making the movie immediately. In consequence, Arthur hired Dick Beals (Speedy Alka-Seltzer TV commercial character) to sing "Why Can't the Animals Smile?" in *The Little Drummer Boy*. "I thought he did an excellent job of capturing my voice. He made me look good!" Eccles told Goldschmidt.

After completing his first book, Goldschmidt befriended Beals, who had forgotten he worked with Rankin/Bass Productions. "I actually reminded him that he sang the song," Goldschmidt noted.

Today, Eccles goes by Ted, is in his sixties, and is married with a daughter. He's a TV producer and film editor. Years after lending his voice to *The Little Drummer Boy*, Eccles worked for LIVE Entertainment, a production company owned by Jose Menéndez, who was murdered by his sons, which resulted in a famous media trial. As fate would have it, Eccles has also worked on the trailers for *The Little Drummer Boy* and *Frosty the Snowman* video releases. At present, he's milling through ten million feet of Fox Movietone, non-Disney-acquired footage (red carpet and other live events from 1948 to 1973).

Meanwhile, Goldschmidt concluded: "Ted's performance as Aaron in *The Little Drummer Boy* is cherished by many fans; in fact, the special is one of Rankin/Bass's finest!"

The Little Drummer Boy, however, has its detractors. Robert S. Ray, for one, was "somewhat put off by Rankin/Bass's attempt to turn to something closer to the biblical Nativity story, by the fact that the lead character, the Drummer Boy, is unlikeable until the very end, with a constant scowl on his face and a sharpness in his voice. José Ferrer's Ben Haramad, who kidnaps the Drummer Boy and forces him into child labor, did not endear me to the story either. But it's a moving tale, perhaps too mature for its intended audience. The regal voice of Greer Garson as the narrator also made this one seem like a school assignment rather than something to be embraced. After a few years, this one, like *Mr. Magoo's Christmas Carol*, drifted into semi-obscurity until it turned up on Rankin/Bass Christmas video collections."

Commencing in the early 1990s, some viewers protested the production for its less than positive presentation of Arab characters. Detroit TV station WJBK halted screening the special after public scrutiny from Arab-American viewers in the area.

In early October 2023, ScreenRant.com's Zachary Moser said such "complaints stemmed from what [viewers] saw as a racist portrayal of the characters and a stereotypical charge at Arab people of being wealth desiring, child abductors. The response to backlash against *The Little Drummer Boy* by completely removing it from the air is a touch more active than how some studios respond to backlash regarding older films in the modern era. In the era of streaming, when dealing with inappropriate content, many streamers have elected to provide a warning at the front of their film."

An earlier report was documented by UPI on December 13, 1991. Carolyn Wofford, WJBK's program director, said: "We serve the community and we have a large population of Arab-Americans in Detroit. One of their concerns is that it gives negative connotations to Arabs just as the (Arab-Israeli) peace talks are going on."

Arabs complained to WJBK that the special depicts Arabs as heavy, unattractive, hook-nosed abductors who take a Jewish boy named Aaron after his parents are murdered by Arab bandits. As Jack Shaheen, then a communications professor at Southern Illinois University in Edwardsville, told UPI at the time, "What these two Arabs do is try to exploit Aaron to make a buck. They think they can be rich if they make Aaron play the drum for a crowd in the marketplace. They then force Aaron to sell his camel and they take the money."

The Arab characters Ben and Ali, Shaheen said, are never allowed to alter their evil behavior. He said Ben is described as having "gold and silver on his mind and mischief in his soul." In place of *The Little Drummer Boy* that year, WJBK screened, *Yes, Virginia, There Is a Santa Claus.*

CHAPTER 20
FROSTY'S EVOLUTION

"Happy Birthday!"

—Frosty, as spoken by Jackie Vernon in *Frosty the Snowman*

Due to the increasing popularity of the NBC-turned-CBS small-screen classic *Rudolph the Red-Nosed Reindeer*, Rankin/Bass Productions was called upon by the latter network to adapt *Frosty the Snowman*, another pop Christmas tune, as a television special.

Premiering on December 7, 1969, *Frosty the Snowman* was based on the holiday music hit composed by Jack Rollins and Steve Nelson and performed and made popular by Gene Autry in the 1950s. But whereas *Rudolph* was created as a one-hour special with stop-action photography, TV's frothy *Frosty* became a thirty-minute production drawn in traditional animation. That happened mostly because the show sought to present the look and feel of a Christmas card come to life. Traditional cel animation also allowed for techniques that were challenging to create and showcase with Animagic, such as having Frosty, upon coming to life, leap about when he utters his first famous words, "Happy Birthday!"

Penned by Romeo Muller, *Frosty* more than capably rides on *Rudolph's* deer-tails. Considered Rankin/Bass's second most successful special to air on "old-school" TV broadcast channels, *Frosty* is the longest-running animated TV special to have consecutively aired annually on its original network. In a further mimic-nod to Rankin/Bass colleagues Burl Ives on *Rudolph* before him and Fred Astaire in *Santa Claus Is Comin' to Town* after him, entertainer Jimmy Durante serves as narrator on *Frosty the Snowman*. The story of the title character, voiced by Jackie Vernon, goes like this:

In 1969, on Christmas Eve, when many students still attended school, a band of doe-eyed schoolchildren are bored in class by the mishap magic of Professor Hinkle (voiced by Billy "Busy, busy, busy" De Wolfe). Fascinated, and near obsessed with the first snow of Christmas (which later plays a magical part in their lives) via their old-fashioned schoolhouse window, the children are eager to go outside and play in the Christmas-vacation snow. Led by Karen (June Foray), the young troupe construct a snowman they name Frosty. By the magical winds of change, they unknowingly place what turns out to be Professor Hinkle's magic hat on Frosty's head. As a result, Frosty comes to life.

Soon after, Karen, Frosty, and the gang make their own kind of happy music, until that is, everyone notices the winter air's hot temperature by way of an oddly placed outside thermostat. Feeling the heat and fear that Frosty's very life would melt away, he, Karen, and Professor Hinkle's wayward rabbit Hocus Pocus trek to the North Pole to derail any potential real deep freeze. But the villainous Professor Hinkle is hot on their trail and will stop at nothing to retrieve his magic hat for evil purposes. And that includes locking Frosty and Karen in a greenhouse.

However, despite the sad greenhouse effect's temperature scene in which we see Frosty melt into a crystal blue puddle of water, and Karen subsequently crying, Santa Claus arrives to save the day (as he usually does). With an enchanting gust of twirling wind, Frosty's core water crystals, made of that magical first Christmas snow, are revived. Alive once more, Frosty re-utters his famous first words ("Happy Birthday!"), and he, with Karen in tow, return to her hometown. There he leads a parade of happy citizens, including an apparently transformed Professor Hinkle.

In formulating *Frosty the Snowman*, which *TV Guide* once ranked as No. 9 on its 10 Best Family Holiday Specials, Rankin/Bass envisioned a Christmas card motif. The team hired Paul Coker Jr., a greeting card and *Mad* magazine artist, to design the core, well-drawn character and stunning detailed background images. The actual animation was produced by Mushi Productions in Tokyo, Japan, with Yusaku "Steve" Nakagawa and then-Mushi employee Osamu Dezak (uncredited), among other staff members.

With the *Frosty* special, Jimmy Durante rerecorded the title song, if with slightly different lyrics, years after being the first to initially do so when it was released in 1950. Originally, June Foray voiced Karen, the teacher, and other children. But Karen and the majority of the kids' voices were replaced with those of actual-age children prior to the special's debut. The end credits did not change. In late 2017, some sources began listing Suzanne Davidson as the performer who provided the new voices, while the original voices may still

112

be heard on the original MGM soundtrack, rereleased years later by Rhino. Rankin/Bass stalwart Paul Frees delivers his usually fine performances. Those include his bit as the traffic cop who swallows a whistle after chatting with Frosty and as Santa, who at one point, instructs Hinkle to write, "I am very sorry for what I did to Frosty" one zillion times.

One year after the traditionally drawn *Frosty the Snowman* premiered on CBS, Rankin/Bass returned to its Animagic technique with *Santa Claus Is Comin' to Town*'s arrival on ABC. Frees was back in the fold, this time voicing the villainous Burgermeister Meisterburger. But not only did *Frosty*'s success, and that of *Rudolph*'s and *Magoo*'s before him, inspire *Santa Claus* to come to TV town, the *Frosty* special proved so successful, a few *Snowman* sequels followed, if each somewhat lacking the charm of the original.

Frosty's Winter Wonderland premiered on ABC, December 2, 1976, and was produced by Rankin/Bass, with animation by Topcraft. Romeo Muller wrote the script, which featured character designs by Paul Coker Jr. and music composed by Maury Laws. Jackie Vernon returned as Frosty's voice, while Andy Griffith was the narrator (replacing Jimmy Durante, who had been incapacitated by a stroke three years prior and retired from acting). Other voices in the cast also include those from Shelley Winters and Dennis Day.

The rights to this special are held by Warner Bros. Television Distribution by way of Telepictures, which used to license the show to Freeform. The latter screen the special every year during its 25 Days of Christmas marathon. But then in 2018, the license was attained by AMC. In 2001, Rankin/Bass dissolved, and the TV rights to their library was divided into two sectors (specials produced before and after 1974). As such, *Frosty's Winter Wonderland* was separated from the original *Frosty the Snowman* special.

On November 25, 1979, ABC premiered *Rudolph and Frosty's Christmas in July* (titled on-screen as *Rudolph and Frosty: Christmas in July*, or simply *Rudolph and Frosty*), an American-Japanese Christmas/Independence Day television special produced by Rankin/Bass. It was filmed in Japan with the company's trademark Animagic stop-action animation technique.

This was the last Rankin/Bass special to star Billie Mae Richards as Rudolph and Jackie Vernon as Frosty. Mickey Rooney reprised his role as Santa Claus from 1970's *Santa Claus Is Comin' to Town* and 1974's *The Year Without a Santa Claus*. Additional voices were provided by Alan Sues, Red Buttons, Ethel Merman, and Paul Frees, the latter two reprising their roles as Frosty's wife, Crystal, and Jack Frost from *Frosty's Winter Wonderland*, while Hal Peary reprised his role as Big Ben the Clockwork Whale from *Rudolph's Shiny New Year*.

This was also the final Rankin/Bass special to utilize the Rudolph and Frosty roles. All other specials/films starring the characters were produced by other companies.

On December 1, 1992, *Frosty Returns* premiered on CBS, which by that time now owned the telecast rights to the original *Frosty* special. Consequently, CBS produced *Frosty Returns* as a companion sequel, if with a different cast, style, and production team. *Returns* featured the vocal talents of Jonathan Winters as the narrator and John Goodman, then the main male star on ABC's super-successful *Roseanne* sitcom, in the title lead. This was Goodman's premiere voice-over performance, which led to several more in other TV shows, as well as TV-movies, big-screen motion pictures, and video games.

Produced by Lorne Michaels' Broadway Video, with assistance from *Peanuts* TV veteran director Bill Melendez and Evert Brown, *Frosty Returns* features music by Mark Mothersbaugh and the supporting vocal talents of the great Billy De Wolfe (*The Doris Day Show*) and Rankin/Bass stalwarts Paul Frees and June Foray.

Due to Michaels' involvement, most of the cast consisted of sketch comedians from his other shows: Andrea Martin (*The Hart and Lorne Terrific Hour*), Jan Hooks and Brian Doyle-Murray (*SNL*, on which John Goodman frequently made guest appearances). Since Broadway Video produced this special and owned the 1969 original prior to Golden Books' acquisition of the Videocraft International catalog in 1996, *Frosty Returns* follows the CBS showings of the original and is coupled with the original on most DVD releases; it was not included in the package sold to Freeform's 25 Days of Christmas cable telecasts, nor the package sold to AMC's Best Christmas Ever.

Frosty Returns has not been well-received over the years. In his review on IMDb.com from November 28, 2003, Homer3428 called it, "In a word: awful. . . . This is a story about some greedy bad guys who seek to exploit Frosty and ruin his good name with a terrible product and shoddy politics. . . . The jokes are weak and just not funny. . . . The songs are dreadfully flat. . . . The bad guy is a corporate type who doesn't care if his product is bad for the environment. C'mon, guys—this is a children's special. Frosty is now fashion conscious. There's no Christmas and no Santa."

On December 15, 2005, on IMDb.com, JosephBrando15 labeled his review of *Frosty Returns* as "A mockery of the original classic!" As he went on to explain, "Gone is the lovable, dim-witted, huggable Frosty we remember. He has been replaced by the father on *Roseanne* in both voice and action. He makes sarcastic wisecracks, dances, and doesn't even need his hat to come to life!"

On December 12, 2008, Steve_Nylan12 titled his IMDb *Returns* review as "Appalling." As he went on to delineate: "This has to be the worse holiday special ever, and I've seen *A Louie Anderson Christmas*, which at least had a couple of subtle laughs in it. . . . First off, Christmas is gone, which is odd considering that Frosty is supposed to be a children's Christmas character. They even took his pipe away since we all know that smoking snowmen will be a bad influence on kids. . . . Also, the whole 'miracle' of Frosty's creation is utterly ignored . . . making the choice of Frosty as the focal character arbitrary and meaningless."

On December 14, 2005, TheUnknown837-1 described *Frosty Returns* as "[not] bad at all."

In another entirely different universe, *The Legend of Frosty the Snowman* appeared in 2005 as a direct-to-video animated film produced by Classic Media, Studio B Productions, and Top Draw Animation. Burt Reynolds served as the narrator, with Bill Fagerbakke as the voice of Frosty and Kath Soucie as Tommy Tinkerton. With background music provided by Jared Faber, this was the fifth and final TV special to star Frosty.

Once more, however, none of the *Frosty* sequels compared to the original, 1969 TV special, which includes poignant quotes like this: "There's a certain magic that comes with the very first snow. For when the first snow is also a Christmas snow, well, something wonderful is bound to happen."

CHAPTER 21
THE YEARS WITH AND WITHOUT A SANTA CLAUS

"Put one foot in front of the other . . ."

—Santa Claus, in *Santa Claus Is Comin' to Town*

Since the dawn of Christmastime, Santa Claus has been known by several different names—St. Nicholas, St. Nick, Father Christmas, Belsnickel, and Kris Kringle. The surname of the latter is an Americanized pronunciation of the South German Christlkind or "Christ Child," a relic from a period when the region believed the infant Jesus was the bearer of gifts on Christmas Eve.

Flash forward a few millennia to ABC in 1969 with *Santa Claus Is Comin' to Town*, directed by Bass and Rankin and written by Romeo Muller. With a nod to *Rudolph the Red-Nosed Reindeer*, *Comin' to Town* is another smart Christmas tale that expands on the popularity of a Christmas song. This time, a charming tale is thread around the origins of St. Nick, here voiced by Mickey Rooney. Also along for this TV sleigh ride is big-screen dancing-legend Fred Astaire, serving as narrator, in much the same capacity as Burl Ives performed on *Rudolph* and Jimmy Durante on *Frosty the Snowman*. Astaire portrays the Christmas Mailman, while additional vocal support is heard from Keenan Wynn as the Winter Warlock, Paul Frees as Burgermeister Meisterburger, Joan Gardner, and Robie Lester as Jessica, Kris Kringle's love-interest-turned Mrs. Santa Claus.

However, *Comin' to Town* belongs to the man himself, Rooney's Santa, who the Kringle family of toy-making elves find as an abandoned baby at the door of their North Pole abode. The infant is wrapped in a blanket with only a name tag that says CLAUS. The elves name him Kris, who they adopt into their family and their family business. Eventually frustrated that the elves make toys that ultimately pile up with no children to give them to, Kris ventures through the frigid woods, faces head-on the diabolic Winter Warlock, and eventually makes his way to the Christmastown to distribute the toys to children.

In the process, Kris Kringle, trim and slim with a red beard, and as a not-yet-fully christened Mr. Claus, meets his future wife, Jessica, a young schoolteacher. At first, Jessica objects to what she views as his outlandish behavior, until Kris charms her with a special present of her own: a China doll.

The two fall in love and get married by the Winter Warlock, and a revisionary tale of how Kris Kringle becomes completely Santa continues to unfold. The Winter Warlock (like Bumble, the Abominable snow monster in *Rudolph the Red-Nosed Reindeer*) reforms his diabolical ways, while the tyrant Burgermeister Meisterburger eventually passes away. It's the Warlock's magic that helps Santa's reindeer fly on the first Christmas Eve, visually and poignantly represented with a shining star in the sky and the image of Kris kneeling. With an ever-so-brief visual nod to *Rudolph*, *Santa Claus Is Comin' to Town* goes down in TV history as the second most popular entry from the Rankin/Bass stable of Animagic specials.

Robert S. Ray observed: "In 1970, Rankin/Bass returned to familiar *Rudolph the Red-Nosed Reindeer* territory with *Santa Claus is Comin' to Town*. It slavishly follows the formula set by *Rudolph* with a lighthearted expansion of a popular holiday secular song into a tale complete with Santa, his soon-to-be wife, reindeer, elves, and a villain who lurks in the woods, threatening our heroes until he's redeemed before the story's end. We had seen it all before in *Rudolph*, but what it lacked in originality it more than made up for with its spirited animation and a collection of catchy and sometimes genuinely moving songs."

By the time *Santa Claus Is Comin' to Town* originally aired, Ray was "getting a bit older, and getting somewhat immune to the charms of the stop-motion specials. But that's my loss, for *Santa Claus Is Comin' to Town* is one of the better holiday specials and rightly deserves its place in the canon of holiday treats still airing over airwaves on ABC and elsewhere."

Four years after Kris Kringle first jingled on ABC, he came back to the network with *The Year Without a Santa Claus*. Bass and Rankin also came back as directors, and Mickey Rooney returned as Santa, this time joined by Shirley Booth (from TV's *Hazel* sitcom) as Mrs. Claus in a witty romp that may be subcoded, *Santa Takes a Holiday*. In the script, penned by William Keenan and based on the novel by Phyllis McGinley, Santa's physician makes him feel obsolete. As a result, the Jolly One doesn't feel so jolly and decides to keep a low profile and take a year off this Christmas Eve. Aghast, Mrs. Claus sends two elves, Jingle and Jangle, to find proof that people still believe in Christmas. In the end, they do just that, and Santa joyfully returns to his rotund duties with a new vigor.

A sophisticated animated tale, with character textures never so fully seen before, *The Year Without a Santa Claus* presents an astounding message with a lovely story, elevated dialogue, and poignant and pristine dialogue.

Said Robert S. Ray: "In 1974, Rankin/Bass returned to the tried-and-true *Rudolph* formula once again with this story of what happens when Santa decides to take a year off from his annual trek. Oscar-winning actress Shirley Booth is engaging as Mrs. Santa Claus, but the threads of the successful Rankin/Bass formula are really starting to show here. Younger boomers may fondly remember this one for its somewhat campy 'Snow Miser–Heat Miser' feud accompanied in songs sung by Dick Shawn and George S. Irving, but it's all rather forced and lacking in the charm of the earlier successes."

This cartoon proved so impressive it spawned a live-action TV-movie. On December 11, 2006, NBC (not ABC) premiered the remake with the same title, *The Year Without a Santa Claus*, which was produced by David L. Wolper and Warner Bros. The following day, the film, which largely followed the same plot as the original animated special, was released on DVD. The redo boasted a stellar cast including John Goodman as Santa Claus, Delta Burke as Mrs. Claus, Michael McKean as Snow Miser, Harvey Fierstein as Heat Miser, Carol Kane as Mother Nature, and, among others, Jack LaLanne as Hercules.

By this time, Goodman's name had almost become synonymous with Christmas specials. In 1992, he offered his vocal rendition of Frosty for the *Frosty Returns* sequel (replacing Jackie Vernon in the original). In 1997, Goodman led another strong cast (including Jim Broadbent, Mark Williams, and Celia Imry) for a live-action feature-film adaptation of *The Borrowers* (directed by Peter Hewitt).

However, as Paul Mavis once noted for the now-defunct DrunkTV.com, the 2006 live-action remake of *The Year Without a Santa Claus* is "a nauseating, angry, joyless little holiday confection sure to poison any child unlucky enough to chance upon it. This hate-filled stocking stuffer has nothing but contempt for its intended audience, promoting the worst possible beliefs about people, while cloaking itself, incredibly, in the fake guise of a meaningful lesson about the holidays: the gall that the cretinous makers of this film have is really quite audacious."

On December 13, 2008, ABC Family aired *A Miser Brothers' Christmas*, a direct-to-video one-hour sequel to the original animated *Year Without a Santa*

Claus produced by Warner Bros. Animation and Cuppa Coffee Studios. This follow-up not only utilized the famed stop-action technique, but a by-then-eighty-eight-year-old Mickey Rooney reprised his role as Santa, while George S. Irving, at age eighty-six, revitalized his vocal cords for a return performance as the Heat Miser. Juan Chioran and Catherine Disher replaced Dick Shawn (who died in 1987) and Shirley Booth (who died in 1992) as Snow Miser and Mrs. Claus.

CHAPTER 22

ALASTAIR'S ALTERNATE *SCROOGE*

"God bless us, everyone."

—Tiny Tim

On December 21, 1971, a new animated half-hour British-American Christmas special premiered on ABC. Unlike NBC's hour-long *Rudolph the Red-Nosed Reindeer*, or CBS's thirty-minute *Frosty the Snowman*, this particular special was not based on a beloved Christmas *song* but a Christmas carol, literally, as in Charles Dickens' *A Christmas Carol*.

A serious drama with wry humor, as opposed to previous animated specials with broader humor sprinkled with dramatic elements, the ABC special (which, technically, clocked in at twenty-two minutes) was directed by Richard Williams, with a visual style by Ken Harris, who is credited as "Master Animator." It was Harris who teamed with legendary Looney Tunes Warner Bros. animated legend Chuck Jones for what became the longest partnership between an animator and a director at the studio.

Jones oversaw production of *How the Grinch Stole Christmas!* TV special, served as executive producer on ABC's 1971 *A Christmas Carol*, which was produced by Zoran Janjic and written by Michael Robinson. This special further distinguished itself with the vocal prowess of Alastair Sim as Scrooge and Michael Hordern as Marley's Ghost. Both actors had reprised their vocal expertise in those roles from the 1951 live-action movie adaptation of *A Christmas Carol*, originally titled *Scrooge*. In key critical sectors, that film is considered the ideal screen interpretation of the Dickens classic.

However, it is the Williams/Janjic/Robinson animated TV special that introduced the Dickens tale to a mainstream viewership of all ages. For many children, up until this point, "cartoons" meant merely watching *Scooby-Doo, Where Are You?* and *The Archies* on Saturday morning or the aforementioned *Frosty* and *Rudolph* specials in prime time.

Unlike other previous animated adaptations of *A Christmas Carol*, the 1971 ABC special includes scenes of miners and sailors singing carols that were left out in previous adaptations. Animation for the unique half hour was created by multiple pans and zooms and unexpected scene transitions. The visual style was inspired by nineteenth-century engraved illustrations of the original story by John Leech and the pen-and-ink renderings by illustrator Milo Winter that illustrated the 1930s editions of the book. The film's dark tone and visuals led some to label it the most frightening of any Dickens adaptation on the big screen or small, animated or live.

According to what TV viewer Peter McCulloch observed on TVParty .com: "Aside from the usual classics like *Rudolph* and *Frosty*, one of my fondest childhood Christmas memories was an animated version of *A Christmas Carol* produced in 1971 that aired for a few years thereafter and featured the voices of Alastair Sim and Michael Redgrave. This was a superbly animated and very creepy version with a very unique Victorian animation style."

One year after its TV debut, the 1971 UK/US hybrid proved so popular it was released as a theatrical feature film. Subsequently, in 1972, it was nominated and won an Academy Award, which proved to be a controversial choice. More than a few in the industry complained because the film had made its TV debut and should not have been recognized by the Academy as a feature. The Academy responded by changing its policy, disqualifying any future works initially shown on television eligibility.

In his book *A Christmas Carol and Its Adaptations*, author Fred Guida writes that the TV special "is widely considered the best animated version" of the story, praising the animation and the return of Sim and Horden, noting that "tribute is being paid to the (1951) film," noting the mannerisms of the animated Scrooge and the deception of Old Joe being a "dead ringer for . . . (1951 performer) Miles Malleson." Despite criticizing the special's brevity, Guida called the special "one of the most faithful of all adaptations," noting it includes scenes often left out of adaptations, in particular the Ghost of Christmas Present showing Scrooge how Christmas is celebrated on a remote lighthouse and on a ship at sea.

The special's director, Richard Williams, who died in 2019, was a Canadian-British animator, voice actor, and painter. A three-time Oscar winner, Williams is best known as director of *Who Framed Roger Rabbit* (1988), for which he won two Academy Awards, and as the director of the unfinished feature film *The Thief and the Cobbler* (1993). His other work includes the title sequences for *What's New Pussycat?* (1965) and *A Funny Thing Happened on the Way to the Forum* (1966), the title and linking sequences in *The Charge of the Light Brigade*, and the intros for two of the later *Pink Panther* movies. From 2008 he worked as artist in residence at Aardman Animations in Bristol, and in 2015, Williams received both Oscar and BAFTA nominations in the best animated category for his short film *Prologue*.

However, it was Williams' work on *A Christmas Carol* of 1971 that earned him his first Academy Award, that being for the Best Animated Short Film of 1972.

In addition to Alastair Sim, the 1971 animated *A Christmas Carol* also featured the vocal talents of Diana Quick as Ghost of Christmas Past, Joan Sims as Mrs. Cratchit, Paul Whitsun-Jones as Fezziwig/Old Joe, David Tate as Fred/Charity Man, Felix Felton as Ghost of Christmas Present, Annie West as Belle, Melvyn Hayes as Bob Cratchit, Mary Ellen Ray as Mrs. Dilber, and Alexander Williams as Tiny Tim, though uncredited.

Williams, the son of director Richard Williams, went on to work as an animator for Disney and DreamWorks, gaining more than thirty years of eclectic experience working on films *Who Framed Roger Rabbit*, *The Lion King*, and the final three *Harry Potter* films.

In 2012, Williams founded an online animation school, Animation Apprentice. He also founded the world's first online-based MA in animation at Buckinghamshire New University, beginning in September 2015. His students have gone on to work in the animation industry at studios such as ILM, Blue Zoo, BBC Studios, Discovery Channel, Jellyfish, Cloth Cat, and many others in the expanding global animation industry.

In recalling his working experience on *A Christmas Carol* of 1971, Williams said: "We may as well have done the whole thing on fast forward." Williams was only three-years-old when he lent his voice for the special. "I do remember them giving me ice cream as a reward for my doing the recording. It is hard to record with kids. But I was the right age and had the right voice.

"It means a lot to me," he went on to say, "because I was in it and it was Dad's work and he won an Oscar for it. I think, if you read Dickens, there is brilliant language. Very powerful. It is hard to believe we can boil the whole book down to twenty-two minutes. That is incredible. To animate the style of the nineteenth-century engraving is difficult work. You can see where Dad has gone over the drawings as well."

Williams' father was also responsible for the title and linking sequences in *The Charge of the Light Brigade* (1968) and the intros of the cartoon feline for two of the later *Pink Panther* films. Those were *Return of the Pink Panther*

(1975) and *The Pink Panther Strikes Again* (1976), and he also worked on *Who Framed Roger Rabbit*, released in 1988.

Beyond his father's *Christmas Carol* adaption, Williams noted other animated Christmas TV favorites, such as *A Charlie Brown Christmas* (which he labeled as "lovely") and *The Snowman*, a British import that PBS aired in America. Of the latter, he said: "It may not play that much in the US. But it features a famous song called, 'We're Walking Through the Air.' The special is widely known in the UK."

Although not classified as a Christmas special, *Mr. Rogers' Neighborhood* featured many holiday episodes. Williams acknowledged the show for personal reasons: "My mother was from Virginia [Rogers' home state], and I did spend some time in the US."

Today, Williams is still working in animation and visual effects. "It is fun work. I got to start the department from scratch. I am teaching it in the way that it should be taught, focusing on outcomes and useful skills."

Of his involvement with *A Christmas Carol*, he concluded: "What I do recall is just how hard I had to work" [in doing the voice-over]. With animation, in general, he added, "There are so many standards that go into that detail. So much labor. It takes a lot of time. Old-school, hand-drawn TV animation. Since no two drawings are exactly the same, it has a glimmer effect."

All of which worked for the tone of his father's animated edition of *A Christmas Carol*. "The drawings were sufficiently good. You need that Victorian type of work to take you back in time. The music was great. So was the narration [by Sir Michael Redgrave]."

CHAPTER 23

WHEN *THE ANIMALS TALKED* AND *VIRGINIA* WAS RIGHT

"When what to my wondering eyes did appear . . ."

—Clement Moore

I n 1823, the poem "A Visit from St. Nicholas" was anonymously published for a newspaper in Troy, New York. Though eventually best known as "'Twas the Night Before Christmas," as written by Clement Clarke Moore, some sources have claimed Henry Livingston Jr. composed the rhythmic tale.

However, the original "Visit" was inspired by Washington Irving, who, along with his cousin Pintard, was one of the founding members of the New York Historical Society (and who at one point suggested making St. Nicholas the patron saint of New York). "Old Santeclaus with Much Delight," an illustrated children's poem from 1821, also proved to be an influence for "Visit."

For example, "Delight" established several Claus-connected familiarities, including his alliance with winter and reindeer and his arrival on Christmas Eve, as opposed to St. Nicholas Day. Moore later added his own elements to the Claus mythology, including Santa's roof-landing sleigh and chimney-sliding agility with a sack of toys across his back. Except for Rudolph, Moore created the names for each of Santa's reindeer and aligned Mr. Claus/St. Nicholas with Christmas and a jovial personality.

Approximately one hundred years later, the animated TV adaptation, *'Twas the Night Before Christmas*, debuted in 1974 in the more than capable creative hands of the talented directing team of Rankin/Bass. As written by Jerome Coopersmith and based on the poem by Clement Moore, *'Twas* was steered away from stop-action animation (*Rudolph, Santa Claus Is Comin' to Town*) and headed into the then-more traditional animatronics of the era. What's more, it's also told in a thirty-minute format (as opposed to the aforementioned sixty minutes, though first completed a few years before with *Frosty the Snowman* in 1969). But their style is still evident, especially drawn in the eyes and "heart" of each character. The result: a sweet narrative delivery of a perfect holiday rhyme featuring the voices of Patricia Bright, Scott Firestone, George Gobel (*Hollywood Squares*), Broadway giant and film legend Joel Grey, and Tammy Grimes (the original choice for Samantha on TV's *Bewitched*).

Directed by Shamus Culhane and written by Peter Fernandez, Jan Hartman, and others, this unique special was just about as far away from Dr. Doolittle as you can get. We learn what the animals were thinking at the birth of Christ. They are granted the gift of gab—and we are granted the gift of insight. Mind-boggling—and eons ahead of its time, this special featured the voices of Pat Bright, Ruth Franklin, Bob Kaliban, Len Maxwell, Joe Silver, Frank Porella, and others.

According to Bob Barnett:

> *The Night the Animals Talked* is a reminder that animals, just like humans, have their own voices, even if we don't always understand them. It's like the unspoken bond between people and their pets—that deep connection that goes beyond words. And then, there's the Christmas angle. The story, set on a magical night, resonated with the spirit of Christmas. Christmas, as I've come to understand, isn't just about the material gifts under the tree. It's about the gift of unity, love, and understanding. The animals talking on that special night symbolized that unity, reminding us that we can all come together, no matter our differences.
>
> In a way, it's just as with the biblical Christmas story and the birth of Jesus. It's about hope, love, and the idea that even in the humblest of settings, something extraordinary can happen.

Along the same vein arrived a simple letter to Santa Claus that became a national sensation by way of Francis Pharcellus Church's famed newspaper editorial, "Yes, Virginia, There Is a Santa Claus." In 1897, eight-year-old Virginia O'Hanlon sent a letter to the editor of New York's *The Sun*, requesting to validate the existence of Santa Claus. Veteran journalist Pharcellus composed a response so well-received that it continues to this day to be published in newspapers around the globe every Christmas. In an interview four decades after the fact, O'Hanlon described the response as "overwhelmingly convincing"—as, undoubtably, have the countless children who have transformed the letter, validating Santa's presence.

Eighty years later, in 1974, CBS aired the animated special *Yes, Virigina, There Is a Santa Claus*, based on the editorial. Directed by Bill Melendez (*A Charlie Brown Christmas*) and written by Mort Green, this special featured the vocal talents of Jim Backus (*Mr. Magoo's First Christmas*), Susan Silo, and Courtney Lemon.

Thirty-five years after that, on December 11, 2009, CBS aired a new TV rendition, titled, *Yes, Virginia*, which was created by Wayne Best and Matt MacDonald and produced by JWT Productions, The Ebeling Group, and Starz Animation, with sponsorship from Macy's. This time, the vocal prowess was provided by Bea Miller as Virginia O'Hanlon and Neil Patrick Harris as her father, Philip.

However, as entertainment historian Bob Barnett clarified, it is the 1974 animated special that leaves the highest impact. Growing up in rural Oklahoma during the 1960s and 1970s, the initial small-screen adaptation of *Yes, Virginia, There Is a Santa Claus* resonated with him:

The movie's portrayal of Virginia's earnest inquiry into the existence of Santa Claus mirrored the innocent curiosity that defined my own childhood. The scenes depicting her journey to uncover the truth evoked a sense of familiarity, capturing the essence of small-town life in a way that felt intimately connected to my upbringing in rural Oklahoma.

The editor's heartfelt response, assuring Virginia of Santa's existence, echoed beyond the screen, tugging at the strings of sentiment woven through the holiday seasons of my youth. The special, with its attention to detail and sepia-toned charm, brought to life not just a story but the ambiance of a bygone era, where the spirit of Christmas was embraced with a genuine warmth that transcended the tiny cinematic frame.

CHAPTER 24
CHRISTMAS IN BEDROCK

"They're a couple of bumblers, but their hearts are in the right place."

—Santa Claus, in reference to Fred and
Barney, in *A Flintstone Christmas*

he Flintstones stands in the history of television as a solid, well-written, funny animated sitcom, which has stood the test of time, prehistorically and historically. Originally airing on ABC from September 30, 1960, to April 1, 1966, the series features the voices of Alan Reed as Fred Flintstone, Jean Vander Pyl as his wife, Wilma, Mel Blanc as neighbor Barney Rubble, and Bea Benaderet (and later Gerry Johnson) as his wife, Betty.

A popular staple on Friday nights, *The Flintstones* encouraged viewers to take their vitamins (a show spin-off in real life) and to drink Welch's grape juice (a show sponsor), while in some sectors of the world, Flintstones gummy bears are still available today. With its alternate Stone Age premise and funny dinosaur bone comedy, the show's appeal remains timeless, even if some of the pop culture references are, well, dated. Special guest-star appearances include Ann-Margrock, Cary Granite, Tuesday Wednesday, and so on, in movie-star-of-the-day episode nods to Ann-Margret, Cary Grant, Tuesday Weld, and others. Even animated versions of *Bewitched* stars Elizabeth Montgomery and Dick York appear on the *flint-com* (expanding in a sense the opening animated sequence of their successful 1960s supernatural sitcom).

Within the context of *The Flintstones*, Fred, Barney, Wilma, and Betty are drawn as *real* people. They laugh, cry; and become angry, love, and forgive, with Barney the most carefree and even-tempered of the group. Nothing really riled him. He was a good guy. Certainly, Fred was a good person, too. Like Archie Bunker on *All in the Family*, Fred wallows before he compromises, but he eventually comes around to his senses. He is nowhere near the bigot Archie is, but rather an uneducated and ultimately lovable poor soul, much also like Ralph Kramden on the live-action 1950s–1960s series *The Honeymooners*, which influenced *The Flintstones* (and to some subsequent extent, *All in the Family*, too).

Like any good series, animated or otherwise, *The Flintstones* plays according to the logic it creates. As with Ralph and Alice on *The Honeymooners*, Fred and Wilma invite us into their self-contained world and make us feel welcome, even though we are the outsiders and, in this case, live-action figures.

Before *The Simpsons* conquered the animated world, *The Flintstones*, with its 166 episodes, was documented as the longest-running animated series in prime-time history. The show's prehistoric ways remain ageless, mainly because of the intelligent and time-honored segments such as "Christmas Flintstone," which originally aired on December 25, 1964, as episode fifteen in the show's fifth season. The plot for this holiday adventure, which is also known, on VHS, as "How the Flintstones Saved Christmas," is as follows:

Fred does such a good job of slipping into Santa's suit and boots for a department store at Christmastime that the real deal calls upon his services from the North Pole for an all-important trip around the world on Christmas Eve.

It's a charming episode with two little songs, "Christmas is My Fav'rite Time of Year" and "Dino the Dinosaur," and was followed by three later-day *Flintstones* Christmas TV-movies, all of which feature Henry Corden's lauded performance as Fred replacing Alan Reed (who passed away on June 14, 1977), and two with Frank Welker as Barney (in place of Mel Blanc, who died on July 10, 1989).

The extended-length holiday sequels include: *A Flintstone Christmas* (which originally aired on NBC, December 7, 1977), *A Flintstone Family Christmas*, a.k.a. *The Flintstones: Christmas Misdemeanors* (ABC, December 18, 1993), *A Flintstones Christmas Carol*, a.k.a. *The Flintstones: A Christmas Carol*, and *The Flintstones: In Charles Dickens' A Christmas Carol* (syndication, November 21, 1994).

A Flintstones Christmas Carol is based on Dickens' 1843 novella *A Christmas Carol*, and after its premiere, it was rerun in later years by Boomerang and Canada's YTV. Turner Home Entertainment released the special on VHS as part of their Turner Family Showcase on September 26, 1995, when it ranked twenty-fourth among children's video rentals in America the following October. On October 2, 2007, Warner Home Video released it on DVD in Region 1 and included the *Christmas* Flintstone episode from the original series as a bonus extra.

The special received a Film Advisory Board Award, but *TV Guide* gave it only two stars. The magazine claimed the story-within-a-story premise is flawed by "the continual cutting away to backstage incidents that turn the careful momentum of Dickens's narrative into jagged stops and starts," adding "how can these prehistoric folk be celebrating the birth of a messiah not due for several millennia?"

ABC's 1993 movie, *A Flintstone Family Christmas*, was nominated for a Prime-time Emmy Award in 1994 for Outstanding Animated Program (For Programming Less Than One Hour). It features the singular appearance of Stoney (a character voiced by Christine Cavanaugh) and the final appearance of Pebbles and Bamm-Bamm in their adult forms, along with their own kids, Chip and Roxy.

From there on in, Hanna-Barbera periodically produced new *Flintstone* adventures (including two feature films), but within the confines of the original show's initial timeline.

All of that brings us to *A Flintstone Christmas*, the 1977 animated entry, which is closest to the original TV show's timeline, if with just a few slight bumps on the Bedrock road. As the second Christmas-themed story in the franchise following the 1964 series episode "Christmas Flintstone," *A Flintstone Christmas* pretty much tells the same story as that initial segment, but more extensively:

Fred, Barney, Wilma, and Betty (now voiced by Gay Hartwig) and the gang are prepping Christmas. Wilma wants Fred to play Santa for the Bedrock Orphanage Christmas party, which will also be attended by a new pre-teen Pebbles (Vander Pyl) and Bamm-Bamm (Lucille Bliss). But Fred objects until his boss, Mr. Slate (John Stephenson), convinces him otherwise. Shortly after, he and Barney meet the real Mr. Claus (Hal Smith, Otis from *The Andy Griffith Show*), who's suffering from a sprained ankle and a bad cold, which means he can't make the rounds this Christmas Eve.

Barney suggests Fred should step up to the plate. Loving the idea, Santa employs his magic and transforms Fred into a jolly ol' St. Nick version of himself and Barney into an elf. With a quick review of how to guide the sleigh at night, Fred and Barney commence their journey around the world. A snowstorm throws them off course a bit, and their stash of Christmas presents are lost, until Barney uses the sleigh's handy CB radio to contact Santa, who guides them the rest of the way, which includes a trip to the North Pole to retrieve a batch of new gifts with the help of Mrs. Claus (Virginia Gregg).

Once on their way, Fred and Barney deliver the presents to remaining homes around the globe, and all is well. That is, until Fred goes into panic mode; he forgot about the Bedrock Orphanage Christmas party and because of that, fears he'll lose his job.

But no worries, because Santa saves the day with more magic, speeding up the sleigh's trek back to Bedrock just in the St. Nick of time to have Fred and Barney arrive at the party, which secures Fred's position with Mr. Slate.

Directed by Charles A. Nichols and based on a teleplay by Duanne Poole and Dick Robbins, *A Flintstone Christmas* was later rerun on ABC Family in December 2011, as part of that network's 25 Days of Christmas broadcast.

Previously released by Turner Home Entertainment on VHS, *A Flintstone Christmas* was also released in September 2011 by Warner Archive on DVD in Region 1, along with 1993's *A Flintstone Family Christmas* under the guise of *A Flintstone Christmas Collection.*

In 2005, authors Kevin Cuddihy and Phillip Metcalfe ranked *A Flintstone Christmas* from 1977 as seventh in their Christmas-themed list of "Not-so-Classic Cartoons." Cuddihy and Metcalfe applauded Corden and also noted how the shows' prehistoric times transpired prior to the birth of Jesus and subsequently Christmas.

In his *DVD Talk* review, Paul Mavis described *A Flintstone Christmas* as "a rather sweet effort" and called the songs "quite cute." William D. Crump, author of *The Christmas Encyclopedia*, described it as "virtually a remake" of "Christmas Flintstone." Matt Bungard, writing for the *Sydney Morning Herald*, placed it in his top 10 Christmas specials, calling the plot simple but "staple Christmas viewing."

However, in the big-picture, near-surreal prehistoric world of Flintstone mythology, *A Flintstone Christmas* is a winner on several fronts. For one, the optimum optical mark of any great Christmas special, animated or not, is the correct placement and/or inclusion of snow. "Fake" or real snow and snowflakes accent many live variety musical specials, TV-movies, or episodic series Christmas segments. And the seemingly mounded snow as drawn around Fred, Barney, and other characters is done with solid placement in *A Flintstone Christmas.*

At its core, *A Flintstone Christmas* is a "reunion" TV-movie which, over-all, are a challenge for Hollywood creatives to complete, as many such films do not always reflect the original essence of the TV show from which they spring. The disappointing *Mary and Rhoda* film from 1990 comes to mind. Severely lacking in the charm and original format of *The Mary Tyler Moore Show* (the movie was filmed without a studio audience, which encapsulated the set of the original series), *Mary and Rhoda* failed across the board.

But *A Flintstone Christmas* soars, as it remains mostly true to the canon of the original *Flintstone* series, if with just one or two significant mishaps along the way. Although Pebbles and Bamm-Bamm talk and are chronologically and logically older in *A Flintstone Christmas*, they appear much younger than the teenage versions of themselves in *The Pebbles and Bamm-Bamm Show*, which originally aired on CBS Saturday mornings from 1971 to 1972. Both characters don't get much to say in *A Flintstone Christmas*, but at least Bamm-Bamm's super-strength, which was missing from the Saturday-morning show, is returned in the 1977 film.

With regard to consistency, at least from a visual perspective, *A Flintstone Christmas* dots all the TV-viewing eyes. Literally. For one, Barney's peepers are fully-drawn in black, as opposed to the less-aesthetically appealing clear circles he had in the early years of the original series. Wilma's weight, which seemed to increase in the *Pebbles and Bamm Bamm Show*, is back in more trim form with *A Flintstone Christmas* and more closely resembles her appearance in the original series. We see Fred's teeth, and Wilma and Betty's too, which were not always drawn into their mouths on the original show, and Santa isn't presented in Flintstone's raggedy hair and wardrobe as the other characters (including the numerous fake Santas) in the 1977 movie.

The colors of *A Flintstone Christmas* are rich and enhanced, superior to the original series, while the catch-phrases from the iconic prime-time series have their place. Fred's "Yabba Dabba Do," of course, is there, while the various prehistoric talking–employed creatures are still heard saying things like, "It's a Living." [Though we never learn why they would need money in the first place.]

Other items of minutia like the visibility of wristwatches only when characters raise their wrists to check the time (and not otherwise) are back in inconsistent session in *A Flintstone Christmas*. But the relationships between all the characters are spot-on. The circumstances and situations of the original show's first season are more logical within the illogical than latter years, and the holiday "fantasy" aspects add one more wrinkle in a sense to the already altered reality of the Flintstone prehistoric timeline. But somehow it all works in this animated adventure, again, with particular regard to character consistency.

Barney, the brains of the outfit, displays his intelligence by utilizing Santa's CB radio, which was all the rage in the late 1970s. Although it's never explained how he automatically knows that Santa's CB handle is Big Red. With other specific holiday-geared points more logically in place, it all balanced out to make *A Flintstone Christmas* a charming addition not just to the *Flintstone* franchise, but to the animated Christmas special sector overall.

Barney's small stature serves him well with his very workable persona here as a sidekick elf to Fred's replacement Santa; both good casting. Hal Smith delivers an amiable voice-driven performance as the real Santa, who is one of the most magical St. Nicks in the history of the character's interpretation. And all of Santa's eight reindeer are in linear position, which is not always the case in animated Christmas specials (sometimes, there's only four or six, as in *Rudolph the Red-Nosed Reindeer*).

The songs in *A Flintstone Christmas* are terrific and sweet, including "Which One is the Real Santa Claus?" "It's My Favorite Time of the Year," "Sounds of Christmas Day," "Brand New Kind of Christmas Song" (released on 1991's *Hanna-Barbera's Christmas Sing-A-Long* album), and "Hope"—reused in 1980's *Yogi's First Christmas*. Though some of the lyrics of "Hope" sound a little silly. ("Everyone believes in hope because hope believes in Santa Claus"; is "hope" a person or a thing?) But again, that's okay, because as the optimum holiday special in the Fred and Barney universe, and across the board, *A Flintstone Christmas* sings.

Talent agent/author Pierre Patrick nicely summarized the Bedrock Christmas experience: "*The Flintstones* was the first prime-time weekly animation program to bring families together and they certainly did that at Christmas in several wonderful prehistoric ways."

MUSIC/VARIETY

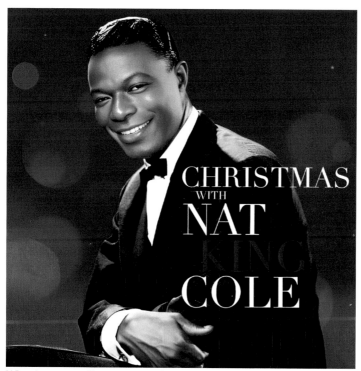

When it comes to Christmas music, the holidays would not be the same without
the vocal and visual charisma of Nat King Cole, who had a short-lived TV variety
show. Classic TV Preservation Society (CTVPS)

Shirley Temple and her Storybook float are
showcased in this 1958 image from that year's
Macy's Thanksgiving Day Parade (broadcast on
NBC). Photofest

Judy Garland and her children (from left): Liza
Minnelli, Joey Luft, Lorna Luft appear in the
December 22, 1963, Christmas episode of The
Judy Garland Show (which lasted only one season
on CBS, 1963–1964). Minelli went on to star
in her own Christmas special, The Dangerous
Christmas of Red Riding Hood (ABC, November
28, 1965). CBS/Photofest © CBS

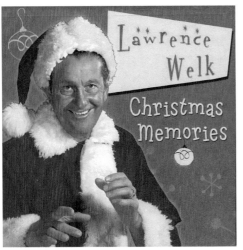

Lawrence Welk and his "musical family" brought countless hours of comfort and joy for decades with annual Christmas TV episodes and specials. CTVPS

Tanya Welk, then-daughter-in-law to Lawrence Welk. Courtesy Tanya Welk

The Welk group reunited at Christmas 2013. Front (l-r): Tom Netherton, Dick Dale, Jack Imel, Jo Ann Castle, Kathy Lennon, Janet Lennon, Mimi Lennon. Back (l-r): Ken Delo, Bob Ralston, Joe Feeney, Norma Zimmer, Mary Lou Metzger, Guy Hovis, Ralna English, Gail Farrell. The Welk Group, Inc./CTVPS

The King Family added group elegance to the holiday season. King Family Archives/Polly O. Entertainment

The King Sisters sing in harmony at Christmas. Pictured: Marilyn (top row) and (from left to right on bottom) Alyce, Yvonne, and Luise. King Family Archives/Polly O. Entertainment

A recent pic of Tina Cole, a member of the King Family in real life and on TV and a cast family member of My Three Sons on TV. Courtesy Tina Cole

Tina Cole and her King Family did Christmas right, in a big way with various specials over the years. In one benchmark moment, her aunt Alycee receives a surprise visit from her son, Tina's cousin, Ric de Azevedo, who was serving in Vietnam. King Family Archive courtesy of Polly O. Entertainment

Mitzi Gaynor, in a recent pic on the right, sang her heart out in her famed 1967 Christmas special. King Family Archives/Polly O. Entertainment

The Kraft Music Hall Mitzi Gaynor Christmas Show *of 1967 is a prime example of everything a music-variety Christmas TV special should be. In top photo, Mitzi jostles joyfully with Ed McMahon in a musical number.* Mitzi Gaynor Archive courtesy of Polly O. Entertainment

Bob Hope's name remains synonymous with "Christmas TV specials." In 1977, Olivia Newton-John was one of his special guest stars. NBC/ Photofest © NBC

In 1991, Bob Hope aired his last military-geared Christmas special, this time helping to bring a little cheer during the Iraq/"Desert Storm" War. NBC/Photofest © NBC

Bing Crosby and David Bowie performing a
medley of the songs "Little Drummer Boy"
and "Peace On Earth" on the set of the
television special Bing Crosby's Merrie Olde
Christmas, which premiered November 30,
1977. CBS/Photofest © CBS

For Bing Crosby, Christmas TV was all about family
with a few prestigious exceptions. The most famous
being David Bowie, who made Christmas TV history
with a special guest appearance alongside Crosby in
1977's Merrie Olde Christmas. The special ended up
being Crosby's final screen appearance. He died shortly
after. CBS/Photofest © CBS

Like Bob Hope and Bing Crosby, Andy Williams
and his Christmas TV specials became
legendary. NBC/Photofest © NBC

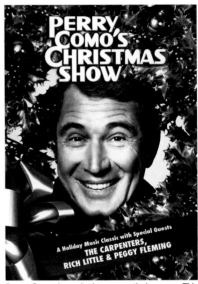

Jackie Gleason paid tribute to Christmas in several TV adventures of the original and reunion episodes of The Honeymooners, as well as The Jackie Gleason (variety) Show. MPI Home Video/Jim Pierson

Perry Como brought his tranquil charm to TV in several Christmas specials over the years, the later editions of which were taped "on location." MPI Home Video/Jim Pierson

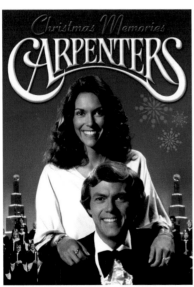

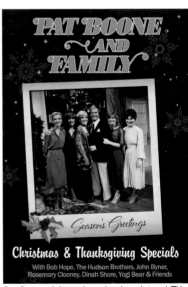

The Carpenters (seen here) and Donny & Marie are two of the most popular sibling acts in musical history. Each presented several Christmas specials in their TV tenure. MPI Home Video/Jim Pierson

Pat Boone delivered top-level traditional TV Christmas specials through the decades. MPI Home Video/Jim Pierson

ANIMATION

Premiering on NBC December 18, 1962, and directed by Abe Levitow, Mister Magoo's Christmas Carol was the first formal animated TV Christmas special to air. Here, we see Bob Cratchit (who was voiced by Jack Cassidy) and Ebenezer Scrooge/Mr. Magoo (starring the vocal talents of Jim Backus). NBC/Photofest © NBC

A now-perennial classic, the touching tale (tail?) of Rudolph the Red-Nosed Reindeer brought elegant poignancy to the small screen when it debuted on NBC in 1964. CTVPS

The groundbreaking animated TV special A Charlie Brown Christmas, with a core spiritual message, premiered on CBS in 1965. CBS/Photofest © CBS

Boris Karloff lent his authoritative voice to The Grinch Who Stole Christmas, *which premiered on NBC in 1966.* CBS/Photofest © CBS

Mickey Rooney voiced the lead in two ABC Santa Claus TV specials for Rankin/Bass: Santa Claus Is Comin' to Town *(1970, pictured here) and* The Year Without a Santa Claus *(1974).* ABC/Photofest © ABC

The original Frosty the Snowman *TV special, featuring the voices of Jackie Vernon in the lead and Jimmy Durante as narrator, paved the way for future* Frosty *sequels that could not compare to the original.* Golden Books/Photofest © Golden Books

Scrooge's lesson

EBENEZER Scrooge, the Dickens character who became literature's most outstanding anti-Christmas symbol, is reformed by one harrowing night and an impoverished but generous family, on "A Christmas Carol," animated adaptation of the Dickens classic to be rebroadcast Saturday on CBS.

In 1971, the esteemed Alastair Sim reprised his live-action, two-hour, big-screen Scrooge/A Christmas Carol role for what has become a treasured, if rarely aired half-hour animated TV classic adaptation of the Dickens tale. Pictured (from top left): promotional ad, director Richard Williams with son Alexander, who voiced Tiny Tim. Courtesy Alexander Williams

The Flintstones *celebrated Christmas like only they could—with several prehistoric holiday episodes and specials over the years.* Hanna-Barbera/Photofest © Hanna-Barbera Prods.

The Simpsons *animated series is renowned for its special Christmas episodes, each with its own relative edge.* Fox/Photofest © & TM Fox

TV-MOVIES

It Happened One Christmas *is TV-legend Marlo Thomas's iconic 1977 remake of Frank Capra's 1947 big-screen classic* It's a Wonderful Life. *CTVPS*

The House Without a Christmas Tree *became so popular on CBS it spawned three sequels, one of which was* The Thanksgiving Treasure *(which took its title from its breakout star Lisa Lucas's real-life horse named Treasure).* CTVPS

The House Without a Christmas Tree, *starring Jason Robards and Lisa Lucas (bottom images) and Mildred Natwick (not pictured), remains one of TV's most memorable and original movies of the week. Pictured top right: Lucas in December 2023 having dinner in New York with Shayne, Sunshine, and Lucas's mother, Bobbi Kay.* Courtesy Lisa Lucas

The success of The Homecoming: A Christmas Story, *a CBS TV-movie based on the real life of Earl Hamner Jr., led to* The Waltons *weekly series. Pictured here: Richard Thomas, who played eldest son, John-Boy Walton, with Patricia Neal (as mother Olivia Walton, replaced in the series by Michael Learned).* CBS/Photofest © CBS

Sebastian Cabot, best known as Mr. French on TV's Family Affair (which did its own share of Christmas episodes), starred as Kris Kringle in a 1973 CBS TV-remake of the 1947 feature-film classic Miracle on 34th Street. CBS/Photofest © CBS

Ed Asner and Maureen Stapleton brought a stark realism to Christmas TV-movies in 1977 with The Gathering, which aired on ABC. It's also important to note that the film was directed by Randall Kleiser, who went on to helm the classic 1978 feature-film musical Grease. ABC/ Photofest © ABC

Henry Winkler, at the height of his popularity as "The Fonz" on ABC's hit Happy Days sitcom, presented a unique spin of a certain Charles Dickens classic in the 1979 TV-movie An American Christmas Carol. ABC/Photofest © ABC

George C. Scott's 1984 TV adaption of A Christmas Carol is considered the best small-screen rendition of the Dickens tale. CBS/Photofest © CBS

Box office king Arnold Schwarzenegger flexed his muscles behind the scenes as a director for the 1992 TV-movie remake of the 1945 big-screen classic Christmas in Connecticut. The TV film stars Kris Kristofferson and Dyan Cannon, both seen here with Schwarzenegger. Entertainment Pictures/Alamy Stock Photo

Shortly after she completed her historic run as Jessica Fletcher on Murder, She Wrote, Angela Lansbury brought her elegance, talent, and gravitas to Mrs. Santa Claus. This 1996 TV-movie musical featured the music of the legendary Jerry Herman and harkened back to the classic feature films of the genre. CBS/Photofest © CBS

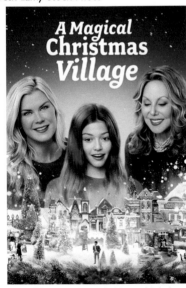

Marlo Thomas (left with Maesa Nicholson in the middle and Allison Sweeney on the left) returned to the land of Christmas TV-movies in 2022 with A Magical Christmas Village, one of the countless charming Christmas TV-movies presented by the Hallmark Channel. CTVPS

A plethora of TV sitcoms have produced their own brand of Christmas episodes from the early days to the present. MPI Home Video/Jim Pierson

The Adventures of Ozzie and Harriet (ABC, 1952–1966) celebrated Christmas with new episodes almost every year it was on the air. MPI Home Video/Jim Pierson

Lucy did Christmas like only Lucy could, shown here with (from left): Vivian Vance, Desi Arnaz, and William Frawley, in the sole holiday episode of I Love Lucy (CBS, 1956). CBS/Photofest © CBS

David and Ricky Nelson celebrate an early TV Christmas with their on-screen and real-life mom Harriet Nelson in the promotional image from The Adventures of Ozzie and Harriet. MPI Home Video/Jim Pierson

The cast of Father Knows Best (from left, Billy Gray, Elinor Donahue, Laurin Chapin, Jane Wyatt, and Robert Young) appeared in several holiday adventures on the series, including two later-day TV-movie sequels from 1977. NBC/Photofest © NBC

Danny Thomas as Danny Williams celebrates Christmas with two of his TV children: Sherry Jackson, who played Terry, and Rusty Hamer as Rusty on Make Room for Daddy, which later changed its title to The Danny Thomas Show. ABC/Photofest © ABC

Marlo Thomas appeared in each of the four categories of Christmas specials: the variety show format (with her father, in an animated segment, Cricket on the Hearth), two Christmas episodes of That Girl (as seen here), the 1977 TV-movie It Happened One Christmas, and more recently in 2022 in A Magical Christmas Village, one of the Hallmark Channel's signature series of Christmas TV-movies. ABC/Photofest © ABC

Doris Day transferred her big-screen Christmas charm in three small-screen holiday episodes of The Doris Day Show (CBS, 1968–1973). MPI Home Video/Jim Pierson

ABC's TV version of The Odd Couple (starring Tony Randall and Jack Klugman, both seen here) adapted what became one of the first retakes of A Christmas Carol in the history of episodic television. ABC/Photofest © ABC

Bewitched Christmas episodes include: "A Vision of Sugar Plumbs" (w/Billy Mumy), "Humbug Not to Be Spoken Here" (w/ Charles Lane), "Santa Comes for a Visit and Stays and Stays" (w/Ronald Long), and "Sisters at Heart" (seen here w/Elizabeth Montgomery, Erin Murphy, Venetta Rogers/ Venetta T. Rowles). ABC/Photofest © ABC

My Favorite Martian actor Ray Walston and Bewitched's "second Darrin" Dick Sargent were guest stars in "A Bionic Christmas Carol" episode The Six Million Dollar Man (which also featured from left Adam Rich [Eight Is Enough], Quin Cummings [The Goodbye Girl/Family], and Natasha Ryan [the 1976 miniseries Sybil]). CTVPS

Happy Days, and its hit spin-off Laverne & Shirley, showcased many Christmas celebrations on ABC. ABC/Photofest © ABC

The Jeffersons "moved on up to the East Side" with several Christmas episodes. From top left: Franklin Cover, Roxie Roker, Paul Benedict, Marla Gibbs, Ned Wertimer, Sherman Hemsley, Berlinda Tolbert, Zara Cully, Isabel Sanford, and Damon Evans. CBS/Photofest © CBS

Julia proved groundbreaking, especially at Christmas with the episode "I'm Dreaming of a Black Christmas." From left to right: Michael Link, Paul Winfield, Stephanie James, Michael Wajacs, Marc Copage. Back, left to right: Hank Brandt, Betty Beaird, and Diahann Carroll. 20th Century Fox TV/Kobal/Shutterstock

Frasier, considered by some as one of the last great sitcoms, if not the last great sitcom, gifted viewers with annual Christmas adventures. CTVPS

A Classic Christmas, hosted by Marion Ross (Happy Days) and Gavin MacLeod (The Mary Tyler Moore Show/The Love Boat), premiered on PBS on November 30, 2019. Produced by Jim Pierson and executive-produced by TJ Lubinsky, this was a contemporary showcase of rare, archived Christmas footage from the 1950s through the 1970s. MPI Home Video/Jim Pierson

CHAPTER 25

CHRISTMAS IN SPRINGFIELD

"Come on, Dad, if TV has taught me anything, it's that miracles always happen to poor kids at Christmas. It happened to Tiny Tim, it happened to Charlie Brown, it happened to the Smurfs, and it's gonna happen to us."

—Bart Simpson, *The Simpsons Christmas Special* (1989)

With its history a bit sketchy (sorry) and continuity nonexistent, *The Simpsons* is an anomaly. As the most popular family animated series in the history of television, following *The Flintstones*, *The Simpsons* has become a cultural phenomenon.

Introduced as a segment of *The Tracey Ullman Show* in 1990, *The Simpsons* feature the vocal prowess of Dan Castellaneta as father Homer, Julie Kavner as wife Marge, and their children Bart, Lisa, and Maggie, voiced by Nancy Cartwright and Yeardley Smith. Usually, animated series don't follow the rules of live-action programs with regard to characters aging and the like. But *The Simpsons* has broken all the rules in any category, if on demand due to its ongoing popularity, marked at nearly an unheard of forty seasons. That's a longer run than any TV series, animated or not. *Gunsmoke* used to hold the trophy as the TV show to clock more seasons and episodes than any other. But not since *The Simpsons*, which within its wheelhouse of episodes, has there been a show that has produced more Christmas episodes.

Unlike *The Flintstones* or any other family-geared animated series, *The Simpsons* is not warm or friendly but rather a little dark and edgy. In the show's early seasons, there was more of, if not happy endings, at least sweeter endings. Such is not the case in the later and continuing years. Again, like *The*

Flintstones, many guest stars of the day make guest appearances or are somehow drawn (sorry again) into the story. But while *The Flintstones* frequently celebrated movie stars of the 1960s, *The Simpsons* periodically lambast them in one passive-aggressive way or the other.

However, *The Simpsons* is obviously doing something right for it to be in production for decades. Amid, too, its countless seasons, the show has managed to incorporate various holiday episodes, so that's indeed cause for celebration. That also designates the show's Christmas episodes as a worthy inclusion in this book.

The Simpsons December holiday gatherings began with the fifth episode of *The Tracey Ullman Show*'s third season, airing December 18, 1988. Although the Simpsons' first Christmas is not technically part of the series, their initial December holiday adventure offers a solid glimpse into the family's key character traits. Within the clever reframing of Clement Moore's *'Twas the Night Before Christmas* poem, Bart serves as narrator, as he seeks to unwrap his gifts before Christmas.

After that initial *Ullman Show* adventure, *The Simpsons* began their own series, which featured the following Christmas segments:

Season 1, Episode 1, "Simpsons Roasting on an Open Fire" (December 17, 1989): As TV fate would have it, *The Simpsons* began their regular weekly life with a Christmas-themed episode. Amid the family's holiday economic challenges, Homer finds part-time work as Santa Claus at the mall. As with TV shows of every format, *The Simpsons* was still trying to find its way in the initial years, while this first Christmas adventure is a good representation of its off-color humor. A heartwarming ending introduces the family's pet, Santa's Little Helper.

Season 7, Episode 11, "Marge Be Not Proud" (December 17, 1995): Bart is up to his borderline personality disorder ways by shoplifting a video game just prior to Christmas. Marge is despondent, while her son deals with his enormous guilt. A few humorous moments lead into another happy ending.

Season 9, Episode 10, "Miracle on Evergreen Terrace" (December 21, 1997): As with *The Tracey Ullman Show* Christmas episode, Bart makes every effort to get an early glance at his Christmas gifts, but this time, the presents are destroyed. He falsely blames a burglar, while the family earns Springfield's support. *The Simpsons* richer character textures are explored here with a few shades of humorous insight.

Season 11, Episode 9, "Grift of the Magi" (December 19, 1999): Bart and Lisa's school closes, a toy manufacturer takes the reins, and the kids create Funzo, a new Christmas toy. It's an odd episode, even for *The Simpsons*, but features a cameo by Gary Coleman and somehow manages to work.

Season 12, Episode 8, "Skinner's Sense of Snow" (December 17, 2000): Though not technically a Christmas adventure, this episode still has its moments. On the last day of school before Christmas vacation, Principal Skinner finds himself stuck in school with many angry students. Homer and Ned's funny rescue efforts to save the kids end up saving the episode.

Season 13, Episode 6, "She of Little Faith" (December 16, 2001): Lisa goes Christmas AWOL and converts to Buddhism, while Marge hopes to reconvert her daughter back to Christianity amid the Holiday Spirit. A solid entry with a message about the importance of cultural diversity.

Season 15, Episode 7, "'Tis the Fifteenth Season" (December 14, 2003): After indulging himself with a lavish Christmas gift, a contrite Homer transforms into Springfield's most affable guy, much like Scrooge's metamorphosis in *A Christmas Carol*, though also much to Ned Flanders' dismay.

Season 17, Episode 9, "Simpsons Christmas Stories" (December 18, 2005): The first of the show's holiday anthology episodes, this entry offers a retelling of the birth of Jesus, *The Nutcracker*, and Grampa Simpson's original WWII Christmas story, with a creative musical finale.

Season 18, Episode 9, "Kill Gil, Volumes I & II (December 17, 2006): Gil Gunderson, Springfield's Danny-Downer, loses his job and becomes the "thing that wouldn't leave" after Marge invites him to spend the holiday with the Simpsons.

Season 22, Episode 8, "The Fight Before Christmas" (December 5, 2010): Another anthology episode that offers a trilogy of Christmas tales, this time represented by separate family member dreams.

Season 23, Episode 9, "Holidays of Future Passed" (December 11, 2011): In this stellar episode, which some hardcore fans of the show have said would have made an ideal series finale, the Simpsons journey into the Christmas future. There, Bart is a deadbeat father, Lisa is wed to Milhouse, and Maggie is a singing star.

Season 25, Episode 8, "White Christmas Blues" (December 15, 2013): Global warming comes into play, as America, all except Springfield, consequently faces a lack of snow for Christmas. As a result, the town becomes a tourist attraction, with the Simpsons home a key pay-per-visit stop.

Season 26, Episode 9, "I Won't Be Home for Christmas" (December 7, 2014): This Christmas Eve, Homer hopes to please Marge by arriving home early, but after a car accident, he is derailed at Moe's. He finds Moe despondent and opts to comfort his friend as opposed to spending Christmas with his family. Homer finally arrives home, and he and Marge argue, but then he leaves to roam the streets of Springfield. In the end, both Homer and Marge are despondent with his decision.

Season 28, Episode 10, "The Nightmare After Krustmas" (December 11, 2016): Krusty the Klown's daughter Sophie returns to Springfield for the holidays as a Christian convert, leaving her Jewish roots behind, and her father in shock.

Season 19, Episode 9, "Gone Boy" (December 10, 2017): With the holidays around the corner, Bart is missing and trapped in an underground bunker. Sideshow Bob learns of Bart's predicament and breaks out of prison. Not a very Christmasy episode at all.

Season 30, Episode 10, "'Tis the 30th Season" (December 9, 2018): Marge makes every effort to have an ideal family Christmas.

Season 31, Episode 10, "Bobby, It's Cold Outside" (December 15, 2019): After Sideshow Bob escapes from prison (again), he's hired as a mall Santa Claus. He's accused of stealing Christmas gifts and sets out to find the true culprit. Like "The Nightmare After Krustmas," this episode is not one of the show's best holiday efforts.

Season 31, Episode 22, "The Way of the Dog" (May 17, 2020): This is another Christmas-geared episode that did not actually air near the holiday. But it's the story of Santa's Little Helper's challenging past infested with the spirit of the season, all the more so with a reference to *The Simpsons* initial Christmas episode.

Season 32, Episode 10, "A Springfield Summer Christmas for Christmas" (December 13, 2020): This episode takes a few humorous jabs at the Christmas TV-movies presented on such networks as the Hallmark Channel and Lifetime. As the essential Simpson-less story goes, once a producer of those kinds of Christmas movies is coerced into filming his latest production in Springfield. In the process, and in keeping with the premise of many such films, her life transforms into a Christmas TV-movie when she falls for Principal Skinner.

Season 32, Episode 16, "Manger Things" (March 21, 2021): With a flashback sequence to a situation never before seen, Marge tells the story of how Homer, once more contrite, tries to redeem himself after mortifying his wife at the office Christmas party.

Season 35, Episode 10, "Do the Wrong Thing" (December 24, 2023): In the most recent Christmas episode, which received mixed reviews, Homer and Bart bond over cheating while Lisa applies to university camps.

PART 3
THE MERRY M.O.W.

Countless Christmas TV-movies have been produced and aired through the decades. It's a tradition that contemporary networks such as Lifetime and the Hallmark Channel have excelled at in recent years, with combined airings of more than forty new films every season.

One of the first Christmas TV-movies was an adaptation of *Babes in Toyland*, the Victor Herbert musical that continues to be a favorite attraction at Christmastime, in new stage productions. According to entertainment historian Randy Skretvedt, author of *March of the Wooden Soldiers: The Amazing Story of Laurel & Hardy's Babes in Toyland*, the initial stage production debuted in Chicago in 1903 and then on Broadway. "The original story was surprisingly violent, with an attempted drowning, a death by poison, stabbings, and a plunge into a fiery volcano," Skretvedt explained. "As a result, while many of the charming songs are retained [including 'Toyland,' 'Castle in Spain,' and 'March of the Toys'] the plot has been rewritten multiple times. The story usually involves evil miser Silas Barnaby wanting to do away with his orphaned niece and nephew so that he can obtain their inheritance."

Two of the best-remembered versions are the 1934 Laurel and Hardy film, retitled *March of the Wooden Soldiers* (thus the subtitle of Skretvedt's book), and the 1961 Disney movie starring Annette Funicello, Tommy Sands, and Ray Bolger. In between, however, were actually three TV productions. Skretvedt continued:

"Max Liebman, who created the groundbreaking comedy-variety series *Your Show of Shows* with Sid Caesar and Imogene Coca, also produced a series of 'Spectaculars' for NBC. On December 18, 1954, a new version of *Babes in Toyland* aired in a ninety-minute timeslot. One of the first shows broadcast in 'compatible color,' meaning that people with black-and-white televisions could also receive it, the production starred Dennis Day and Jo Sullivan, with rotund, bombastic comedian Jack E. Leonard as evil Silas Barnaby, meek and mild Wally Cox as toymaker Grumio, and the Bil and Cora Baird puppets as various animals."

With a script co-written by Neil Simon, the show offered plenty of wit along with the music. Hosted by the drily funny Dave Garroway (the original host of NBC's *Today*) as a department store Santa Claus, the program was so popular that a second live production aired on December 24, 1955. "The leading lady this time around was Barbara Cook," Skretvedt said, "and a couple of specialty numbers were different, but otherwise the show was a twin to the 1954 edition, if a bit more technically proficient. Both shows survive only in black-and-white kinescopes [and are available on a DVD from Video Artists International]."

Shirley Temple, who had been hugely popular as a child star in 1930s movies, came to television in January 1958 with a one-hour anthology series of children's stories in newly written productions. Titled *Shirley Temple's Storybook* and then *The Shirley Temple Show*, the series produced fifty-five episodes through July 1961. The new edition of *Babes in Toyland*, broadcast on December 25, 1960, also emphasized comedy. Jonathan Winters starred as a very unusual Barnaby, with bumbling cohorts Jerry Colonna, Joe Besser (later in *The Joey Bishop Show*), and Carl Ballantine (best remembered for *McHale's Navy*).

"The Babes this time around," said Skretvedt, "were little Michel Petit, who was very active in early 1960s television, and Angela Cartwright, by special permission of *The Danny Thomas Show*." Oddly, the cast had no well-known singers apart from Shirley Temple, who sang "Toyland" and, in a surprisingly wacky performance as a Gypsy witch, "Floretta." Angela Cartwright did her best with "Go to Sleep," and Tony Charmoli's dancers traipsed through "March of the Toys." Directed by Bob Henry and written by Jack Brooks and Sheldon Keller, the fast-paced hour was produced on videotape in color and is available today in a very nice transfer on DVD from Genius Entertainment.

Other than *Babes in Toyland*, only a few chosen TV-movie classics from the past remain true perennials in the present. Those include: *Homecoming: A Christmas Story* (the pilot for *The Waltons*), *It Happened One Christmas* (the 1977 remake of *It's a Wonderful Life* starring Marlo Thomas), *The House Without a Christmas Tree* (starring Jason Robards, Mildred Natwick, and Lisa Lucas), *Father Knows Best: Home for Christmas* (NBC, 1977), *A Christmas Carol* (the 1984 CBS edition starring the Oscar-winning George C. Scott),

An American Christmas Carol (ABC, 1979, with Henry Winkler), *Miracle on 34th Street* (the 1973 CBS edition starring David Hartman), *The Gathering* (ABC, 1979, starring Ed Asner and Maureen Stapleton), *Christmas on Division Street* (ABC, 1991, with Fred Savage), *A Very Brady Christmas*, *Christmas in Connecticut* (the 1992 TNT version directed by Arnold Schwarzenegger), and more.

One of the most fondly recalled Christmas TV-movies from the past is not technically a TV-movie in the traditional larger-budget sense. Like *The House Without a Christmas Tree* and *Father Knows Best: Home for Christmas*, NBC's December 6, 1969, Hallmark Hall of Fame production of *The Littlest Angel* starring Johnny Whitaker (*Family Affair*) and Fred Gwynne (*The Munsters*) was videotaped. But unlike *House* or *Home*, *The Littlest Angel* was a musical, thus combining variety-show elements with a narrative teleplay.

The Littlest Angel TV-movie is based on the children's book of the same name by Charles Tazewell and illustrated by Katherine Evans, which was released by Children's Press in 1946. That same publishing house reissued the book with different illustrators in 1962, before NBC's TV version, and again in 1991, when *School Library Journal* called the book a "classic Christmas story."

The story is about a four-year-old boy who arrives in Heaven but is unable to adapt to the ethereal existence. He's not gifted with the ability to sing like the other angels, he's frequently late for prayers, and his robe and halo are always soiled. He annoys his fellow angels and is subsequently unhappy and lonely. Finally, this relatively lost little angel is introduced to the Understanding Angel (adapted to be Patience, the Guardian Angel), who wonders how he can help. That's when the Littlest Angel requests to receive the box of childhood treasures that he held hidden underneath his bed on Earth.

The Understanding Angel grants the request, and the Littlest Angel becomes content and angelic, his true heavenly and destined personality. At which point, the birth of the Christ Child is announced and all the angels prepare their finest gifts for him.

The Littlest Angel decides to give the Christ Child his own box of boyhood favorites, which pleases to no end God, who mounts the gift in the sky, where it transforms into the Star of Bethlehem.

This remarkable and touching story had been adapted into films before and after the NBC Hallmark production. A semi-animated edition of the story (with the majority of the motion created by panning the camera across the artwork) was produced in 1950 by Coronet Films and widely distributed in 16mm for church and school showings. In 2011, an animated edition was produced, starring the voices of Caleb Wolfe as the Littlest Angel, Ed Kelly as his dog, and Ron Perlman as God.

However, it is NBC's Hallmark presentation that was repeated for multiple subsequent Christmas seasons. The film is enhanced by Johnny Whitaker's poignant performance in the title role, Fred Gwynne as the Understanding Angel, and other cast members including Cab Galloway, John McGiver, Tony Randall, George Rose, Connie Stevens, and E. G. Marshall as God. The soundtrack companion album to the special peaked at #33 on Billboard's *Best for Christmas* album chart on December 26, 1970.

A few years later, another classic Christmas TV-movie tale based on a classic narrative tale made a musical connection with a well-known small-screen personality. In 1978, ABC aired a TV-movie adaptation of O. Henry's "The Gift of the Magi," about a turn-of-the-last-century rich girl in a soon-to-be-arranged marriage. Titled, *The Gift of Love*, the ABC production starred Marie Osmond, who, alongside her brother Donny, was then enjoying the success of their popular ABC weekly variety show.

The Gift of Love also starred Timothy Bottoms, who had recently gained fame from such prestigious feature films as *The Last Picture Show* and *The Paper Chase*, a pre-fame James Woods, and June Lockhart, another film and TV icon, then and still best known from *Lassie*, *Lost in Space*, and *Petticoat Junction*. According to Telly Davidson, *The Gift of Love*, like *The Littlest Angel*, was apparently a match made in Heaven. He described it as "the epitome of a great holiday movie," a "benchmark" production that was even allowed a preview as one of rival network NBC's Bob Hope's Christmas specials that year.

That was indeed a significant development, one of which had not trans-pired since ABC allowed its *That Girl* icon Marlo Thomas, if just with her voice and in animated form, to appear with her father, Danny Thomas, on the *Cricket on the Hearth* segment of the latter's NBC musical variety program. "For all the people who'd written off Marie Osmond as just a too-cute, grown-up child actor, this was a real revelation," Davidson said. "We really got to see what 'pretty little Marie' was capable of, not only singing and being maternal and big-sisterly, but holding her own" opposite Bottoms, Woods, and Lockhart. "It was done with subtlety and good taste and could still stand up alongside today's Hallmark-style movies and other older holiday classics."

Meanwhile, also in 1978, on December 20, CBS aired the notable TV-movie *A Christmas to Remember*, which was filmed in Rush City, Missouri. Starring Eva Marie Saint, Jason Robards, Joanne Woodward, and George Perry, this movie was directed by George England and adapted from the 1977 novel *The Melodeon* by Glendon Swarthout.

The story: Rusty McCloud (Perry) is sent by his economically strapped mother (Woodward) to live on his grandparents' farm one winter during the Great Depression. The grandparents, Daniel Larson (Robards) and his wife, Emma (Saint), are still grieving the loss of their son in World War I, while Daniel is at first especially resentful toward his grandson. However, in time, Rusty and Daniel form a bond, which culminates at Christmas as they work to deliver a melodeon left by the dead son to the local church as a surprise gift.

Two years after that, CBS aired *A Christmas Without Snow*, starring Michael Learned of *The Waltons* and John Houseman. Learned plays Zoe Jensen, a divorced woman who moves to San Francisco to start a new life. She joins the choir of a local church and is inspired by the choirmaster, Houseman's Ephraim Adams, a perfectionist and curmudgeon. As Christmas approaches and the choir practices for a performance of Handel's "Messiah," issues of racism and ageism, accusations against a young choir member, and the director's health issue threaten to undermine the performance.

One decade or so later, *Christmas on Division Street* debuted on ABC in 1991. Directed by George Kaczender and written by Barry Morrow, this film features *The Wonder Years* star Fred Savage, who delivers a fine performance as the privileged offspring of wealthy parents who learn the true meaning of Christmas from their son (who learns it from a homeless man played by Hume Cronyn). Hint: it doesn't have anything to do with buying lots of expensive, materialistic gifts for people on Black Friday. *Christmas on Division Street*, which offers one of the sweetest endings this side of *It's a Wonderful Life*, also stars Badja Djola, Cloyce Morrow, Kenneth Walsh, Kahla Lichti, and Virginia Bagnato.

The list of notable Christmas TV-movies goes on and on, as just a select few are now explored in the following pages.

CHAPTER 26
ONE *MIRACLE* AFTER THE OTHER

"Christmas isn't just a day, it's a frame of mind."

—Kris Kringle, *Miracle on 34th Street*

I n 1947, 20th Century Fox released *Miracle on 34th Street*, the now-classic Oscar-winning black-and-white feature film directed by George Seaton, who also wrote the screenplay. The film, set between Thanksgiving and Christmas in New York, stars Maureen O'Hara as Doris Walker, a Thanksgiving Day parade event coordinator and widowed single parent to a very young Natalie Wood. John Payne is their neighbor Fred Gaily, an attorney; a vocation that comes in handy when Edmund Gwenn's once-inebriated Kris Kringle requires a strong defense for sanity in court after Doris hires him as a department store Santa Claus for Macy's.

The film was then remade three times for television and once more for the big screen.

On December 14, 1955, a one-hour black-and-white television adaptation of the movie, titled *The Miracle on 34th Street*, originally aired as an episode of the *20th Century Fox Hour*. In this production, directed by Robert Stevenson, Thomas Mitchell (of TV's *The O. Henry Playhouse*) portrayed Kris, Macdonald Carey (*Days of Our Lives*) was Fred, Teresa Wright played Doris, and Sandy Descher was cast as Susan. This production, which was later rerun with the title *Meet Mr. Kringle*, eliminated the inebriated element of Santa's personality.

A few items: Mr. Gimbel was portrayed by Herbert Heyes, who reprised his role from the initial big-screen movie. Of the five main *Miracle* adaptations, this is the only one that was filmed entirely in California (not counting stock footage or process shots).

In the EastWest DVD Co. iteration, this movie is paired with a bonus animated short titled *Little Gray Neck*, a British-dubbed Russian tale that was released in 1948.

Meanwhile, this *Miracle* from 1955 is included in the bonus material for the Fox DVD release of the original 1947 motion picture.

As to the 1955 production itself, significant scenes and plot lines are cut, while much of the actors' performances are hurried to fit into what was an hour-long time frame.

Four years later, on November 27, 1959, yet another *Miracle* occurred, minus the "the" in the title and as a color Christmas episode of *NBC Friday Night Special Presentation*. This show was an anthology series that featured drama, comedy, and musical entertainment produced by TV legend David Susskind and occasional special news reports (all of which alternated monthly with another color series, *The Bell Telephone Hour*, a musical show).

This time, Ed Wynn played Kris, Peter Lind Hayes was Fred, Mary Healy portrayed Doris, and Susan Gordon was Susan. For this adaption, which was broadcast live and in color the day after Thanksgiving, NBC made a kinescope, most likely for broadcasting opening night on the West Coast. The copy was in a large collection of kinescopes donated in 1986 by NBC to the Library of Congress and was thought to be lost. That is, until it was later recovered by Richard Finegan, who reported his experiences in the December 2005 issue of *Classic Images*.

The program was sponsored by Westclox; commercials were presented live by Betsy Palmer. Of the five main adaptations, this is the only *Miracle* that was produced completely in New York and not to present scenes of the Macy's Thanksgiving Day Parade.

A special screening of this adaption was held at the Library of Congress in December 2005 with Susan Gordon, who played Susan Walker in the program, attending. She was able to watch her performance for the first time.

All of this brings us to the 1973 CBS TV-movie edition of *Miracle on 34th Street*, directed by Fielder Cook (*The Homecoming: A Christmas Story*, 1971) and written by Valentine Davies and Jeb Rosebrook (among others). It's nowhere near the elegance of the original 1947 feature-film classic, but it's far superior to the 1955 and 1959 editions and more touching than the overblown remake from 1994.

Now, it's Sebastian Cabot (Mr. French from TV's *Family Affair*) who plays Kris Kringle, David Hartman (soon to be an early-rising staple on

ABC's *Good Morning, America*) is cast as Fred, Jane Alexander (who's just about to find super fame playing Eleanor Roosevelt in a series of TV-movies for ABC) as Doris, and Suzane Davidson as Susan.

In solid supporting roles: Roddy McDowall, Jim Backus (*Gilligan's Island, Mr. Magoo*), James Gregory (*Barney Miller*), Conrad Janis (*Mork & Mindy*), Roland Winters, and David Doyle (*Charlie's Angels*) and Tom Bosley (*Happy Days*), who have been cross-identified by viewers for years, and who appeared on-screen together for the first time.

Despite what could have been a higher production value, for its time, and with its noble elements and efforts for nostalgia, a straight-forward "logic within the illogic" script, this film becomes everything a Christmas TV-movie (or any TV-movie for that matter) should be.

Some anecdotes:

For starters, the opening credits of this movie include this disclaimer—*The persons and events in this film are fictitious. Any similarity to actual persons or events is unintentional.*

Sebastian Cabot had to shave off his famous beard for this movie and don an artificial one after makeup artists were unable to whiten and enhance his real beard in order for him to look like St. Nick.

Robert Wagner and Natalie Wood were approached to play Fred and Doris, with Wood's daughter Natasha Gregson Wagner set to portray Susan. However, Wood rejected the offer, believing her daughter was too young for the role and that she wanted Natasha to have as normal a childhood as possible.

Melissa Gilbert, soon to become a pop culture legend of her own as the star of *Little House on the Prairie*, wanted very much to play Susan but lost the part to Suzanne Davidson.

David Doyle, who was cast as Mr. Macy, had previously played the psychologist Dr./Mr. Sawyer on Broadway in the musical adaptation of *Miracle on 34th Street*, titled, "Here's Love."

The year before this *Miracle* took place, Doyle had played Meredith Baxter's father on the short-lived but heralded TV sitcom *Bridget Loves Bernie*, and he was just three years away from finding fame on TV's *Charlie's Angels*. On that super successful female detective show of the 1970s, producer Aaron Spelling cast Doyle as Bosley, a little inside joke knowing of Doyle's similar appearance to actor Tom Bosley (who was one year away from making his own TV mark on *Happy Days*).

Two decades after the 1973 TV edition of *Miracle on 34th Street*, the story returned to the big screen with Richard Attenborough as Kris Kringle,

Elizabeth Perkins as "Dorey" Walker (instead of Doris), Dylan McDermott as Bryan Bedford (instead of Fred), and Mara Wilson, whose character kept the original name of Susan Walker.

CHAPTER 27
CHRISTMAS ON *WALTONS'* MOUNTAIN AND *THE PRAIRIE*

"If John doesn't get home soon with money, all we'll have for Christmas dinner is my applesauce cake.

The only Santa Claus I wanna' see is your Daddy walking through the door."

—Olivia Walton, as played by Patricia Neal in *The Homecoming*

Before Ralph Waite and Michael Learned stepped into their Emmy-winning roles as John and Olivia Walton on *The Waltons* (CBS, 1972–1981), the acclaimed family series began with the TV-movie *The Homecoming: A Christmas Story.* This film, which premiered on CBS December 19, 1971, featured Patricia Neal and Andrew Duggan as parents to John-Boy Walton, the central character played by Richard Thomas in both the original *Homecoming* TV-movie and subsequent *Waltons* weekly series.

The Homecoming, adapted from Earl Hamner Jr.'s novel of the same name, was a ratings and critical success. Creative writer, high-technological maestro, and entertainment enthusiast Christopher Pufall offered his insightful perspective on the initial movie:

> The movie is set in 1933 and relates an Earl Hamner story, inspired from his life, of a family desperately awaiting the return of their father for Christmas Eve, after he had taken needed work out of town. Not knowing if the harsh snowy weather had caused his unexpected delay, or worse an accident, the mother sends her oldest son out on a hero's journey to find his father. Patricia Neal plays the anchoring foundation

of this family household that includes seven children and two grand-parents. Nominated for an Emmy and winning the Golden Globe, Ms. Neal so authentically embodied this role of Olivia that her performance could be likened as Oscar-worthy.

The Homecoming was actually the second film of Hamner's autobio-graphical writings committed to the screen, the first being *Spencer's Mountain* (1963) as a film sourced in the same material and starring Henry Fonda and Maureen O'Hara. For context of the eventual Waltons TV journey, the series saw the casting return of all seven children, additional to the grandmother. Also returning to each episode's ongoing tradition was the pitch-perfect ending started in *The Homecoming*, that of each family member declaring their "Good Night" across the household as the last light flickered off in that warmly caring home.

This is a humble story, distilled down to the pure essence of Christ-mas, where profound and gentle offerings lovingly shared from the heart outlast the transient fragility of material gifts. *The Homecoming* celebrates this through the dynamics of a family strengthened by hardships during the Great Depression and by their bootstrapped self-sufficiency with living off the land nestled along Walton's Mountain. The film conveys principles where religious expression and spiritual conviction are neces-sarily balanced against a more humanistic way of life, firmly roughened and honed by discipline and practicality—when maturity obviates the nudging aside of innocence early within a child's life.

When John senior, the Walton's father, finally returns home late Christmas Eve, we witness a vital myth unfolding anew for how the family sees their father, as he relates a tale of wrestling the immortal Santa for a stash of wrapped gifts finely tuned to each recipient's heart. Of particular note are the writing tablets given to John-Boy, the oldest child, who is on the cusp of full adulthood and hoping to cultivate his desire for becoming a writer.

According to entertainment journalist Melissa Byers, *The Homecoming: A Christmas Story* left its mark:

It's become such an incredible . . . and integral part of American cul-ture. 1971 was a fraught time in American history, yet this simple tale of a bygone era captured the imagination of the public, and we took the Waltons into our hearts. Papa Walton trying to get home to his family, and the family at home hoping and praying that he would make it, reflected all the families waiting for their loved ones to come home from the war. *The Waltons* were a large, boisterous family, with the usual squabbles among the children, but they remained close and the love they had for one another was palpable. It was a necessary film for the time, and it gave America a perfect Christmas card.

On November 28, 2021, as part of a fiftieth anniversary celebration to *The Homecoming: A Christmas Story*, The CW Television Network (CW) aired a remake of the film, which was retitled *The Waltons: Homecoming*. Original John-Boy and Emmy-winning-actor Richard Thomas introduced and narrated the film. As he told the Television Academy and Emmys.com at the time, about *The Waltons* in general, "The staying power it has is . . . astonishing."

As Christopher Pufall noted earlier, *The Waltons* saga began with *Spencer's Mountain*, Hamner's novel about a poor West Virginia family struggling to make ends meet during the Great Depression. Published in 1961, the book became a 1963 motion picture of the same name starring Henry Fonda and Maureen O'Hara as Clay and Olivia Walton, and James McArthur (*Hawaii Five-O*) as their oldest son, Clay-Boy, a sensitive young man with dreams of being the first in his family to go to college.

In his teleplay for the original *Homecoming*, Hamner changed the family surname to Walton, Clay to John, and Clay-Boy to John-Boy. In addition to Patricia Neal's portrayal of Olivia and Andrew Duggan's initial take on John Sr. and Thomas's John-Boy, Ellen Corby and Edgar Bergen played paternal grandparents Esther and Zeb. When CBS launched *The Waltons* series in 1972, Michael Learned and Ralph Waite stepped in as Olivia and John Sr., Will Geer replaced Bergen as Grandpa Zeb, and Corby continued as Grandma Esther. The same young performers from *The Homecoming* played the other six Walton children in the series: Jon Walmsley as Jason; Judy Norton as Mary Ellen; Mary McDonough as Erin; Eric Scott as Ben; David Harper as Jim-Bob; and Kami Cotler as Elizabeth.

After ending its original run in 1981, *The Waltons* cast reunited for several popular TV-movies in the 1990s, including *A Walton Thanksgiving Reunion*, *A Walton Wedding*, and *A Walton Easter*.

Fifty years later, for the new CW version of *Homecoming*, John-Boy is played by Logan Shroyer, who became familiar to television audiences for his role on *This Is Us*. The rest of the cast includes Bellamy Young and Ben Lawson as Olivia and John Sr., Christian Finlayson as Jason, Marcelle LeBlanc as Mary Ellen, Tatum Sue Matthews as Erin, Samuel Goergon as Jim-Bob, and Callaway Corrick as Elizabeth. Rebecca Koon plays Grandma Esther and

Alpha Trivette is Grandpa Zeb. Music superstars Marilyn McCoo and Billy Davis Jr. make cameo appearances.

Reflecting on the original *Homecoming* telefilm, Thomas recalled on Emmys.com: "This is not like anything else on TV. Who knows if it will fly?"

But fly it did—across generations. "The idea of the family structure of all those different demographics coming together in one show was kind of a big deal and very different," Thomas said. "So, that's how the audience sort of coalesced. And the critics got behind it. *The Waltons* certainly was a show in which familial love and a sense of community were the ground on which it was built," he added.

The series became so popular that it was parodied in *Mad* magazine and on *The Carol Burnett Show* in a sketch titled, "The Walnuts." Thomas was nothing but flattered by the Burnett segment in particular: "It was such an honor," he said.

"It's all been such a blessing . . . such a gift," said Mary McDonough, who played middle daughter Erin. "Earl Hamner's incredible writing in *The Homecoming* captured a snapshot of Christmas. It was, and remains, a story about the bonds of family and community. It's the same thing that made the show so great."

McDonough also credited original *Homecoming* director Fielder Cook for guiding her through the process. "He encouraged us to just be ourselves," she said.

Judy Norton, who played tomboy Mary Ellen, agreed. Cook "was lovely," Norton said. "Very easy to work with, he was great with all of us kids."

Kami Cotler, who charmed audiences as the youngest Walton, Elizabeth, said Fielder "was able to invite me into the idea that we were pretending, and we were pretending in an authentic way.

"It was so realistic with such texture," Cotler continued. "In *The Homecoming*, and in the first couple of years of making the series, it was a bit more like a movie from the 1940s or 1950s than like a 1970s television series."

Playing a close-knit family created bonds among the cast members off-screen, as well. Eric Scott, who played business-minded middle son Ben, invited his fellow TV siblings to his bar mitzvah. It was at that event that Scott and his fellow youthful peers learned from his agent that the *Homecoming* telefilm had been greenlit as a series. "That was an amazing day," he said.

Before that happened, however, the original *Homecoming* cast was cautioned to take things slowly with Patricia Neal, who had suffered a stroke shortly before filming. As Scott recalled: "I was told by my mom, and by everyone on the crew, 'You have to be gentle with her.' She had issues with her speech, but in the end, it's clear she delivered a terrific performance."

Edgar Bergen, who achieved fame as a ventriloquist in films and early television shows with his wooden sidekick Charlie McCarthy, also "seemed pretty fragile to me," Scott said. "But he was very sweet and had a great sense of humor. And he was so good in his performance, especially because he had never performed on TV [in a dramatic role]."

Jon Walmsley, who played musically gifted Jason, also remembered Bergen fondly. "He was a sweet, lovely man. In Jackson Hole [Wyoming, where *Homecoming* was shot], he did some of his ventriloquist act for us—sitting in front of a fireplace and 'throwing his voice,' talking up to Santa, who literally sounded as though he were calling back down the chimney. It was remarkable, I'll never forget it."

As for Neal, Walmsley said, "She struck me a bit like royalty, in a way. It wasn't until many years later, on a Waltons cruise, that I was exposed to her mischievous, playful side and her wicked sense of humor!"

Norton described Neal as "astounding," while adding that Michael Learned and Ralph Waite "were just magic together."

"Michael has often talked about how easy it was for her to play Olivia because of Ralph," Norton said. "All she had to do was show up and play the scenes with him because he gave so much. And Ralph—I always felt was sort of the bedrock of the show. Neither he nor Michael had a false moment. You just believed that relationship, and they brought the audience in. When any of us played scenes with them it was just so easy because they were everything you would want in a set of parents. They were firm, but they were fair; they were compassionate, and yet they weren't overly permissive."

Learned remained close friends with Waite over the years. "I was devastated when he passed [in 2014], and I adored Patricia [Neal, who died in 2010]," she said. Though Learned's Olivia was not as lenient as Waite's John Sr., hers was a less stern performance than Neal's. "I knew that I couldn't be quite as tough on a weekly basis. There were certainly some moments where Olivia was tender and warm. So, she managed to walk that line, where you knew she loved her kids, even though she was strict with them."

In the 2021 CW production, Olivia and John Sr. were brought back to life by Bellamy Young and Ben Lawson, loving parents to Shroyer's remolded John-Boy. As fate would have it, Richard Thomas was grandfather to Shroyer's childhood best friend.

In the process, the new *Homecoming* aligned with Hamner's original vision. Or, as Judy Norton said of the first *Homecoming* and *The Waltons*: "Earl felt that there needed to be that spice to offset the softer stuff."

The consistent aesthetic thread and approach were guided in the reboot by producer Sam Haskell, a former longtime talent agent at the William

Morris Agency. In recent years, Haskell became synonymous with heart-warming television productions that centered around Christmas. These include a series of TV movies starring Dolly Parton, including Netflix's *Dolly Parton's Christmas on the Square*, which won the Emmy for Outstanding Television Movie in 2021.

To bring a fresh perspective to the new *Homecoming*, Haskell reunited director Lev L. Spiro and writer Jim Strain, who performed those respective duties on the 2019 telefilm *Dolly Parton's Heartstrings*.

Among Strain's tweaks to Hamner's original teleplay were Thomas's direct-to-camera introduction and the interspersing of narration throughout. It's a voice-over presence that Thomas had sought to provide in the original telefilm and series, but that job went to Hamner.

Five decades later, however, "I finally did that," said a delighted Thomas. "And it's all come full circle."

Similar appreciation for the original *Waltons* was shared by David Harper, who played Jim-Bob, the youngest Walton son. "I loved working on the show," he said. Harper recalled how the Family Research Council "bombarded the studios" in the early 1970s with pleas for programming suitable for all ages.

Beyond both editions of *The Homecoming*, *The Waltons* presented other Christmas episodes, including "The Best Christmas" (December 9, 1976), "The Children's Carol" (December 8, 1977), "Day of Infamy" (December 7, 1978), and "The Spirit" (December 20, 1979). The show also sprouted several Thanksgiving segments, including (for NBC) *A Waltons Thanksgiving Reunion* movie from 1993 and CW's 2022 rebooted *Waltons Thanksgiving* sequel to the second *Homecoming*.

When CBS scored strong ratings with the original *Waltons* series, Harper said, "It started a boom. Shows like *Little House on the Prairie* [NBC, 1974–1982] piggybacked on us the next year, much the way *I Dream of Jeannie* piggybacked off *Bewitched* [in the 1960s]."

In like manner, several *Little House on the Prairie* Christmas episodes celebrate the message of the season. Like *The Waltons*, *Little House* has a strong following that continues to pull on their heartstrings. Also, like *The Waltons*, *Little House* was based on a best-selling book, this time, a series of autobiographical tomes by Laura Ingalls Wilder. Wilder's stories were told from the heart, echoing the real-life adventures of a family, friendship, and the daily life of pioneers in the nineteenth century.

The cast of *Little House* included Michael Landon as Charles Ingalls, following his long run as Little Joe on NBC's *Bonanza*; Karen Grassle as Landon's TV wife, Caroline Ingalls, and Melissa Sue Anderson and Melissa

Gilbert as their daughters Mary and Laura Ingalls, respectively; twins Lindsay and Sidney Greenbush sharing the role of youngest daughter Carrie Ingalls; Victor French as Isaiah Edwards, Alison Arngrim as Nellie Oleson, and among others, the co-leading man Dean Butler as Almanzo Wilder, who eventually marries Laura.

Eight Oscar-winning actors and actresses appeared as guest stars on various episodes: Ernest Borgnine, Burl Ives (from *Rudolph the Red-Nosed Reindeer*), Red Buttons (from *The Year Without a Santa Claus*), Eileen Heckert (the later-day *Honeymooners* Christmas special), Louis Gossett Jr., Ralph Bellamy, Sean Pean, and original *Waltons* mother Patricia Neal.

On October 13, 2020, journalist Courtney Campbell explored a few key points of the *Little House* Christmas episodes for WideOpenCountry.com:

Season 1, Episode 15, "Christmas at Plum Creek" (December 25, 1974): "The first Christmas episode on the series came in the very first season of the beloved show. If there's ever an episode of a TV show to get you in the Christmas spirit, this is it. Everyone in the Ingalls family becomes secretive as they plan what to get each other for the upcoming holiday. Charles and Caroline get extra jobs to be able to afford gifts for their loved ones and Laura tries to work out a deal to sell her horse Bunny to Mr. Oleson [Richard Bull] so she can afford a new stove for her mother. It's a story of selfless love and the true meaning of the season. You'll never forget seeing little Carrie understand what it's all about at the end of the episode as she puts the topper on the tree."

Season 3, Episode 11, "Blizzard" (January 3, 1977): As Campbell explained, this episode was set on Christmas Eve. "A snowstorm is headed for Walnut Grove so Miss Beadle [Charlotte Stewart] lets the children out early as the snow has already started falling. When some of the women come to the schoolhouse and find the children gone, the entire town comes together with a search party. Mr. Edwards and his children Alicia [Kyle Richards] and Carl [Brian Part] are still missing on Christmas morning after the blizzard has ended so the town goes out to help locate them. Even Harriet Oleson hands out coats to volunteers. Though the search party does result in a loss for some, it is a favorite Christmas episode. Charles Ingalls dramatically ends the episode by reading the Christmas story from the Bible to everyone."

Season 8, Episode 11, "A Christmas They Never Forgot" (December 21, 1981): Campbell called this adventure "one of the fan-favorite holiday episodes" that "follows an adult Laura who is pregnant, joined by her husband Almanzo, the Ingalls family, and the newly adopted Cooper children as they all spend Christmas together. Hester Sue [Ketty Lester] also brings Mary and Adam [Linwood Boomer] as a Christmas surprise for everyone. While the family is snowed in, they sit around and recount their best Christmas memories together. Laura remembers a holiday when the family still lived in Kansas together and it turns out to be the perfect way to pass the time together under the Christmas tree."

According to *Little House on the Prairie* historian Lisa Kavarian Hiatt, the "Blizzard" episode is the best of the bunch:

This is my favorite Christmas episode, as it includes almost the entire cast members, which makes it all the better to watch and love. I love all the snow and classroom scenes. My favorite scene is between Willie [Jonathan Gilbert] and Miss Beadle. It's touching to see how Willie is so very sad about what happened. It's probably one of the only times that Willie is sad for someone else.

This storyline is from real-life events that happened in 1888 called "The Children's Blizzard," which hit the US Great Plains when several children died during one of most horrific winter storms of all time.

For this episode, I don't believe that Michael Landon wanted to be harsh and have children die on-screen and therefore, he had the adult [Ted McGinnis] played by [John Carter] pass away instead as he was looking for his son [Henry] played by [Johnny Timko] in the blizzard.

CHAPTER 28
THE HOUSE THAT ADDIE BUILT

"Why won't you buy me a tree, Dad? I'll settle for a small one."

—Addie Mills

"I want that tree out of my house . . ."

—James Mills

"She's more than your daughter, she's a human being."

—Grandma Mills

T he *House Without a Christmas Tree* is another gem in the jewel pool of Christmas TV-movies. Premiering on CBS December 3, 1972, *The House Without a Christmas Tree* was directed by Paul Bogart and based on a story by the special's producer Alan Shayne (today, in his late nineties) and Gail Rock, with an Emmy-winning teleplay by Eleanor Perry. Artist Norman Sunshine (in his mid-nineties, and Shayne's husband) won an Emmy for the illustrations he created for the show's opening credits and his design of the tree-top star shown in the special.

The impeccable cast of this period piece, set in the 1940s, includes acting veterans Jason Robards and Mildred Natwick and the scene-stealing newcomer Lisa Lucas. The movie was so successful it inspired three CBS sequels: *A Thanksgiving Treasure* (January 1, 1974), *An Easter Promise* (March 26, 1975), and *Addie and the King of Hearts* (in celebration of Valentine's Day, February 25, 1976).

Lucas was only twelve years old when she appeared in the initial *Christmas* movie and fifteen by the end of the miniseries of specials.

Shayne later became president of Warner Bros. and went on to write several books about his and Norman's life together, including *Double Life*, which was a bestseller, and *The Minstrel: A Christmas Story*, which was the first book he ever wrote, and which Norman illustrated. Shayne has also authored a novel called *Finding Sylvia* and recently published his memoir.

For Lucas, "Alan Shayne is my hero. He discovered me. I never would have had my career without him." As she went on to explain, "This is the story of how *The House Without a Christmas Tree* came to be":

> One night, Alan and Norman were having dinner with Eleanor Perry and Gail Rock, both of whom Alan or Norman had never met. They all started talking about Christmas stories. Gail mentioned her childhood, and Alan then came up with an idea about someone who wouldn't allow his daughter to have a tree. Alan said, "That would make a great Christmas movie."
>
> So, he wrote the story, and Eleanor wrote the teleplay, and then Gail wrote the book, which was published two years after *The House Without a Christmas Tree* aired. Gail did not create the original idea for the movie, but she wound up writing four consecutive novels that were adapted and published after each special. To be clear, there was no book until two years after the premiere of the first movie, *The House Without a Christmas Tree*.

A simple but beautiful story, *The House Without a Christmas Tree* is eloquently and intricately told and performed:

James Mills (Robards) has grown bitter and distant over the years following the loss of his wife ten years prior. He no longer celebrates Christmas and refuses to put up a tree. But this is no run-of-the-mill take on Scrooge—especially after watching Jaime's young daughter Addie (Lucas) drag a decorated tree through town and into the Mills' living room. Natwick as James's mother and subsequently Addie's grandmother serves as the go-between driving force of reason who helps to bring peace to a house at subtle war over the holidays. *Tree* was produced on videotape, which ultimately lends to the movie's poignant reality.

Mainstream relatable in several ways, this delicate film features a familiar house, neighborhood, school, and characters with exquisite simplicity and nostalgia.

Lucas recalled several moments of playing Addie, including some uncomfortable ones. Namely, the schoolhouse auditorium sequence involving

Addie's performance in a Christmas pageant. "That was a night shoot," Lucas recalled. "I suddenly got sick. I had a fever and felt horrible. And I got these bumps on my forehead, so we stopped shooting and they called the doctor.

"They could not cover the bumps with makeup," Lucas continued. "It was just so funny. But there was nothing anyone could do about it. You can see my bumps in the earlier scenes with Millie [Natwick] when she is sewing my dress, and when we're in her room, in bed."

To have it all make logistic sense within the confides of the story, and to explain the bumps, Lucas said, "They had to write a scene where Addie got into a fight" [with another student, who called her grandmother a "character"].

The fight sequence occurred in the schoolhouse cloakroom which, along with everything else in the film, was realistically presented. Addie's courageous and bold defense of her grandmother, as Lucas continued to explain, "was true to her character. She was like that."

As fate would later have it, Lucas faced another physical challenge when filming *The Thanksgiving Treasure*. "You can see my limp in that movie because I had broken my ankle. I fell off a horse and broke my leg in seventeen places."

However, it's the initial *House Without a Christmas Tree* special that remains seamlessly unbroken, and fondly remembered. "I still get fan mail," Lucas said, "starting at Thanksgiving and going through Christmas, every year. It has been over fifty years now. I get more fan mail today than I did then. I used to just get letters [in the regular mail]. Now, I get emails and Facebook messages. It is usually all these guys close to my age. They had a crush on me. I just bristled every time I had to wear those pigtails and glasses, which I still have. Most people said they have watched it their whole lives . . . every year with their entire family."

As a period piece, and one of the only post–*TV Golden-Era* movies-of-the-week to be videotaped, *The House Without a Christmas Tree* became what could be termed in big-screen jargon as a *sleeper hit*. In making the film, neither Lucas or anyone else associated with the production ever imagined the long-lasting welcoming effect it would have and retain, much less that it would ignite a series of sequels. "We never thought we would do more than one," Lucas observed. "We never thought we would become a cult phenomenon."

That "we" included director Paul Bogart, who, at the time, was also helming episodes of the network's TV-changing comedy *All in the Family*, which, like *Tree*, was a three-camera production. According to Lucas, Bogart "was amazing. Just a big teddy bear."

The director also knew how to work a room, literally. The interiors used for the small house in the special were, according to Lucas, "like a regular sitcom set. It had four spaces including those for the kitchen, the living room, and those that doubled for the various bedrooms, and the attic. The exteriors used for the house and the school were taped in Canada, whereas the house where Addie brought the tree was right around the corner. That was pretty much all the locations we did."

The interior scenes at the kitchen table were a challenge to tape. "It was cold," Lucas said. "And we did a lot of baking and decorating." Such moments and others were rehearsed and taped at CBS Television City on Fairfax Avenue in Hollywood next to the famed Farmer's Market. "I just loved Farmer's Market," Lucas recalled. "I would roller skate all around it with my little autograph book."

Lucas brought that book everywhere, as when she was rehearsing for another production, this time, on the Warner Bros. studio lot, which has always housed several different movies and TV shows at once. It was on that lot where, as Lucas recalled, "I saw Robert Redford. He was shooting a scene from *The Way We Were* on the outside of the sound stage on a set of stairs. I made sure to get his autograph. And Groucho Marx was sitting at the table in the commissary, eating eggs. He said, 'I will sign your book if you give me a kiss.' And so, I did, and he kissed me with eggs in his mouth. I was grossed out. But I wanted to do it because it was *Groucho Marx*!"

On the *House* set, however, Lucas felt a more sincere kind of love from the *Christmas* cast. "We were like a family. I didn't know who Jason Robards was. I didn't know who Mildred Natwick was. I figured it out later. But I didn't understand the weight and importance of these people." In her recollection, the entire *House* cast "was a dream to work with," particularly Robards and Natwick. "I thought of them as my father and my grandmother for four years. Jason and Millie. They were not prima donnas at all. They loved me. They were my family.

"Jason would even make me paper airplanes with weights in the front," Lucas continued to observe. "I kept one. He was joking a lot at the time. I know that now, but I didn't know at the time."

When the cameras began to roll, the playing field was leveled productively and naturally, indeed just like family. "It sounds like a cliché," Lucas said, "but we all really did get along. I always wanted to know everyone's name and their family. And I have a good memory, but that got me in trouble," she mused. "I'd memorize the script on the way out to L.A. [she lived in New York]. I read everyone else's lines. If Jason would forget a line, the precocious-little-twelve-year-old that I was, would tell him his line."

However, each time Lucas *coached* Robards, as she recalled, "He said, 'Thank you.' He was always wonderful to me. He kind of stayed in character in the first [film], so I was intimidated. He was gruff. I think he purposely did that. He didn't give me advice, but I just watched him. I have always been good at learning from others . . . what not to do, especially, more so than what to do. I hadn't done a heck of a lot at that point."

Lucas's favorite sequence in *House* occurs near the movie's end where Robards' James lifts Addie to the top of the tree to place a star upon it. According to Lucas, her scenes with Robards hit home the most because she, too, like Addie, had a challenging relationship with her father in real life. In watching the scene recently, Lucas teared up, just like Addie did on-screen in her father's arms. Though that pertinent sequence took some doing, with precise coordination for it all to happen in a timely fashion. Lucas explained:

"When James finally goes and gets the star that her mother made and lifts Addie up so they can put it on the tree together, I cried. Paul Bogart wasn't on the floor on the set. He was up in a booth. It was very difficult. I just wasn't doing the scene right. So, Paul started yelling at me through the speaker. And I just stormed off the set. I was sobbing. I told my mother, 'I'm not doing this anymore!' Paul finally came into my dressing room and calmed me down and convinced me to come back and do the scene again.

"Of course, I did the scene well," Lucus noted, "because I had been crying for half an hour. He yelled at me on purpose."

Such theatrical tactics might not seem appropriate or acceptable by today's strict Hollywood standards, but Lucas was quick to defend Bogart. "He didn't do anything bad," she said. "It wasn't traumatic or anything. He knew I was having trouble with the scene, and that I needed something to help me.

"Paul was very sweet to me," Lucas clarified. "I was good at getting angry. But I wasn't so good at crying [on cue] and tapping into that emotion for the camera, because [doing so] made me uncomfortable."

Lucas had saved the tree-top star for more than four decades, and even made copies of it to give to family members. Though she in recent years lost track of the original star, Lucas noted: "At least I still have the original pair of glasses which as it turned out were inaccurate for the time period. They were aviator glasses, but they didn't have aviator glasses in the 1940s."

Another of Lucas's favorite on-screen *House* moments is also memorable for the audience; the heart-wrenching scene when Addie drags a Christmas tree through the streets. Earlier in the movie, she won the tree in a lottery during her classroom Christmas party at school, using a numbers game technique she learned from her father. With the help of Addie's young friend

Carla Mae, played by Alexa Kenin, she brought the tree home, much to the dismay of her father. Upon learning the tree reminds him of his dead wife and Addie's mother, Addie drags the tree back out of the house and up the street to the home of Gloria (Gail Dunsome), her less-fortunate opponent and classmate in the lottery. As Lucas had mentioned earlier, "I didn't have to go too far to drag the tree," as the location-shoot for that scene was close by to Addie's house. "And while Addie was very unemotional in that scene," Lucas said, "I get emotional now whenever I see it or think of it, because of Lexi [Kenin]."

Kenin, with whom Lucas remained close off-screen into adulthood, died when she was only twenty-three years old. "We were best friends and room-mates when she passed away," Lucas recalled. "She was amazing . . . and talented. And unlike me, she knew how to cry on-camera."

Kenin's real-life mother, Maya Kenin Ryan, also appeared in the movie, playing Gloria's mother in the pivotal scene when James delivers Christmas cookies made by Natwick's character. Upon entering Gloria's house, he notices the tree that he readily assumes Addie has delivered with a note signed by Santa Claus.

Other *House* moments proved charming for Lucas, including Addie's interactions with her school crush, Billy Wild, played by Brady McNamara. In this case, life imitated art, as Lucas, too, had "a little crush" on McNamara. Addie worked hard not to show her true feelings for Billy, who ends up having her name for the Christmas Secret Santa gift exchange in class. He gives her a necklace, which Addie ultimately wears. "He was so cute," Lucas said of both Billy and Brady.

House originally succeeded, spawned sequels, and remains popular today because, according to Lucas, it presents "a relatable story . . . a difficult father relationship. James punished Addie because he couldn't handle the memories of his wife. The show was so well-written. They show [Natwick] standing up for what is right. What got me crying was when he played a mean-spirited water trick on Addie. My real-life father would do things like that."

A similar tone threaded each of the subsequent *House* sequels, including *Addie and the King of Hearts*, in which Addie is jealous of her father's girl-friend. Each film showcases "the true nature of the father-daughter relation-ship," Lucas said, specifically *The House*, which "strikes different chords in different people. For some people, it's about the nostalgia from their youth. They say things like, 'My Dad was like that.' It reminds them of how they grew up. For people of my age, it was wanting to be like Addie. She eventu-ally left a small town and went somewhere big. She was precocious and coura-geous. She fought with boys and was kind of a tomboy. But she wanted to be like a girl and liked boys. She showed a typical adolescence in such a natural way. It was like people got inside the head of the little girl. It went into a deeper layer of adolescence, in dealing with family issues. It presented heavy issues. 'My father hates me. What did I ever do? I was born. My mother died. I felt safe with grandma.'"

In discussing how other Christmas TV specials of any genre, including the animated sector, relate to *House*, Lucas said, as a child, "I wasn't a huge *Charlie Brown* fan, but I love the Halloween special [*It's the Great Pumpkin, Charlie Brown*, CBS, 1966]. And I love *Rudolph* [*the Red-Nosed Reindeer* special from 1964]. That was my favorite. I loved its [stop-action animation]. I didn't like the [traditionally drawn] cartoons too much as a kid.

"Rudolph was kind of like Addie," Lucas continued, "because, like him, she was different and an outsider. She didn't even belong with her own father and family. She was an outcast. So, she had to become strong to make something of herself and get what she wanted. Rudolph was a lot like that. Pull yourself up by your bootstraps and come out stronger on the other side. That kind of thing. Both Addie and Rudolph were like that. It sounds silly, and I never thought to make an analogy with a reindeer, but Addie and Rudolph have a lot in common."

As a child, Lucas also enjoyed classic and modern movies, *The Sonny & Cher Comedy Hour*, and *The Carol Burnett Show*. She also "watched a lot of Johnny Carson. I always wanted to marry Johnny. He had four wives. I wanted to be number five."

"My only problem with the movie is that I mumble throughout, to the point of sometimes error. I was almost too natural."

Certainly, contemporary audiences have grown accustomed to mumbling dialogue in new TV shows and movies, some of which are drowned out by special effects and poor sound mixing. More often than not, today's actors in films and TV shows are too darkly lit for scenes in which they speak too softly, while booming background music or sound effects are heard, competing for the audience's attention. As Lucas herself noted, "I have to turn the television up so loud. I have to keep readjusting. I watch a lot of old movies. In today's shows, they are either over the top and too articulate, or it is mumbled."

Lucas never took an acting class until she was in her twenties, "But that was it." As such, just like the *House* film itself was a slice-of-life production, presented with a solid sense of realism, the then-twelve-year-old Lucas was indeed a "natural" when it came to acting. Many child actors, or former child stars, upon reaching adulthood, do not retain their aesthetic appeal or talent for roles. More often than not, when young actors rise into adulthood, their talent does not always grow with them. They either seem to forget how to act or they may have never understood the actual technique and craft of acting in the first place. As kids, they are many times just that: kids, unaware of acting as a craft and the abilities it requires to make a character or a scene work.

Those like former child star Richard Thomas, pre–*The Waltons*, always knew, studied, appreciated, and respected the craft of acting. He then grew into adulthood, and subsequently, deeper into his craft with an Emmy-winning career.

In like manner, Lucas has retained her diverse theatrical talents, while she continues to explore other vocations and lives a fascinating life. "In my twenties," she recalled, "I went to France and went to Cordon Bleu and became a chef. I came back in 1992 and made one more movie, called *Heart and Souls* (1993). I still audition occasionally."

Today, Lucas would still consider acting, possibly in a sequel to *The House Without a Christmas Tree*, though she now classifies herself as a writer. "I have been doing short stories and pilots."

Lucas, not to be confused with the Lisa Lucas who works in publishing, was once an investigative reporter for the New York *Daily News*. "I spent a lot of time in Haiti after the quake [January 12, 2010] because I was living in Florida at the time and I speak French. I spent about three months and got malaria. But the New York *Daily News* wouldn't send me there. So, I went on my own."

When not working, Lucas enjoys sports, like snow-skiing and pickleball. "And I am a huge tennis fan," she said.

However, it's the love she feels to this day from *The House Without a Christmas Tree* that keeps her on her game. Whenever a fan names *The House Without a Christmas Tree* as their favorite Christmas special, Lucas responds in awe, and takes pause with a simple, and poignant audible "aw." She is continuously astonished when fans approach her and express how much the film means to them. "I have one family friend whose mother just passed and it is his favorite show.

"It makes me cry," she said.

CHAPTER 29
IT'S A WONDERFUL TV-MOVIE

"Merry Christmas, Mr. Potter!

        —Mary Bailey, *It Happened One Christmas*

On Sunday, December 11, 1977, a kind of miracle transpired on television. ABC aired the TV-movie *It Happened One Christmas*, starring and executive-produced by the network's *That Girl* icon. A remake of director Frank Capra's 1946 big-screen classic, *It's a Wonderful Life*, starring Jimmy Stewart and Donna Reed, *It Happened One Christmas* was miraculous in a Hollywood way. More often than not, remakes, reboots, and the like tend never to live up to the original on which they are based. However, such is not the case with the small-screen reimagined *It Happened One Christmas*. Directed by Donald Wrye, with a teleplay by Lionel Chetwynd, *Happened* equals if not surpasses the big-screen *Wonderful* template that gave it life.

It's a Wonderful Life itself was adapted from previous material; Philip Van Doren's self-published short story and booklet, *The Greatest Gift*. When published in 1943, *Gift* itself was loosely based on previous-released material, Charles Dickens' 1843 novella *A Christmas Carol*.

Chetwynd's *Happened* TV script from 1977 varies little from the *Wonderful*'s 1946 big screenplay (by Capra, Frances Goodrich, and Albert Hackett, with additional dialogue by Jo Swerling), which makes its female-geared reimagining all the more fascinating, compelling, and groundbreaking from an equal gender–friendly point of view. Thomas reworked *Wonderful* with a female twist that led to impressive results.

The film's premiere was the fourth-most-watched prime-time TV program for the week (with a Nielsen rating of 27.5, or twenty million homes), airing as an entry for *The ABC Sunday Night Movie*, which usually showcased first-network runs of theatrical films (as opposed to first runs of new movies made specifically for TV).

Happened's casting also played an important role in the spectrum of its success. Each actor gives 100 percent to their portrayals, including Thomas as Mary Bailey Hatch (the female counterpart to Stewart's George Bailey); Wayne Rogers (*M*A*S*H*) as her love interest George Hatch (whereas Reed's Mary played opposite Stewart's George); the legendary Mercury Theatre stage and film actor/director Orson Welles as Henry F. Potter/Mr. Potter; Cloris Leachman (*The Mary Tyler Moore Show*) in her Emmy-nominated role as Clara Oddbody (the angel, the female counterpart to Clarence Odbody—with only one initial "d"—played by Henry Travers in *Life*); Doris Roberts (*Everybody Loves Raymond*) as Ma Bailey (Beula Bondi's *Wonderful* role); Christopher Guest as Harry, Mary's brother (who Todd Karns played in *Wonderful*); Barney Martin (*Seinfeld*) as Uncle Willie (Thomas Mitchell was *Wonderful*'s Uncle Billy), along with other characters played by such stalwarts as Dick O'Neill, Cliff Norton, C. Thomas Howell, and more, each a resilient resident of their fictional upstate New York hometown: Bedford Falls.

The timeless story goes something like this:

In the late 1930s and early 1940s, the trailblazing, career-minded Mary Bailey has big aspirations of world travel. However, due to responsibilities and developing circumstances, she ultimately is forced to remain in Bedford Falls. There, she lives a more traditional life; marrying her high school sweetheart George Hatch, with whom she raises a family. However, Mary is still a fierce go-getter who oversees her family's business, the local Building & Loan.

All seems stable for a few years into her resettled life, until something very special "happens one night." On the wintery, slippery Christmas Eve of 1945, following a series of traumatic events, Mary's life, career, and disposition begin to change. It's all because Uncle Willie has misplaced the Building & Loan's funds and left Mary with insurmountable debt to the entire town. She becomes frantic, loses her temper, and lashes out at her husband and children. Once known and beloved for her generous and amiable spirit, Mary is now a lost, desperate soul. She's always had a solution for every dilemma, but this time, she sees no way out, except one.

In her direst moment of consequential financial crisis and near utter emotional collapse, a severely despondent Mary contemplates suicide. Though just as she's about to take a fatal leap over Bedford Falls' main town bridge, Mary is rescued by her guardian angel; an off-center, wing-seeking, jovial sort, aptly named Clara Oddbody.

With a mysterious journey to an alternate Bedford Falls, Clara shows Mary what life would be like had she "never been born." The town's name has been changed to Potterville, following its acquirement by the wealthy tyrant Mr. Potter; her husband George is a slug; Mary's mother runs a tenement house, and her brother Harry has died.

Harry's demise hits Mary the hardest; the straw that breaks the camel's back in this newfound lost world that has deserted her. As children, in the Bedford Falls life she had once known, they went skating on thin ice. Mary was there to save him from falling through a crack in the surface. But this time, in the alternate town of Potterville, she never existed; she wasn't there to rescue him from drowning.

Fortunately, with Clara's divine intervention and earnest motivation to win her wings, Mary ultimately sees the proverbial light at the end of the tunnel. She is returned to her original Bedford Falls universe, whose recognizable residents, despite dealing with their own financial duress, band together at Mary's home, with a deluge of countless dollars. Uncle Willie's fiscal fiasco could not derail them from remembering all that Mary had done for each of them at one point in their lives. Even the federal bank inspector throws his two cents into the pot.

Amid the smiles of abundant and grateful hearts, a tiny bell is heard ringing from an angel ornament upon the Bailey home's Christmas tree. That's a sure sign that Clara has earned her Heavenly wings and that for Mary and Bedford Falls on Earth, all's well, that end's well.

The idea for the movie was generated by ABC's then-programming chief, Fred Silverman. As Thomas remembered, Silverman called her and said: "I would like you to do a Christmas special for us." To which Thomas replied: "Oh, Freddie, thank you . . . but I am not right for that. What can I do? I would have to sing and dance, and I could barely do either. And I can't be Ed Sullivan and introduce other people. I just really have never been a part of the musical variety world. I am not a musical person. Everything I have done has been a story [in scripted, narrative form]."

Silverman, however, was persistent. "You don't have to do any singing and dancing," he told Thomas. "You just bring me a Christmas special."

At which point, music supervisor Bruce Hart, married to Carol Hart, Thomas's producing partner, stepped into the picture and suggested a remake of *It's a Wonderful Life*. "I didn't even know the movie," Thomas acknowledged. "In 1977 it wasn't the cult classic that it became."

The conversation began with Thomas and Hart's tossing around ideas, "talking about what we could do," she recalled. "It was just so stuck in my head that a Christmas special was supposed to include music and was confounded about doing one any other way. But then we just ran with Bruce's idea and got very excited. And what was so revealing, especially to me, since this was 1977, was that when we wrote the script, we hardly had to change any of my lines from *It's a Wonderful Life*. My character said the same things that Jimmy Stewart's character said."

However, an entirely new storyline and character was injected for George Bailey, as played by Rogers. Even though his role shared the same name as Stewart's character in the original *Wonderful* film, Rogers' character was completely different in *It Happened One Christmas*. "We had to create a whole other storyline for Wayne to play my husband, and that was fascinating."

The *Wonderful Life* screenplay's transformation into the *Happened* teleplay had more to do with the fleshing out and development of other Bedford Falls citizen characters. When George, Harry, and other residents go off to fight in WWII, each write Mary detailing their experiences and are shown in uniform, interspersed with actual war footage. Another brief scene depicts wounded George attempting to readjust to civilian life after the war has ended.

Because women were not drafted in WWII, the TV remake does not cause *Happened*'s Mary to lose her hearing in one ear; a theatrical device initially used to justify *Wonderful*'s George's 4F classification and his inability to escape Bedford Falls, even in a world war. This TV version did return to the same Los Angeles high school gymnasium for the scene where they fall into the pool.

The population of Bedford Falls is noticeably less in the TV movie than in the original feature film, evidenced by fewer people in the high school graduation scene and the desperate run on the Building & Loan. While this was likely due to budgetary restrictions, a sparser group of residents enhances the more effective vision of Bedford Falls as a small town which, in turn, contributes to Mary's desire for larger, greener pastures.

The look of the film was enhanced by the talents of art director John J. Lloyd and Oscar-winning cinematographer Conrad Hall. "That was one of our big secrets," Thomas said. "We built that entire town, the whole square, the drug store, everything. It was a costly production."

One that paid off in the long run, as Lloyd and set decorator Hal Gausman both received Emmy nominations for Outstanding Art Direction for a Miniseries or Movie. Costume designer Connie Hall also played a pertinent part in the motif of *It Happened One Christmas*. Hall worked intensely with

Thomas on the various set colors for walls, as well as the selection of wall-papers, props, and the like. The wardrobe, too, spanning thirty years, also enhanced the film's visual aesthetic. "They had planned the costumes and colors as Mary aged," Thomas recalled. "I was in white, then in pink, then in burgundy, and powder blue, all in pale colors during her younger years until she married and had children and was running the Building & Loan."

For Thomas, behind and in front of the camera, the experience of working on the film was "a dream." A multi-award-winning actress herself, Thomas was "flabbergasted" to be sharing the screen with those such as the Oscar- and Emmy-winning Cloris Leachman. "Cloris was great as Clara, and so wonderful to work with, as was Orson Welles, Christopher Guest, Doris Roberts, Barney Martin, and Wayne Rogers," all of whom have since passed away. "Wayne was a terrific acting partner. I just adored him. We became dear friends."

As with the kind of transcendental association that transpired between the TV audience and the musical and comedy families presented on *The Lawrence Welk Show*, *The King Family* series, *The Andy Williams Show*, *The Carol Burnett Show*, and *Donny & Marie*, a similar and strong sense of camaraderie amid the actors behind the scenes of *It Happened One Christmas* played into their roles on-screen, and ultimately bled into and was transmitted to the home viewers. In this way, Marlo Thomas's original concerns about not being musically inclined fade away as *It Happened One Christmas* continuously plays to the beat of its unique drum—across the decades.

CHAPTER 30
GATHERING THOUGHTS

"I accept most of your preamble about the rich, full life to which I've been blessed. The plain and unbiased truth is I need time. . . . Certain aspects of my life are not in order."

—Ed Asner's Adam Thornton, in *The Gathering*

The Gathering raised the bar not just for Christmas TV-movies, but for TV-movies in general. Unique on several levels, *The Gathering* premiered on ABC, December 4, 1977. A product of Hanna-Barbera Productions, which was known mostly for children's animated fare, *The Gathering* was directed by Randal Kleiser. Kleiser later guided *The Blue Lagoon* and *It's My Party*, as well as the TV-movie *The Boy in the Plastic Bubble*, John Travolta's first starring role, which led to the actor's breakout performance on the big screen in John Badham's *Saturday Night Fever* and to Kleiser's even larger mega-hit musical *Grease*.

Written by James Poe, *The Gathering* stars Ed Asner as the gruff executive Adam Thorton. Because he's dying, Adam arranges a final Christmas reunion with his estranged wife Kate, played by Maureen Stapleton, and adult children and their spouses. One particularly challenging relationship is that of Adam with Bud, his Vietnam War–draft-dodging son played by Gregory Harrison (then of *Trapper John, M.D.*).

The film inspired a 1979 sequel, *The Gathering, Part II*, which picked up the story two years after Adam's demise and focused on Kate's relationship with a new love in her life played by Efrem Zimbalist Jr. Hanna-Barbera Productions returned behind the scenes, but Kleiser opted instead to helm

Grease, leaving *The Gathering II* in the capable hands of director Charles S. Dubin.

From Randal Kleiser's perspective, he was hired to direct *The Gathering* due to *Peege*, a similarly themed short film he guided in 1973, when he was a film student at USC. Into the mix, Kleiser, who grew up in Philadelphia, experienced many of the Christmas traditions that he incorporated into both *The Gathering* and *Peege*, the latter plot of which goes like this:

On Christmas Day, a suburban couple, played by William Schallert and Barbara Rush, and their children; Bruce Davison as Greg, Barry Livingston as Damion, and David Alan Bailey as Jerry, embark on their annual journey to visit Peege, their fraternal grandmother, portrayed by the remarkable Jeanette Nolan. The once vibrant elderly woman (she loved horror movies and had a wicked sense of humor) now resides in a senior home, isolated, suffering from dementia; she's visually impaired, has lost her teeth, is incontinent, and subsequently depressed.

For her family, their visits are awkward and uncomfortable, all except for Greg, the more sensitive, eldest son who's now a grad student. Via flashbacks, we see his immersion in memories of happier days with Peege, while the rest of the family would prefer to leave as soon, and respectfully, as possible.

There's little if any hope for Peege's recovery, but by the movie's end, it's clear just how much an uplifting impact the more caring and compassionate Greg has made in her life, most likely for the last time.

One of the most realistic films of its time, of any length, in any format, and of any premise, *Peege* is a fiercely realistic film; a slice of life in the most poignant terms. For anyone who has served as a primary caregiver to any elderly or ill parents, relative, or friend, the film proves intensely moving.

The cast is impeccable. Barbara Rush (who died at 97 in 2024) had been a film star for years and would continue to act on television for decades to come with appearances on sitcoms such as *The New Dick Van Dyke Show* to sci-fi adventure dramas such as *The Bionic Woman*. William Schallert, another veteran of countless TV and film appearances, notably as Patty Duke's father on *The Patty Duke Show* and then Caryn Richman's dad on *The New Gidget*, plays well opposite Bush. Barry Livingston, so earnest as the newly adopted middle child Ernie on *My Three Sons*, delivers another spot-on performance. David Alan Bailey is also solid and sincere.

However, *Peege* belongs to Davison and Nolan, who, comparatively, paved a slight path for Gregory Harrison and Ed Asner's relationship in *The Gathering*. *Peege* is intricately linked to *The Gathering*, which was based on the real-life experiences of its writer, James Poe (who died in 1980).

The casting for both films was key to their success. Kleiser would cast Davison again in *The Gathering*, while he would later many times work with Harrison. Casting director Joel Thurm was responsible for most of the casting for *The Gathering*, as well as other films by Kleiser (including *Grease*).

Asner, however, was reluctant to work with Kleiser simply because he was unfamiliar with his work. But then Asner saw *Peege*, and that all changed.

In the process of making *The Gathering* as realistic as possible, Kleiser took great care during rehearsals with the actors. For example, the group scenes around the dinner table benefited from the extensive improvisation sessions Kleiser held during rehearsals with the actors. "For the large crowd scenes," he recalled, "I sat all the actors down and went through who was related to who, and worked on the improvisations with them so that when they were all talking, they'd look real. Every one of the actors were terrific."

Overall, Kleiser said, "We respected the writer's intention to tell his story. Every family faces death at one point, and that's what we tried to show as a way to deal with that situation.

"*The Gathering* and *Peege*," Kleiser continued to explain, had "a similar vibe and feel." And undoubtably, *Peege* paved the way for *The Gathering*. The former became one of the few student films that has been entered into the Library of Congress, which each year selects twenty-five movies to represent American culture. According to Kleiser, those who love *The Gathering* will feel the same way about *Peege*, which he described as "almost a companion piece to *The Gathering*."

Television and film historian Ken Gehrig discussed *The Gathering* and *Peege*, their not-so-obvious cross-pollination, and the personal effect both movies had on him:

On paper, *The Gathering* sounds like an attempt to merge the tear-jerking qualities of *Love Story* or *Brian's Song* with a Frank Capra–style family reunion film. Ed Asner plays a man who finds out at Christmastime that he doesn't have long to live. He's separated from his wife, played by Maureen Stapelton, and out of touch with his four adult children. As a tough businessman he clearly drove his loved ones away and now hopes to reunite them for Christmas without inviting pity by telling them of his condition.

Watching it again, I am struck by how it begins a lot like the above premise might suggest. I know that watching it when it was new, I was engrossed, but I think that maybe the early scenes always bordered on being a little depressing. However, the sheer honesty of its dialogue and the performances of Edward Asner, Maureen Stapelton, and John

Randolph [as the physician who gives Asner the bleak prognosis] ease one into the hopeful aspect of the family reuniting. When Asner and Maureen, as his wife, take steps to welcome whichever of their children may show (and they are indeed unsure who will), a sweetness emerges that gives the story an optimistic momentum (even John Barry's score has an uncharacteristic jaunty fairy tale quality at this point)!

By the film's end, sure there are tears and an expected reuniting of family. However, the intelligence of James Poe's script keeps it from seeming predictable.

CHAPTER 31

FATHER'S THANKSGIVING AND CHRISTMAS REUNIONS

"Home is wherever the family is . . . [and] grown-ups cry, too . . ."

> — Jane Wyatt's Margaret Anderson, in *Father
> Knows Best: Home for Christmas*

In November and December 1977, NBC aired two *Father Knows Best* TV-reunion movies: *The Father Knows Best Reunion*, which was a Thanksgiving story written by Paul West and directed by Marc Daniels; and *Father Knows Best: Home for Christmas*, directed by Norman Abbott and written by West and original series creator Ed James. Like *The House Without a Christmas Tree*, both reunions were videotaped (whereas the original *Father* series was filmed). But little matter; the stories were homespun-made-for-TV, and the scripts, characters, and all the original actors were in place and dynamite. Those being Robert Young (*Marcus Welby, M.D.*) as Jim Anderson; Jane Wyatt (Spock's mom on *Star Trek*) as his wife, Margaret; Lauren Chapin as Kathy "Kitten" Anderson, Billy Gray as James "Bud" Anderson, and Elinor Donahue as Betty "Princess" Anderson.

The original series produced two Christmas episodes, both of which were incorporated as flashbacks in the *Father Knows Best: Home for Christmas* movie. The first was titled "The Christmas Story," which originally aired on December 19, 1954, and was reworked with a new opening and closing on December 15, 1958. The second Christmas episode was "The Angels Sweater," which premiered December 19, 1956.

In "The Christmas Story," Jim is flabbergasted with Betty, Kathy, and Bud's materialistic view of Christmas, so he plans an old-fashioned holiday. That involves a family drive to the mountains, where they can chop down their own tree. But when a snowstorm derails his plans, the family comes upon a closed-up lodge as a haven. In the process, each of the Andersons discovers the true meaning of Christmas through the eyes of Kathy and a friendly older homeless man (Wallace Ford), who pretends he's the grounds-keeper, but who Kathy assumes is Santa Claus.

In "The Angels Sweater," Kathy struggles with the arrival of the spinster-like Aunt Neva (Katherine Warren), before an elderly Mr. Fixit handyman (Ludwig Stossel) shares with her a poignant Christmas tale.

In a rare new interview, Elinor Donahue discussed *Father Knows Best* in general, the two Christmas episodes, in particular, and the 1977 reunions, specifically *Father Knows Best: Home for Christmas*. She was especially complimentary of Billy Gray, who is also known for several big-screen classics, including *The Day the Earth Stood Still*, released in 1951; and two holiday movies with Doris Day: *On Moonlight Bay*, also released in 1951, and *By the Light of the Silvery Moon*, released in 1953 (though some sources document its release as 1952).

> Billy was the best actor . . . the most efficient. He was not only talented but multi-talented. I think Lauren and I were fine and good. She certainly was adorable. But [our theatrical abilities at the time] we were limited in what we could do. Generally speaking, every week each episode featured a particular character within the family.
>
> The first Christmas episode ["A Christmas Story"] was kind of magical. Wallace Ford is wonderful as the homeless man who breaks into the cabin and doesn't want anyone to know that he's there. Kathy is unhappy because she thinks that Santa Claus isn't going to be able to find her. But then she looks out the window and sees an elk go by and then Wallace Ford . . . who's somewhat chubby and round and he's dressed in warm clothes and wooly hat. And she thinks he's Santa Claus.
>
> The second Christmas episode we did ["The Angels Sweater"] features Ludwig Stössell, a fine European actor, and Katherine Warren as Aunt Neva, who Kathy doesn't like and sulks about. But then, in an elaborate dream sequence, Aunt Neva turns out to be like the Christmas Fairy . . . and Ludwig is an elf. He was just so charming and adorable in the role.

Two decades later, Donahue regrouped with the original show's cast for the reunion films, including *Father Knows Best: Home for Christmas*. During production for the latter, Donahue was extremely busy. "In show business you're hot [that is, popular] or you're not," she said. "And the minute I turned forty years old I got really 'hot' for a couple of years. We had completed an initial *Father Knows Best* reunion [as a Thanksgiving special that premiered one month before], and that did very well in the ratings. So, we were rushed into production for the Christmas reunion."

However, before the Thanksgiving reunion, Donahue had appeared in the pilot-movie for *Mulligan's Stew*, a short-lived family series for NBC. The ratings for the initial *Mulligan's* movie, as Donahue noted, "went through the roof."

At which point, NBC also rushed into producing *Mulligan's Stew* as a weekly series, while it hurried into production for the second *Father Knows Best* reunion, which was the Christmas special. "We all wished we could have been given more time to do the second reunion," said Donahue, "particularly Robert Young."

More time to produce the movies, Donahue added, may have resulted in a continued series of *Father Knows Best* movies. "But because NBC rushed me into *Mulligan's Stew*, that meant I was unavailable to fully participate in the *Father Knows Best* Christmas reunion. And that's why my part is relatively small in the second film."

But no less impactful. In the movie, Jim and Margaret decide to sell their home; the kids are grown; they're living in an empty nest. And now, at Christmastime, their hopes to reunite the family are dashed; Bud, Betty, and Kathy are all adults now with lives of their own spread around the country. Everyone got together just four weeks prior for Thanksgiving, but Christmas is a little more hectic, especially for Betty, whose husband, Frank (Jim McMullan), is an airline pilot. Bud and his wife, Jeanne (Susan Adams), and son, Robbie (Christopher Gardner), arrive, as does Kathy and her boyfriend, Jason (Hal England), who has a broken leg. However, Betty's two young daughters have arrived early: Jenny (Cari Anne Warder) and Ellen (Kyle Richards, sister to Kim *Nanny and the Professor* Richards, with whom she much later becomes a TV reality-show star).

Betty finally makes it to the reunion, but she and all the Andersons soon learn her husband's small plane is caught in a snowstorm. He then ultimately arrives safely, though not before Betty nearly falls apart, and she even scolds a few Christmas carolers to "go away!"

In the end, however, the expanded Andersons share a beautiful Christmas together, as Jim shares the "bad" and "good" news. The house is sold, but it's Bud who buys it! He and Jeanne have been searching for that "something else," and now they found it; it's been in front of their eyes all along. As such, the cherished Anderson residence remains in the family, now housing Bud, his wife, and son, while Jim and Margaret travel across the country in a Winnebago.

Through it all, Donahue's screen time was brief, and while her grown-up "Princess" character may not have appeared until the movie's latter half hour, her performance was key to the story. And as Donahue recalled with a smile, Robert Young told her, "You better be good because we waited five days for you to get here."

Off-screen, Donahue was married to Screen Gems TV executive and former CBS network head Harry Ackerman. Together they had four sons: James, Chris, Peter, and Brian Ackerman.

Raising four boys is a challenge for any parent and, as Donahue recalled, meant frequently instructing her son Peter to, "Pull up your trousers please and put a belt on."

"I was on him a lot about that," she laughed.

"So, one day," she continued, "I came home from the grocery store and he and the boys were watching reruns on television and it happened to be *Father Knows Best*. And as I walked through the room, Margaret says to Bud, 'Will you pull up your pants. I don't like them down on your hips!' And we all just roared because that scene obviously rang so true to us.

"The plots on the show," Donahue continued, "had to do with every day ordinary things . . . nothing too big and melodramatic . . . but real. And a lot of it had to do with the writing of course and Gene Rodney" [the show's producing partner with Robert Young].

"Robert Young was very keen on keeping things real," Donahue said. "If he saw anything in the script during the table read that didn't ring true to him, he would contact Mr. Rodney and discuss it . . . and changes would be made."

Donahue's son, author Peter Ackerman, offered this additional insight into the *Father Knows Best* universe, including the reunions:

How exciting it was during this period to hear from her that *Father Knows Best* was coming back for two television movie specials. For the first reunion show, I remember a lot going on before she asked me to help with her dialogue. As the first script was delivered to our home, what excited me most was the possibility that I could go onto the set of a show that was from my mother's past."

CHAPTER 32
CAROL-ING WITH THE STARS

"Another sound from you—and you'll keep your Christmas by losing your situation."

> — George C. Scott's Ebenezer Scrooge, in
> *A Christmas Carol* (CBS, 1984)

Charles Dickens' classic 1843 novella *A Christmas Carol* has been adapted countless times for the stage and screen over the decades. The 1971 animated rendition (with lead voice-over work by Alastair Sim, star of the optimum 1952 live-action feature) is considered the best cartooned *Carol* (on TV or otherwise).

However, there are at least four notable live-action interpretations that have aired on the small screen, including those starring Henry Winkler, Patrick Stewart, Kelsey Grammer, and George C. Scott, the latter of which proved to be the most memorable. But first, let's look at the previous three editions.

On December 16, 1979, Winkler starred in ABC's *An American Christmas Carol*, a modern-day tale directed by Eric Till and loosely based on the Dickens classic.

In Depression-era Concord, New Hampshire, it's Winkler's miserly businessman Benedict Slade who is visited by the three spirits who resemble those whose possessions he had seized for outstanding loans.

In addition to Winkler, the cast includes Dorian Harewood, Susan Hogan, Cec Linder, R. H. Thomson, David Wayne, Tammy Bourne, and others.

A few sidenotes:
It required five hours to apply the old-age makeup on Winkler and one hour to remove it.

In one flashback, dated four decades earlier, Slade is seen as a teenager, which would mean he was only in his late forties or early fifties in the main story, seemingly too youthful to be as wrinkled and white-haired as he appears. This coincides with Dickens' original tale of Scrooge, who, while frail, was seemingly meant to be not yet in his sixties.

One of the places Slade visits to repossess the furniture has a copy of *A Christmas Carol* on which this is based.

Entertainment historian David Laurell described Winkler's *Carol* as "a Great Depression–era version of the Charles Dickens classic. This film is a wonderful reminder that the spirit of *A Christmas Carol* lives on, always reminding us of the joy of the season, the compassion we must show to those who have no joy, and the love, respect, and dignity we must give as a daily gift to everyone we encounter."

On December 5, 1999, Sir Patrick Stewart (mostly everybody's favorite *Star Trek* captain) starred as Scrooge in a British-American made-for-TNT TV adaption of *A Christmas Carol* that was directed by David Jones.

During the 1990s, Stewart wrote and starred in a one-man play based on *A Christmas Carol*, performing it in several locations throughout the United States and the United Kingdom. He performed it again for the survivors and victims' families of 9/11, and again in 2005. In the play, he performed more than forty different characters.

That was not the case for Stewart's 1999 TV film adaptation for TNT, which featured Richard E. Grant as Bob Cratchit, Joel Grey as the Spirit of Christmas Past, Ian McNeice as Albert Fezziwig, Saskia Reeves as Mrs. Cratchit, Desmond Barrit as the Spirit of Christmas Present, Bernard Lloyd as Jacob Marley's Ghost, Dominic West as Fred, Kenny Doughty as Young Scrooge, Laura Fraser as Belle, Ben Tipper as Tiny Tim, Claire Slater as Martha Cratchit, Tim Potter as the Spirit of Christmas Future, and Rosie Wiggins as Fran, Scrooge's sister, among others; while Liz Smith reprised her role as Mrs. Dilber from George C. Scott's 1984 adaptation of *A Christmas Carol*.

The dialogue between Scrooge and the undertaker on "what is particularly dead about a doornail," when having a drink with the priest immediately after Jacob Marley's burial, is exactly the opening lines of Dickens' book, which ends with "I am inclined to believe that a coffin nail is the deadest piece of ironmongery in the trade."

After departing Bob Cratchit's home, the Spirit of Christmas Present shows Scrooge different groups of people singing "Silent Night" during scenes with a lighthouse, coal miners, and sailors on a ship at sea in the United Kingdom (particularly Wales). Almost every other screen adaptation, except the heralded 1971 animated edition, omits these moments.

On November 28, 2004, Kelsey Grammer starred for NBC in *A Christmas Carol: The Musical*, which was directed by Arthur Allan Seidelman and written by Lynn Ahrens. In addition to Grammer, the cast includes Jesse L. Martin, Jane Krakowski, Jennifer Love Hewitt, Geraldine Chaplin, and Jason Alexander.

This *Musical* version is based on a play that was performed in New York for several years before being filmed. It is a noble, if somewhat overblown and overdone production, with several Easter eggs of sorts that make it noteworthy:

During the opening credits, a top-hatted urchin picks a gentleman's pocket, stealing his pocket watch. He then passes the watch off to a full-coated man standing close by.

For those familiar with Dickens' entire body of work, this is an obvious nod to the author's Artful Dodger and Fagin from *Oliver Twist*; the boy Scrooge calls upon for the prized turkey is based on the appearance of the Artful Dodger especially with the top hat, while the beadle seen at the Exchange is based on Mr. Bumble, another character from *Oliver Twist*.

In the Christmas Past segments, Scrooge's father is seen going to prison and Scrooge is working at the boot factory, both moments of which are from Dickens' real-life childhood and not from *A Christmas Carol*.

Scrooge meets all three Christmas Ghosts in human form before meeting them as spirits; a unique moment in *A Christmas Carol* history; similar to the scene with the three Kansas farm workers, Miss Almira Gulch, and Professor Marvel in *The Wizard of Oz* from 1939.

Forty-five years later, on December 17, 1984, on CBS, *A Christmas Carol* was reborn once more, this time as a British-American TV-movie starring George C. Scott. Released theatrically in Great Britain and filmed in the historic medieval county town of Shrewsbury in Shropshire in the English Midlands, this *Carol* is considered the optimum live-action TV adaption. It's an upscale production directed by Clive Donner, who served as an editor of the heralded 1951 feature-film classic *A Christmas Carol/Scrooge* (starring Alastair Sim, who again, voiced the acclaimed 1971 animated edition).

With teleplay scribe Roger O. Hirson's pristine interpretation of Dickens' original words and story, *A Christmas Carol* (1984) also stars Frank

Finlay, Angela Pleasence, Edward Woodward, David Warner, Susannah York, Roger Rees, and several other refined thespians. Comparatively speaking, with what time and money would allow, there is little doubt that this small-screen 1984 *Carol* is equal in elegance and quality to the big-screen 1951 presentation. In each case, casting is the key, certainly with regard to the leading role. As Melissa Byers explained: "So many versions of *A Christmas Carol* have been made over the years, but the idea of casting the ultimate curmudgeon, George C. Scott, was a stroke of genius. Scott's gravelly voice, his patented scowl, and his imposing presence brought a depth to Ebenezer Scrooge that went beyond caricature. Watching Scott's gradual thawing and final glee was mesmerizing. A worthy addition to the *Christmas Carol* canon."

Novelist and essayist Louis Bayward, writing for Salon.com, described this adaptation as "the definitive version of a beloved literary classic" and praised its "fidelity to Dickens' original story, the strength of the supporting cast, and especially Scott's performance as Scrooge."

Additional behind-the-scenes insight was offered by IMDb.com. For example, Scrooge's headstone prop can still be visited at Saint Chad's Churchyard in Shrewsbury, where the cemetery sequence was shot. The production team found the stone, apparently blank, and gained permission to have it inscribed. This was left in place at the end of the shoot.

The 1984 film is most likely the only adaptation of *A Christmas Carol* in which Scrooge wears dress slacks with a dress shirt, vest, and smoking jacket instead of his nightshirt, slippers, and cap. Allegedly, George C. Scott openly reeled at the very thought of portraying Scrooge under such conditions, especially in an English winter. In the book, Scrooge wears his shirt, pants, vest, dressing gown, and slippers. Scott's clothing is very close to the book.

At one point, Dickens lost the rights to *A Christmas Carol* in a lawsuit filed by several impostors claiming the tale was their creation. Following the suit, Dickens wrote *Bleak House*, an equally successful novel about corruption in the English courts.

As documented on Wikipedia.org, the scenes set in the Cratchit family house were filmed in a wine merchant that still exists. The particular building was next door to a car garage. The scene in which Scrooge visits and learns of Tiny Tim's demise had to be refilmed, due to an extractor fan drowning out the actors' speech from the body shop on the other side of the wall.

The film's American TV debut was sponsored by IBM, which purchased all of the commercial spots for the two-hour premiere. The film won its time slot in the ratings (20.7/30 share, ranking #10 for the week). The film was marketed with the tagline "A new powerful presentation of the most loved ghost story of all time!" Scott was nominated for an Emmy for Outstanding Lead Actor in a Limited Series or a Special for his portrayal of Scrooge.

The movie has aired in American syndication on local channels since its premiere in 1984 and was released on VHS in 1989 (in the United Kingdom) and to DVD in 1999. This was because Scott himself (and later his estate through Baxter Healthcare, to whom the Scott family donated their copyright) owned the rights to the production.

On November 25, 2007, Scott's *Carol* reemerged on AMC for the first time since its CBS debut, and the network continues to show it each December under license from the Scott estate and 20th Century Studios/Walt Disney Television (the latter's distribution rights the result of their owning the video rights).

In 2009, the Hallmark Channel also aired the film shortly following Thanksgiving, amid that network's (among others) several additional adaptations of *A Christmas Carol*. That same year, Fox rereleased Scott's *Carol* with revised box art but the same menu and features as the previous DVD release.

In December of 2010, Fox released the film on Blu-ray.

CHAPTER 33

A VERY BRADY CHRISTMAS MOVIE

"O Come, All Ye Faithful . . ."

> — Florence Henderson's Carol Brady, singing in the
> original *Brady Bunch* episode "The Voice of Christmas"
> and in the 1988 TV-movie *A Very Brady Christmas*

When it premiered on December 18, 1988, not many believed *A Very Brady Christmas* would become one of the highest-rated TV-movies in history (alongside 1985's *I Dream of Jeannie: 15 Years Later*).

However, the story of *A Very Brady Christmas* begins with a first-season episode of the original TV series, *The Brady Bunch*, titled, "The Voice of Christmas," which aired on December 19, 1969.

The entire *Brady Bunch* originally ran on ABC from 1969 to 1974 and showcased TV's first blended family. Widower Mike Brady, played by Robert Reed (*The Defenders*), with three young sons (Barry Williams as Greg, Christopher Knight as Peter, Mike Lookinland as Bobby) meets, falls in love with, and marries widow Carol, played by Florence Henderson (*The Song of Norway*), who has three young daughters (Maureen McCormick as Marcia, Eve Plumb as Jan, Susan Olsen as Cindy). The family's housekeeper, Alice, played by Ann B. Davis (*The Bob Cummings Show*) and held over from Mike's initial household, joins the family to care for the newly combined brood.

In "The Voice of Christmas," the Bradys celebrate their first Christmas together, and Carol is all set to perform a solo of "Come All Ye Faithful" at a Christmas church service. But those plans are thwarted when she contracts laryngitis. Naturally, everyone's disappointed, especially Cindy, the "youngest one in curls," played by Olsen. So, upon seeing Santa, she asks him to heal her mother's voice. To Mike and Carol's surprise, Santa, who's a little thrown by the request himself, hesitantly consents. In the end, Cindy's wish comes true, all is well, and Carol's voice is restored like it only could be in TV land.

Decades later, the Brady cast reunited for *A Very Brady Christmas*, except for Susan Olsen. Instead, Jennifer Runyon took over the role of Cindy in a movie that presents the extended Brady family, including Jerry Houser (as Marcia's husband, Wally) and Ron Kuhlman (as Jan's spouse, Phillip), carried over from the short-lived NBC series sequel *The Brady Brides* (which itself was a follow-up to the initial NBC *Brady* 1981 TV reunion movie, *The Brady Girls Get Married*). Also along for the *Very Brady Christmas* sleigh ride was Caryn Richman, as wife Nora to Williams' Greg, Carol Huston as Valerie, Knight's on-screen love interest, among several other new younger Bradys.

For Houser, working on *A Very Brady Christmas* was surreal. "There I was on the set with all of those wonderful actors who I had watched for years on the original series, and now I was working with them. It was magical."

The movie features several references to the original show's episode "The Voice of Christmas," most notably the scene in which the Brady kids find themselves congregating in the middle of the night on Christmas Eve, drawn together by their shared pain: their father Mike is stuck in a mine. In the original episode, they converge around the Christmas tree, whereas in the reunion they bond around the kitchen table and near the mine shaft. It's at the latter location where Carol ignites another heart-wrenching rendition of "O Come All Ye Faithful," this time eventually performed by the entire family as a group prayer to have Mike found safe and sound, which of course, he is in the end.

A few behind-the-scenes tidbits:

At the start of filming, Robert Reed, Barry Williams, Christopher Knight, and Mike Lookinland each had grown mustaches. Producer/creator Sherwood Schwartz (*Gilligan's Island*) requested that at least two of them shave, or else, he joked he'd have to retitle the movie *A Very Brady Moustache*. Knight and Lookinland gave way to the request; Reed and Williams did not.

When Alice is meeting various family members at the airport, she initially approaches a young woman, who she mistakenly assumes to be Cindy; a little inside joke and nod to the Susan Olsen–Jennifer Runyon casting switch.

It's been previously reported that this film marks the first time Lookinland did not dye his hair brown for the role of Bobby. However, that is not true. He retains his original red hair throughout the entire fifth and final season of the original series.

Due to the overwhelming success of *A Very Brady Christmas*, several sequels, reboots, remakes, and even a stage adaptation followed, including

HGTV's *A Very Brady Renovation* reality series from the fall of 2019—which helped to celebrate the original show's fiftieth anniversary by rebooting the actual physical on-location home to match the architecture of the show's original interior set.

Other *Brady* re-formations have included replacement actresses, Geri Reischl as Jan Brady in ABC's 1977 short-lived and quite bizarre *Brady Bunch Variety Hour*, and Leah Ayres as Marcia Brady for NBC's 1990 and also short-lived *The Bradys* (a *Thirtysomething*-esque dramedy).

In November 1992, Paramount Home Video released *A Very Brady Christmas* on VHS. In April 2007, the film was included as a bonus feature on *The Brady Bunch: The Complete Series* twenty-one-disc DVD set by CBS/Paramount, who then released it as a stand-alone DVD on October 10, 2017. Two years later, CBS/Paramount rereleased it on DVD as a part of *The Brady-est Brady Bunch TV & Movie Collection* as a further commemoration of the original show's fiftieth anniversary.

CHAPTER 34
CHRISTMAS IN CONNECTICUT
BUT ON A SMALLER SCALE

"Well, here we are in my living room except this isn't my living room.
This isn't even my house. Uh, you see, we're in Connecticut."

— Dyan Cannon's Elizabeth, in *Christmas in Connecticut*

n 1994, another unique production emerged in the annals of Christmas TV
specials. Actor, Hollywood icon, and former Mr. Universe Arnold Schwarzenegger, while starring in that year's *True Lies* on the big screen, took on
the enormous feat of remaking the 1945 *Christmas in Connecticut* feature film
for the small screen.

In another stunning development for the history books, Arnold's *Connecticut*, which aired on TNT, ended up being the first and only movie he ever
helmed. But not for lack of trying or talent; his or anyone else's involved with
the film, which stars Dyan Cannon, Kris Kristofferson, Tony Curtis (whose
daughter, the now-Oscar-winning Jamie Lee Curtis, co-starred with Arnold
in *True Lies*), Richard Roundtree (*Shaft*), and Kelly Cinnante.

In the somewhat parallel tradition of Alfred Hitchcock, if with a shock-
horror bent, Arnold has a cameo in *Connecticut*, seventy-six minutes into the
film. There, he's seen outside sitting at a table and speaking into a cell phone
in front of TNT's satellite uplink truck.

As the story goes, Cannon's Elizabeth Blane is the star of a popular
cooking TV series and the author of several cookbooks. One day watching
the news, her manager, Alexander Yardley (Curtis), sees a heroic forest ranger
named Jefferson Jones (Kristofferson) talking about how he lost his cabin in a
fire and pining for a home-cooked Christmas meal. Alexander then arranges
for Elizabeth to host a special live Christmas episode of her show, where

she will make Jefferson's dream come true. But that's a bit of a challenge, as Elizabeth can't even boil water, let alone cook an entire Christmas dinner, which places her in quite an awkward position with Jefferson or her live TV audience.

As journalist Jonathan Norcross observed in a contemporary review of *Connecticut* on Collider.com:

> *Christmas in Connecticut* aims to be a Hallmark-esque holiday film with familiar themes of finding love, appreciating family, rejecting superficiality, and embracing wholesome values. For Arnold, an Austrian immigrant who longed to be an American, it's easy to see why he finds these themes appealing. The film is very much of the Reagan/Bush era. It celebrates traditionalism and conventional gender roles. It's not exactly a shock that the director of such a film would go on to become a Republican politician.
>
> *Christmas in Connecticut* is an interesting glimpse of Arnold Schwarzenegger's sensibilities beyond just pumping iron and being an action star. His decision to cast Kristofferson and Cannon in the lead roles demonstrates that he has a good eye for talent and knows how to work well with actors. The overall concept of the film isn't totally off-base. With a rewrite and director change, *Christmas in Connecticut* might make for a solid Lindsay Lohan/Netflix-style holiday rom-com. For all these reasons, the film deserves to be seen by anyone interested in this one-of-a-kind weightlifter turned actor turned politician. Arnold Schwarzenegger is one of the most unique figures in American cinema and his sole directorial outing is nothing if not an interesting experiment.

In other news, FixedQuotes.com, offered this review: "While the film might not have reached the legendary status of [the original *Christmas in Connecticut* movie] . . . [the remake] is still a wonderful experience filled with vacation cheer, romantic tension, and humorous deceptiveness covered in an unforgettable serving of situational funny. The film got blended evaluations, however, succeeded in using a lighthearted, holiday-themed watch that still remains in the heart of audiences."

CHAPTER 35

THE CHRISTMAS BOX AND OTHER PACKAGED TV-MOVIES

"The first gift of Christmas was love. A parent's love. Pure as the first snow of Christmas. For God so loved His children that He sent His son, that someday we might return to Him."

—Richard Paul Evans, author of *The Christmas Box*

As discussed elsewhere in this book, countless Christmas TV-movies have been produced over the years; entries that would fill an entire library of books. For example, a chosen random few from the 1990s include *The Christmas Box* (1995), *Borrowed Hearts: A Holiday Romance* (1997), *Saint Maybe* (1998), and *A Season of Miracles* (1999). With too many more to mention, let's at least begin with *The Christmas Box*.

Years after Richard Thomas of *The Waltons* fame first played John-Boy in *The Homecoming* TV-movie of 1971 and the subsequent original series, he appeared in several Christmas TV-movies, notably, *The Christmas Box*, which premiered on CBS, December 17, 1995.

The film is based on the 1993 self-published novel of the same name by Richard Paul Evans, an advertising executive. He allegedly wrote the book for his children, and he positioned it in a Utah bookstore, where it became a local bestseller. This got the attention of major publishers, who participated in an auction to acquire the book, resulting in a multi-million-dollar publishing contract for Evans. In 1995, Simon & Schuster released a hardcover edition of *The Christmas Box*, which became the first book to simultaneously reach the No. 1 spot on the *New York Times* Best Seller list for both the paperback and hardcover editions.

The TV-movie adaptation, a Hallmark Entertainment production (separate from the future Hallmark Channel offshoot), was written by Greg Taylor, directed by Marcus Cole, and in addition to Thomas, starred Maureen O'Hara, Annette O'Toole, Kelsey Mulrooney, and Lily Gibson in her screen debut.

The premise is this: a ski shop owner (Thomas) reluctantly moves himself, his wife (O'Toole), and their daughter into an estate as live-in help for an elderly widow (O'Hara). While struggling to balance his career and family life, he has recurring dreams about an angel.

As he did with *The Homecoming: A Christmas Story*, creative and entertainment enthusiast Christopher Pufall shared his enlightening, pensive reflections on *The Christmas Box*:

> The central, dynamic force of this story is driven by a mother's steadfast love, in this case not only as exhibited by Maureen O'Hara's role, but amplified further through the compassionate care given to her by Richard Thomas's wife, as portrayed by Annette O'Toole. For many of us, there is a natural resonance with this archetype as a vital, formative aspect within our own mythic experience of life and Christmas. It doesn't escape me that another two of my favorite TV-films for Christmas also have a mother as foundational to anchoring story and resolution: *The Gathering* (1977) and *The Homecoming: A Christmas Story* (1971).

> Ultimately, *The Christmas Box* gives us a message of profound simplicity and importance, namely that the first, most transcendent gift of Christmas was a child, and it heartbreakingly conveys this in a culminating revelation that reshapes the father's priorities from being job-first to being family-first—a cornerstone tenet as relevant to consider as ever. Although key symbols in the story may relate more directly to particular religious traditions, with an open mind and heart I believe any spiritual path can assimilate the film's insight in meaningful and relatable ways, thematically and personally.

Some backstage insight: This was O'Hara's first television film role since *The Red Pony* from 1973. Before retiring, the actress would go on to make two more movies (one in 1998, the other in 2000, as well as *Only the Lonely* on the big screen with John Candy), which is now considered a feature-film Christmas classic (even though it was released in May). Annette O'Toole and Richard Thomas also starred together in *Stephen King's IT*. The film inspired a TV-movie sequel, *Timepiece*, which aired in 1996.

One year later, CBS aired another touching Christmas movie, *Borrowed Hearts: A Holiday Romance*. Directed by Ted Kotcheff, with a script by Pamela Wallace and Earl W. Wallace, *Borrowed Hearts* features Héctor Elizondo, Eric McCormack, pre–*Will & Grace*, and its leading lady of grace: Roma Downey (the film's executive producer and star of the network's then very-popular *Touched by an Angel* series, which, naturally, produced several Christmas episodes).

StudioJakeMedia.com offered this thorough observation about the film:

Borrowed Hearts is a decent holiday film that is sure to make a good date night during the Christmas season. Every once in a while, the nineties provide a hidden gem that is something to enjoy.

Sundrop on IMDb.com agreed, per their review of June 19, 2001, titled, "Fantastic":

I first saw this movie in a rerun and only saw the last half. After seeing the last half, I just couldn't wait to watch it from beginning to end. This is the kind of movie that after you start watching it you just can't leave it for any reason until it's over. All of the actors and actresses just made it so believable that you felt like you were friends with the characters at the end.

I didn't even realize that Roma Downey was playing Kathleen until I'd been watching it for a few minutes. You wouldn't expect her to be good at the part of a struggling single mother, but she really was. It had the perfect casting combination, and the writers also knew what they were doing. It had a great plot, and is a movie that people would enjoy at just about any age. It's rare that you see a movie like this on television today.

One year after *Borrowed Hearts: A Holiday Romance*, CBS aired *Saint Maybe* on Sunday, November 22, 1998. Technically, *Saint Maybe*, another Hallmark Hall of Fame production (before the separate entity of the Hallmark Channel) is not a Christmas movie, but it's so infested with the holiday spirit, that it should be.

Saint Maybe is directed by Michael Pressman and written by Robert W. Lenski from the book by Anne Tyler. The film is nicely documented on TCM.com:

Seventeen-year-old Ian Bedloe lives with his parents and older brother Danny in Baltimore in 1965. When Danny meets Lucy, a divorcée with two children, Ian and his parents are disturbed when Danny and Lucy quickly marry and have a daughter, Daphne, seven months later. Ian wonders whether Danny is really Daphne's father. One night, Ian meddles in his older brother's life, and from that careless moment on, nothing is the same. Following an accident that causes Danny's death, Lucy succumbs to her own unhappiness and takes her own life. Seeking to make amends and haunted by guilt over his brother's death, Ian drops out of college to raise Lucy and Danny's three children, altering his life forever. Ian is also drawn to the Church of the Second Chance, led by the charismatic Reverend Emmett, who convinces Ian that forgiveness doesn't come automatically.

Ray Richmond offered this review of *Maybe* in *Variety*, on November 19, 1998:

In a world of boorish overkill, it's rare when an original telepic is able to make its points poignantly yet calmly. This film achieves it thanks to an eccentric gem of an adapted teleplay from scribe Robert W. Lenski, eloquent work from helmer Michael Pressman, and superbly modulated performances from Blythe Danner, Edward Hermann, the exquisite Mary-Louise Parker, and especially little-known Thomas McCarthy.

Here are some behind-the-camera observations:

The movie was filmed outside Charlotte, North Carolina, by Hallmark Hall of Fame Productions.

Blythe Danner, mother to Gweneth Paltrow, and Tom McCarthy would later co-star in *Meet the Parents* (released in 2000). Danner and Edward Herrmann previously co-starred together in the film *A Love Affair: The Eleanor and Lou Gehrig Story*, which aired on ABC in 1977.

One year after *Saint Maybe*, director Michael Pressman returned to CBS with *A Season of Miracles* on December 12, 1999. Based on the novel of the same name by Marilyn Pappano, this film originally aired as another Hallmark Hall of Fame production (its 203rd). The story is as follows:

Emilie Thompson (played by Carla Cugino) is forced to take charge of her nephew J.T. (Evan Sabara) and niece Alanna (Mae Whitman) when their drug-addicted mother (Laura Dern) overdoses and the children are threatened with foster care. Fleeing the authorities, the trio come across the sleepy town of Bethlehem, Rhode Island, just before Christmas. Even though the authorities have been temporarily left behind, Emilie will need a miracle to keep her family together. A versatile guardian angel (Patty Duke), who assumes a variety of earthly guises, helps, along with the small-town folks who are surprisingly friendly. One "coincidence" after another gives the struggling family a chance at happiness.

Unlike *Saint Maybe*, *A Season of Miracles* has been ravaged by the press. Ray Richmond of *Variety* called the film "a holiday grab bag of improbability stacked atop improbability."

According to Dove.org, *A Season of Miracles* is "Corny and contrived . . . certainly not Hallmark Hall of Fame's finest two hours." Although a little harsh with its tone, the site went on to dispel the movie, which is set in a Southern town called Bethlehem, in this way:

The producers would have done well to watch a segment or two of *Touched by an Angel*. The teleplay does address themes concerning forgiveness, anything is possible, and family unity, but although Auntie Emilie keeps saying lying is wrong, she continues to do it, professing no other option. Patty Duke, a guiding angel, surfaces every twenty minutes or so as a waitress, clerk, or bartender, to solve a problem—by hook or by crook. Ms. Duke is a seasoned professional, but as written, her angel lacks much depth, sincerity, or charm. Rather than the quality we are used to from Hallmark, this is like TV as usual—time filler. Well, at least the commercials will move you.

Despite the professional critical backlash, *A Season of Miracles*, which was Hallmark Hall of Fame's 203rd production, has remained a favorite to viewers who, in the end, ultimately have the last word.

A few other sidenotes:

Director Michael Pressman was an executive producer on CBS's acclaimed drama *Picket Fences* (1992–1996), which starred Kathy Baker, who played Ruth Doyle in this film.

The actor who portrays Mitch, the mechanic who fixes Emilie's car, is not listed in the credits on the DVD and not anywhere else, even though he has several speaking parts and plays a pertinent character.

CHAPTER 36
IT'S A WONDERFUL VILLAGE

"I am so honored to be a part of this movie."

—Marlo Thomas

D ecades after Marlo Thomas executive-produced and starred in the now-classic Christmas TV-movie *It Happened One Christmas*, she returned to the small screen in the Hallmark Channel's charming new holiday tale *A Magical Christmas Village*.

The film, written by Melissa Salmons and directed by Jason Furukawa, also stars Hallmark veteran actress Alison Sweeney, who served as an executive producer, while actors Luke Macfarlane, Maria Meadows, and Maesa Nicholson presented their own brand of likability on-screen.

It's nothing less than magical to see Thomas back on TV, where she starred from 1966 to 1971 on *That Girl*, her groundbreaking ABC sitcom. With *That Girl*, which co-starred the late Ted Bessel, Thomas paved the way for female empowerment, playing aspiring actress Ann Marie, one of TV's first independent career women.

In 2022, with a contemporary take and a dash of nostalgia, Thomas made another lasting impression in *A Magical Christmas Village*. With her pristine comedic timing and wit in razor-sharp shape, she delivered a mesmerizing, near-mystical performance with the perfect balance of sweet drama.

In a romantic tale with a poignant family twist, Thomas plays the idealistic widowed mother to Sweeney's single, more practical-minded daughter, and grandmother to the starry-eyed if slightly cynical Nicholson. In the process, the generational gap not only closes but its dynamic expands for the better—just in time for the holidays.

Colorful and cheery as can be, but not saccharine, *A Magical Christmas Village* brings to light its multilayered message for every age. Modern life and love, in any form, are about patience, authenticity, and economics. The movie takes a realistic approach to storytelling while its measured dose of fantasy gingerly teeters between wish fulfillment and coincidence.

The on-screen result? It takes the entire cast and production team to make *A Magical Christmas Village* work—and work it does.

Off-screen, Thomas is married to TV talk show pioneer Phil Donahue and is the daughter of actor/entertainer Danny Thomas, founder of St. Jude's Children Research Hospital. Today, she carries on her father's legacy with the nonprofit organization that has for years helped countless cancer-stricken children and their families.

In addition to her starring role in *That Girl*, Thomas has made several TV guest appearances on shows such as *Friends* (playing Jennifer Aniston's mom), *Law & Order*, and *The New Normal*, while her feature films include: *L.O.L.* (2012), *Playing Mona Lisa* (2000), *In the Spirit* (1990), *Thieves* (1977), and *Jenny* (1970). Some of her many heralded accomplishments include four Emmys (with a total of nine nominations). She is the recipient of The Peabody, a Golden Globe, and a Grammy; has been inducted into the Broadcasting Hall of Fame; was awarded the 2014 Presidential Medal of Freedom (in recognition of her artistic and philanthropic efforts) by President Barack Obama at a White House ceremony, and was honored with a building in her name as part of St. Jude Children's Research Hospital (with Hillary Clinton presiding at the building's ribbon-cutting).

The talented, also multi-hyphenate Sweeney, is a reality show host, director, and author who is best known for her portrayal of Samantha "Sami" Brady on NBC's long-running daytime soap *Days of Our Lives* (which now streams on Peacock). She played the part from 1993 to 2014 and earned a Daytime Emmy Award nomination, four *Soap Opera Digest Awards*, and a Fan Voted Daytime Emmy Award. After making sporadic appearances since then, she returned to *Lives* as a series regular in 2021. For the last twenty-two years, Sweeney has been married to David Sanov, with whom she has two children.

Of her experience in making *A Magical Christmas Village*, Thomas said: "I love that movie. It's beautiful. It took us sixteen days to shoot, while *It Happened One Christmas* required twenty-one days for filming." For Thomas, *A Magical Christmas Village* was just as "charming" as *It Happened One Christmas*. The film's producer was Frank Bomgard, a friend of Thomas's, who sent her the script. "I was very surprised when I received it," she said. "I have known Frank for a long time. He said, 'I don't know if you want to do something like this, but we would just die to have you.' So, I read it and was surprised at how good it was. A lot of stuff I get isn't that good. And I played the grandmother, but she didn't die. So, that was nice."

In the film, Thomas's character, Vivian Todd, is a throwback to the 1960s hippie persona with which the actress was familiar:

I had a grandmother who played the drums. I always loved her because she was independent. And this was a contemporary grandmother in this film. She had her own life and house. She couldn't be held down by her daughter who had an image of what her mother should be. And we do that to older people. When my grandmother was playing the drums at a beer garden in Pasadena, my father just went crazy (it was my mother's mother). She used to bill herself as "Danny Thomas's Mother-In-Law" during the week and then to get the younger crowd on the weekends, she billed herself as "Marlo Thomas's Grandmother."

I just loved her. Her best friend was this gay guy named Frank Ramy. They used to ride around in his white convertible with leopard-skin seats. My grandfather was alive. This was just her buddy. She was an inspiration to me as much as anybody, in terms of being *free to be*. [a reference to Thomas's groundbreaking 1974 TV special, *Free to Be . . . You and Me*]

Thomas's character in *Village*, her real-life grandmother, and the actress herself share a common trailblazing trait. "A grandmother and granddaughter have a special relationship," she explained. "The grandmother is free to do anything. More than the mother, who has responsibilities."

All of that, and more, played out so very well in *A Magical Christmas Village*, for as SusanMNorth5 noted on IMDb.com, November 5, 2022, in her review titled, "Alison Sweeney Always Shines and Marlo Thomas is Magical":

What do you really need for an enjoyable Hallmark Christmas movie? For me, it's a story that keeps me engaged, good performances, and, oh yes, a little magic. That's why I choose Hallmark. I am a huge Alison Sweeney fan. Her performances are flawless and the chemistry between her and Luke Macfarlane is like watching teenagers navigate the beginning of a relationship. Now add Marlo Thomas. Delightful and whimsical. Her portrayal of Alison's mom and [her] relationship with

Macfarlane's character is where the magic shows up. And the daughter (moving the characters in her gramma's Christmas village) is the thread that ties them all together. Very enjoyable.

PART 4
COPACETIC EPISODIC HOLIDAYS

W eekly television shows have offered their share of holiday-themed episodes, be they drama or comedy, including segments of *I Love Lucy*; *Make Room for Daddy*/*The Danny Thomas Show*; *The Joey Bishop Show*; *The Dick Van Dyke Show*; *The Brady Bunch*; *The Partridge Family*; *Happy Days*; *All in the Family*; *The Odd Couple*; *The Mary Tyler Moore Show*; *The Bob Newhart Show*; *The Jeffersons*; *That Girl*; *The Six Million Dollar Man*; *Reba*; *Beverly Hills, 90210*; *Frasier*; *Julia*; *Moonlighting*; *How I Met Your Mother*; *The Golden Girls*; *The Love Boat*; *The Donna Reed Show*; *Leave It to Beaver*; *My Three Sons*; and even *Murder, She Wrote*, a mystery series, and sci-fi/fantasy shows such as *The Twilight Zone*; *Lost In Space*; *Bewitched*; and many more.

As Brett White once declared on Decider.com, "I love Christmas episodes. They're seasonal delights that hold a mirror up to our own holiday experiences, albeit with way more studio audience laughter, one-liners, and confirmation in the existence of Santa Claus.

"But more than that," White clarified, "Christmas episodes act like a permission slip for sitcoms to indulge a bit. The holiday season lets shows try out new storytelling techniques and it lets performers *perfo*rm like, singing and dancing and all that jazz. And true to life, the holidays raise the stakes as our faves struggle to pull off the best Christmas ever, just like us. They sometimes even let sitcoms get serious, go quiet, and ruminate all existential like. And we allow it because it's Christmas, a season of lengthened night and heightened emotions. These episodes can be comforting and, in 2020, they can keep you company. Watching certain holiday episodes of your favorite show can be as essential a tradition as watching [the feature films] *It's a Wonderful Life* or *Elf*."

Classic television and film preservationist/documentarian Dan Wingate offered another perspective regarding some of the earliest pre-formal-sitcom classic TV shows like those featuring Jack Benny, George Burns, and Gracie Allen, among others (which featured comedy situations within a variety show format). "Even with the holiday theme, 1950s and 1960s comedies retained their basic flavor and format playing the impending event for laughs—with the actual sentimental stuff usually saved for a little cap at the end. The one-camera comedies would often offer more heart-tugging moments—like on *Bewitched* and *Hazel*—or Buster Keaton's appearance as Santa on *The Donna Reed Show* comes to mind."

Along those latter *Donna Reed Show* family lines is a weekly relative sitcom called *The Adventures of Ozzie and Harriet*, which reveled in the holidays with several Christmas-season episodes.

CHAPTER 37

THE HOLIDAY *ADVENTURES* OF *OZZIE* AND *HARRIET*

"Say, isn't this a nice-looking Christmas tree the Nelsons have at their house?"

—Verne Smith

"There's something about Christmas week that sort of brings families together."

—Ozzie Nelson

As the author of the detailed, aptly named biography *The Adventures of Ozzie Nelson*, Professor John Holmes knows his Nelsons. What better source than to have him comment on the Christmas episodes of *The Adventures of Ozzie and Harriet*, the famed family sitcom that aired on ABC from 1952 to 1966.

Holmes's fond recollections of "The Miracle," broadcast Christmas Day of 1953, and "The Busy Christmas," from the week before Christmas 1956, were generalized in his mind as part of a wealth of holiday episodes from the fourteen seasons of the TV show (and eight more before that on radio, where the Nelsons began their all-media takeover). But it was the marketing of just a few episodes of *Ozzie and Harriet* in the decades after the show went off the air that made him think there were more than there were: PBS ran "The Busy Christmas" every December through the 1980s and 1990s, and VHS and DVD copies of "The Miracle" were longtime stocking stuffers every year.

"The truth is," Holmes said, "those two episodes alone had a larger Christmas footprint (stocking-print?) than I realized." In the 1950s and

1960s, before streaming services and even before home videos, reruns of favorite episodes were, as Holmes said, "more of a treat than a nuisance, and Ozzie kept recycling a handful of Christmas shows. The very first *Ozzie and Harriet* Christmas show, "Late Christmas Gift," aired on December 26, 1953, but then reappeared the final season, on December 29, 1965. Half a dozen other shows followed the same pattern, which means that half of the fourteen seasons had no original Christmas program. (More than half, because 1956 had *two*.)

As to the number of actual *Ozzie and Harriet* episodes that could be distinguished, Holmes said:

> It depends on how you define a Christmas episode. Two episodes with "Christmas" in the title aren't really Christmas-themed: "Christmas in October" is about a fall party of Ozzie's, and "The Boys Earn Christmas Money" is tied to Yuletide only by the motive for Dave and Rick's job-seeking. A similar plot when the boys are older involves Rick getting a seasonal job at the Nelsons' favorite store, The Emporium, not to make money for gifts this time, but to get cozy with "The Girl in the Emporium" [which aired December 14, 1960]. But even if we leave out these more commercialized Christmastime shows, that still leaves half a dozen classic episodes that really shine with that elusive "Spirit of Christmas."

Holmes could not think of a better way to recapture the joy of Christmas past than to "settle back in your easy chair," as the show's announcer Verne Smith used to say in the intro to the early episodes, and enjoy these celebrations of Christmases 1952–1966—and one flashback from Ozzie's Christmas of 1919."

In doing so, Holmes cautioned, "let's keep two things in mind. First: remember how much our enjoyment of these classic shows owes to the hard work and sacrifice of Sam Nelson, Ozzie's grandson, who lovingly restored these images so that we can actually see greater detail and fidelity in these episodes than the original viewers could. Second: savor also those Christmas commercials, especially the ones from Eastman Kodak, who sponsored the seasons five through nine [1956–1961]."

Of the seven Christmas episodes chronicled here, six were sponsored by Kodak; "A Piano for the Fraternity" was courtesy of Coca-Cola.

That elusive sentiment that the holiday specials call "Christmas Spirit" takes different forms and offers different lessons in each of the episodes described with detailed information provided and written by Holmes.

Season 1, Episode 13, "Late Christmas Gift" (December 26, 1952; repeated December 29, 1965, rewritten from radio episode of December 28, 1951): Grandma Nelson's Christmas gifts for Ozzie and David arrive the day after Christmas: a massive book called *Biographies of Famous Statesmen* and a flashy checked sport coat. Assuming the coat was for him, Ozzie wears it and enjoys the younger look it gives him. David begins reading the book. After consideration, however, Harriet thinks maybe the book was for Ozzie and the coat for David. When Ozzie gives David the coat his eyes light up; he clearly prefers the coat as a gift. Later Harriet discovers a note from Grandma Nelson they had overlooked: it confirms that the book was intended for David and the coat for Ozzie. Harriet is about to tell David, but Ozzie convinces her not to. David is so pleased with the coat that Ozzie wants him to enjoy it.

Announcer Verne Smith opens the episode with, "Say, isn't this a nice-looking Christmas tree the Nelsons have at their house?"

In the end, the spirit of Christmas shines through as both David and Ozzie take pains to maximize the other's joy in the gifts. David tries to keep his mother from telling Ozzie about the possibility of the switch, and at the end Ozzie does the same for David.

Season 2, Episode 15, "The Miracle" (December 25, 1953; rerun December 23, 1959; rewritten from radio episode of December 26, 1948): Christmas day is over, and Ricky is anxious for a white one. But there is no snow in the forecast. Ozzie reminisces about a similar Christmas when he was Ricky's age (which would have been 1919). Little Ozzie had received skis for Christmas and longed to try them out, but there was no snow in sight. His father promised him snow, and so strong was a boy's faith in his father, that he expected snow, and by a miracle, it came. Taken by his father's story, Rick construes Ozzie's vague supposition about the possibility of the white stuff as a promise of another miracle. The next morning there is no snow. But the Nelsons' neighbor Thorny appears, inviting the boys to go skiing with him up in the mountains—which are topped with the snow Ozzie had "promised."

As Holmes explained: "The scenes flashing back to Ozzie's childhood in 1919 are worth the whole episode. As director, Ozzie has recreated his memories of his childhood Christmas: he plays his father George; Harriet plays his mother Ethel, David plays his brother Al, and Ricky plays young Ozzie. Here is Ozzie's takeaway: 'Oh, I think the decorations on our tree might have been a little different in those days. But the spirit of Christmas was just about the same.' Ozzie peppers the dialogue with 1919 slang ('It's snowing like Sixty!' 'Put on your arctics.') and references to specific locations in his Ridgefield Park, New Jersey, home (Strohmeier's Hill, Hackensack Road, Brewster Coal and Fuel). Watching this episode in the twenty-first century, we get a double Christmas nostalgia, with black-and-white images of Christmas 1953 on top of Christmas 1919."

Season 3, Episode 14, "The Lost Christmas Gifts" (December 24, 1954; rerun December 23, 1955; rewritten from radio episode December 25, 1953): After all the Christmas gifts are distributed—quite a haul for the boys—Ozzie worries that the boys are too caught up in the materialism of the season and are missing the true meaning of Christmas. But when a package arrives that was supposed to go to another Nelson on the other side of town, Ozzie and the boys drive over to deliver the package, and they find a family of children who have just lost their father and will not be getting much for Christmas. Dave and Rick gather a bunch of gifts for the kids; Rick even gives up some of the presents he has just received.

As Holmes noted, the spirit of Christmas is nicely represented early in the episode, when Ozzie says: "You know, maybe it's my imagination, Harriet, but doesn't it seem to you as if the boys are missing the real spirit of Christmas? All they seem to be interested in is the number of presents they receive." This concern is dissolved by the plot, in which the boys give up some of their own presents to make a merry Christmas for a poor family on the other side of town.

Meanwhile, there is a strong family connection that is showcased in this episode. The casting in this episode is a family affair; the children are played by Tony Montenaro Jr. (the son of the show's set decorator), Kathy Nelson and Laurie Nelson (the daughters of Ozzie's younger brother Don, who was a writer on the show), and the mom (the other Mrs. Nelson) by Don's wife, Barbara.

Season 5, Episode 12, "The Busy Christmas" (December 19, 1956; repeated twice, December 24, 1958, and December 23, 1964): Ozzie insists that he is not going to be pressured into scheduling too many activities at Christmastime. With less than a week before Christmas, he has still not bought the tree or put up the lights, but he promises to do both. But then he is maneuvered into agreeing to sing carols with the neighborhood choir. Then Doc Williams needs him to play Scrooge in the town's production of Dickens' *Christmas Carol*. Then Joe Randolph rushes in to tell Oz that Toby McIntyre is unable to play Santa at his lodge's Christmas Eve fundraiser for the orphanage. They need Ozzie to put on the red duds and white beard. On Christmas Eve, Oz is still promising to get a tree and put up the lights, but he is unable to do either. As Oz's fellow singers come to pick him up for caroling—the last event of the evening—Oz laments having disappointed his family. But it turns out

Dave and Rick have put up the tree and the lights. We end with Ozzie joining the choir in a harmonic arrangement of "Deck the Halls." In the 1964 rerun, a musical trailer was added, with Rick singing Mel Tormé's "Christmas Song."

According to Holmes, "One of the nicest Christmas moments in this episode transpires when Ozzie takes a moment to rest during a flurry of Christmas shopping in a crowded department store, and hearing 'Silent Night' on the store's sound system, he shares this memory with fellow shopper Mrs. Brewster. 'You know, every time I hear "Silent Night," it reminds me of a wonderful Christmas Eve years ago when Harriet and I were first married. We'd finished trimming the tree, and we'd opened a few of our presents, and we were just sitting there in front of the fireplace, when all of a sudden, as if from out of nowhere, we heard voices singing "Silent Night." It was a group of carolers. Friends of ours. They had stopped in front of our house to sing for us.'"

As Holmes explained, "This was an actual real-life memory for Ozzie, from Christmas of 1940, when David was four and Ricky only six months old. The carolers were a female quartet known as the King Sisters."

Ozzie trivia: Dickens' *Christmas Carol* was well known to Ozzie. His degree at Rutgers was in English literature, and Dickens was his favorite author. *Variety* reported in October 1943 that Harriet's eighth anniversary gift to Ozzie was a first edition of Dickens' collected works.

Family connection: it was the 1964 rerun, with a musical coda added, featuring Rick singing "The Christmas Song" to his wife, Kris, and their daughter Tracy, and Dave's wife, June, holding their son Danny, that became a PBS holiday broadcast tradition.

Season 5, Episode 13, "The Day After Christmas" (December 26, 1956): Cleaning up the morning after a pleasant Christmas, Dave and Rick fondly reminisce about all the times during their childhood when the family went skating at the lake the day after Christmas. Ozzie and Harriet mistake this wistfulness for a desire to go to the lake now. After Mom and Dad get everything ready, however, it turns out that Dave and Rick both have dates. So, Ozzie and Harriet go to Plan B, Oz bowling with Doc Williams and Harriet playing bridge with the ladies. But Oz can't get a lane, so he goes home and watches TV, where a roving camera is filming the day-after-Christmas skaters at the lake. Ozzie falls asleep and the TV show becomes his dream, with all four Nelsons showing off their skating skills. Waking up, Oz takes the hint and goes to the indoor skating rink. There he finds that the dates Dave and Rick had planned were for skating. And Harriet talked the ladies into playing bridge at the rink. So, all four Nelsons end up skating together the day after Christmas after all.

A few sidenotes involve Harriet, who, according to Holmes, "really was a brilliant skater. In the Winter Carnival at Lake Placid in 1935, Harriet was named the Snow Queen."

As Holmes continued to note: "The challenge to the Spirit of Christmas in this episode is the boys growing up and beginning to lead their own lives without Mom and Dad. The trick is, how to develop that adult independence without losing the connection with family. That tension informs this exchange between Ozzie and Harriet."

It's in this episode where Ozzie states: "There's something about Christmas week that sort of brings families together."

Season 6, Episode 12, "The Christmas Tree Lot" (December 18, 1957): The boys (Dave and Rick and their friends Wally and John) hatch a scheme to rent a vacant lot, fill it with Christmas trees, and make money for Christmas presents. After they lose their lot, however, they strike a bargain with a local real estate agent who lets them have a vacant storefront for free—*if* the boys entertain his nieces. This leads to the standard anxiety over blind dates, but the girls turn out to be beautiful and delightful. Sales are initially slow, but Rick sparks interest by singing his current rock and roll hits.

As Holmes observed: "While selling the Christmas trees, Dave asks one of the nieces 'What are you doing tonight?' But an older and less alluring woman thinks Dave is talking to her, and Dave covers his embarrassment by turning the woman over to Wally. In the final scene we see Wally, dressed as Santa, calling offstage, 'Hurry up, honey! We'll be late for the show.' The older woman appears, saying 'Here I am, Santy Claus!' As she walks off the shot, Wally turns to the camera and delivers the curtain line: 'Well, after all, it's Christmas!'"

Season 9, Episode 13, "A Piano for the Fraternity" (December 21, 1960): Rick and Dave's fraternity plans a Christmas party featuring singing Christmas carols around the piano. There is one catch: they don't have a piano. They finally locate one for sale, but the boys charm the Fergusons, the old couple selling it, so much that they decide to give it to the boys. The boys are equally charmed by the Fergusons. The rest of the episode is a musical record of the party, with the whole crowd singing carols ("Deck the Halls," "Santa Claus is Coming to Town"), and a bonus of "Winter Wonderland" in four-part harmony by The Four Preps.

Ultimately, Dave and Rick, Bruce (one of The Four Preps, Bruce Belland), Glen (another Prep, Glen Larson), and the other fraternity brothers all feel guilty for leaving their parents alone at Christmastime. Hence, they decide to invite the parents to the fraternity Christmas party.

As Dave says at one point: "You know, Mom and Pop were kidding, but we do kind of desert them around Christmastime. . . . You know, it might be a nice idea if we invited the parents to the Christmas party this year."

As Holmes noted: "The theme of making every effort to be with family at Christmas drives this episode, and all of the Christmas episodes, especially as the boys grew older, and it is touchingly represented in this episode as the Fergusons, the elderly couple who donated the piano, find the family they are missing in the fraternity brothers and their parents."

Years after *The Adventures of Ozzie and Harriet* ended its original run, and after the show failed to strike the same kind of lightning magic with the syndicated *Ozzie's Girls* in 1973, the Nelsons returned to TV, if on a local Los Angeles level, in the 1981 KTLA Christmas Special, *An Ozzie and Harriet Christmas*. As Holmes explained: "It is a typical TV reunion show in that it reassembles as much of the original cast as possible, but it also interweaves 1981 reminiscences with scenes from all the original Christmas episodes, 1952–1966. Some of the memories recorded here are not found elsewhere: Lyle Talbot remembering his days in stock theater with Harriet's father, meeting Harriet as a child actress; Harriet's recollections of first meeting Ozzie, with details never mentioned in other interviews. And all are filmed around a Christmas tree on a fair imitation of the original Ozzie and Harriet set (which in turn was a fair imitation of Ozzie and Harriet's real house). The opening dialogue sets the mood (and the cast). Harriet and Dave are trimming the tree.

HARRIET: The tree looks beautiful, doesn't it?

DAVE: Yeah, it sure does. Who all is coming by tonight?

HARRIET: Oh, Mary Jane Croft and Lyle Talbot, and Don DeFore—and your uncle Don.

DAVE: Oh, great! Jim Stacy called, and he's coming over with Kent McCord.

HARRIET: Oh, good! And Parley Baer said he might stop by.

DAVE: Oh, great! It should be a lot of fun. Just like the old days, right? The whole neighborhood is coming over!

HARRIET: Well, that's what Christmas is all about. Family and friendship. Time to get together again with family and friends.

As Holmes explained further: "Rick was unavailable for the filming, and Ozzie had passed away six years earlier, but both missing Nelsons were represented on film, and the special—nominated for a regional Emmy (in the most competitive region in American TV) was superbly edited to give Ozzie a voice in Christmas of 1981."

The host of this special was KTLA celebrity Tom Hatten (1926–2019), who started as an announcer on KTLA the year the Nelson show premiered on television, becomes like one of the family on the show, and serves as a stealth interviewer while seeming to be just another guest.

"Is it hokey?" Holmes wondered. "A little bit. The platitudes are predictable. But that's true of most family Christmas gatherings. So, it feels just right."

CHAPTER 38
CHRISTMAS WITH *LUCY, DONNA,* AND *HAZEL*

"What's the matter, Mr. B., hasn't the Spirit of Christmas touched you yet?"

—Shirley Booth's Hazel, to Don DeFore's Mr. Baxter, on *Hazel*

The household domestic is represented nicely with several characters in the history of television, three of which are uniquely featured in shows that offer optimum Christmas episodes: *I Love Lucy* and *The Lucy Show, The Donna Reed Show,* and *Hazel*.

In *I Love Lucy* (CBS, 1951–1957), Lucille Ball stars opposite real-life husband Desi Arnaz, with Vivian Vance and William Frawley as their neighbors. In *The Lucy Show* (CBS, 1962–1968), Ball was back as a widow with neighbor Vance now playing Vivian Bagley (TV's first divorced female character). *The Donna Reed Show* (ABC, 1959–1966) featured the *It's a Wonderful Life* actress in the leadership role (behind and in front of the camera) opposite Carl Betz as her husband, parenting two children played by Paul Petersen and Shelley Fabares (who were later joined by Petersen's real-life sister, Patty Petersen, after Fabares exited the series). Oscar-winning Shirley Booth led *Hazel* (NBC/CBS, 1961–1966), based on Ted Key's one-panel comic in *The Saturday Evening Post*.

Let's begin with the *Lucy* Christmas episodes, which are explored by entertainment historians Robert S. Ray, a *Lucy* aficionado, and Geoffrey Mark Fidelman, author of *The Lucy Book*.

On December 24, 1956, "The *I Love Lucy* Christmas Show" aired. As Ray explained, this was the only holiday-themed episode of the series.

And it was largely a retrospective episode featuring clips from past episodes, largely focused on Lucy's 1952–1953 pregnancy. For this reason, and possibly because it was felt that a Christmas-themed episode would seem out of place in daily reruns, it was decided at the time the show went into syndication that this episode would not be included in the package. Thus, until December 18, 1989, nearly eight months following Lucille Ball's death, when CBS aired it as a prime-time special, this was considered the "Lost Episode." Since the Christmas aspect only comes into play during the bookend sequences for all the clips, it's a relatively minor entry in the canon of classic TV Christmas outings. And, indeed, the fantasy epilogue, in which the cast breaks the fourth wall to wish everyone a Merry Christmas, is a reworking of a special epilogue used only once during the Christmas Eve 1951 screening of the otherwise non-holiday episode "Drafted."

In both the original tag and in its remake here, the Ricardos and the Mertzes each get the idea to dress up as Santa Claus to surprise the others only to be confounded by the appearance of the real Santa in their midst. As they count the Santas and realize there are five rather than four, the real Santa mysteriously disappears. In the 1951 version, Santa is played by Vernon Dent, a longtime member of *The Three Stooges* short-film series supporting players. In 1956, he's played by Cameron Grant, who had an uncredited bit role in the Lucy-Desi feature film, *The Long, Long Trailer.*

According to Fidelman's book, "The *I Love Lucy* Christmas Show" was the "first ever retrospective for a sitcom, a common practice with TV series today. Included are flashback scenes of Lucy telling Ricky she is pregnant (Episode #45), the barbershop quarter (Episode #47), and the cast taking Lucy to the hospital to have little Ricky (Episode #51).

"The last scene," Fidelman continued, "with five Santa Clauses," is a rewritten version of the one that appeared in the holiday installments during the first three seasons of the series (with Cameron Grant replacing Vernon Dent as St. Nick). Contrary to what has been reported elsewhere, this is not originally a special; it is just another episode of the series. The new scenes are filmed in one day without a studio audience present."

The episode was repeated twice by CBS, Fidelman observed, and as a special, following Ball's demise in 1989, both in black-and-white, and in a colorized edition.

In Fidelman's book, Ball explained how "This episode wasn't sold into syndication with the rest of the show, because CBS thought no one would want to see a Christmas show at the wrong time of the year. Who knew? There is something eerie and spooky about this show. I don't know what it is, but it makes me a little nervous and I do not enjoy watching it."

Next up, *The Lucy Show* segment, "Together for Christmas," which originally aired December 24, 1962, in the sitcom's first season. As Ray delineated:

This was the only time one of Lucy's many series had a 100 percent Christmas-themed episode, with no flashbacks to non-holiday events. It's actually a fairly good entry from what is by far the best season of *The Lucy Show.*

The opening scenes depict a realistic problem that many newly blended families across America could relate to: various family members have many cherished holiday traditions that may conflict with the traditions of those members who are newly part of the family. Should presents be opened on Christmas Eve or Christmas Day? Should a real tree be purchased or an artificial one? Will Christmas dinner include a turkey or a goose? Recently widowed Lucy Carmichael and new roommate Vivian Bagley face this issue as they celebrate their first Christmas under one roof, with their children all gathered as one. This was a dilemma based in reality, and in classic Lucy fashion, the second act takes that relatable premise and whips it into a slapstick "tit-for-tat" fight (this time involving a Christmas tree) worthy of an old Laurel and Hardy comedy. Lucille Ball and Vivian Vance are at their best in the many episodes of all their series in which their characters feud, and this one is no exception.

Fidelman offered his take on the episode:

"Together for Christmas" presents a very insightful script. No one in TV had effectively addressed the idea that families from different backgrounds celebrate Christmas very differently. The cultural and traditional disparities of Americans were almost always homogenized in any holiday show produced by Hollywood. And again, even more background is given here on the Carmichael and Bagley families, including the fact that this Lucy also comes from Jamestown, New York, and that her mother is still alive [matching the reality in both cases of Lucille Ball].

As with *I Love Lucy*, *The Donna Reed Show* produced only one Christmas episode. "A Very Merry Christmas" premiered on December 24, 1958. The episode opens with an anxiety-ridden Donna Stone, who is married to a pediatrician (played by Carl Betz, later of TV's *Judd for the Defense*), with whom she shares two children (played by Shelley Fabares and Paul Petersen). At Christmastime, Donna finds herself all a flutter with last-minute preparations for the holiday, including distributing fruitcakes that no one sincerely welcomes or appreciates, including the paperboy and the mailman. At the department stores for last-minute gifts, she's overwhelmed by the number of manic and rude shoppers. But in the end, all hearts are warmed when Donna, with the help of the handyman at her husband's hospital, organizes a Christmas party for the facility's children who are unable to leave their ward and spend the holiday with their families. In the process, her own children learn the meaning of the season by way of their less fortunate new young friends at the hospital.

According to Brian Cronin of PopCultureReferences.com, "this episode is very much a *Father Knows Best*–esque plot. . . . It's a very adorable, well-told story [and receives bonuses] for no 'maybe Santa Claus *is* real' moments!"

In leaving the sly and happy Stone family of *The Donna Reed Show*, we venture toward exploring *Hazel*, which ran for five years on two different networks (first NBC, then CBS), with two different casts.

In the first four years, the Oscar- and Tony-award-winning Shirley Booth played Hazel Burke, which subsequently brought her a double Emmy win. As a the bold, brassy, and busybody but oh-so-caring housekeeper with a heart of gold, Booth's Burke was dedicated to the Baxter family, headed by Whitney Blake as Missy (whom Hazel cared for as a child), little Harold Baxter (played by Bobby Buntrock, who later died tragically), and father-head Don DeFore (from *It Happened on 5th Avenue*, the beloved 1947 Christmas feature film), whom Hazel affectionately refers to as *Mr. B.*

By the end of its fourth year on NBC, the series had been canceled. But CBS had sought to air the sitcom for the following year. In the process, Booth invested her own money into that fifth season. But by then, DeFore and Blake had signed other contracts for work elsewhere. Cast in their place were Ray Fulmer and Lynn Borden with young Bobby Buntrock retained from the original cast. From a fiscal standpoint, money played a role in the cast changes as well.

With the higher-priced DeFore and Blake out of the picture, literally, Fulmer and Borden were hired at a lower salary. However, they would not be playing the same characters as DeFore and Blake. Fulmer was cast as Steve

Baxter, younger brother to DeFore's George Baxter, and Borden was hired to portray Steve's wife, whereas Blake had played George's wife.

Subsequently, there was a key change in the core premise of the series, ignited by Booth: Hazel would not disagree with Fuller's Steve Baxter as she would with DeFore's George Baxter, and vice versa.

By the end of the CBS fifth season version of the show, *Hazel* was still performing well in the ratings. But Booth's health was declining, and she opted not to continue the series. As such, the show officially ended a second time, but that was because of Booth and not the network's decision to cancel it.

With that explained, the sitcom presented only two Christmas episodes, both with the original cast:

"Hazel's Christmas Shopping," which premiered December 21, 1961, and "Just 86 Shopping Minutes to Christmas," which initially aired December 24, 1964.

In "Hazel's Christmas Shopping," everyone's favorite busybody gets another job at a department store to earn some extra cash for Christmas presents. In the process, Hazel ultimately reminds the family about the true meaning of Christmas, to love the gift giver and not the gift.

Once again, we share more of Brian Cronin's straightforward, spot-on thoughts from PopCultureReferences.com:

"Hazel's Christmas Shopping" had such a simple setup, but the writers of the episode, William Cowley and Peggy Chantler Dick, pretty much put on a master class of sitcom writing in this episode. Nothing extraneous was used, everything served the plot, and it was filled with bits that [were] so effortlessly introduced that you wouldn't think that they *were* going to tie into later plots, but they *all* do. It's just masterful writing. . . . The really cool bit is that we never see anyone actually exchange presents in the episode, and yet the writers have everything so well set up that we know how it'll go, and who'll get what. The economy of storytelling is excellent. Just excellent television.

In "Just 86 Shopping Minutes to Christmas," Dorothy finds a mink coat in the house and automatically assumes it's her Christmas gift from George. But's she's wrong. The gift is for Rita (played by Karen Steel), George's sister, from her husband, Harry (Lauren Gilbert), who asked George to keep it safe and hidden for the holiday.

Unlike *Hazel's* first Christmas adventure, "Just 86" was broadcast in color, to which the series transferred in its second season. In 1994, the episode was packaged within the CTHV VHS release *A Double Holiday Dose of Hazel*, which also included "Hazel's Christmas Shopping." It was later included on Shout Factory's *Hazel: The Complete Fourth Season* DVD set, released on December 11, 2012.

CHAPTER 39

MAKE MERRY ROOM FOR DANNY, SHERIFF TAYLOR, AND DICK VAN DYKE

"The greatest gift you can give to others is your time, attention, and love."

—Danny Thomas

Producer/directors Sheldon Leonard and Carl Reiner were also performers, who never fully abandoned acting, but as their careers continued, each was more likely to be found behind the scenes. Ironically, one of Leonard's earliest film roles was that of Nick the bartender in *It's a Wonderful Life*, which was remade for TV by Marlo Thomas, daughter of Danny Thomas. In switching their careers, Leonard and Reiner often partnered with the father Thomas in bringing to life some of the most popular sitcoms in history.

Those include: *Make Room for Danny*, a.k.a. *The Danny Thomas Show* (NBC, 1953–1964), *The Andy Griffith Show* (CBS, 1960–1968), *The Dick Van Dyke Show* (CBS, 1961–1966), and *Gomer Pyle, U.S.M.C.* (CBS, 1964–1969), starring Jim Nabors. Thomas's sitcom, on which Leonard had a recurring role as Danny's agent, Phil Brokaw, gave birth to Sheriff Andy Taylor, Griffith's alter ego from TV's fictional rural small-town Mayberry from which Nabors' Pyle moved away to join the Marines with his own sitcom. All the while, comedy/variety writer Rob Petrie, Van Dyke's role in his self-named comedy, worked for Alan Brady, who was played by Carl Reiner; though that was not the initial plan.

Reiner had shown Leonard a TV pilot he wrote and starred in called *Head of the Family*. Leonard loved the concept but felt Reiner was miscast, and he suggested Dick Van Dyke for the lead. The *Head of the Family* pilot became *The Dick Van Dyke Show* on which, subsequently, both Leonard and Danny Thomas eventually made guest appearances.

Thomas delivered a cameo performance as the alien, Kolak, from the planet Twilo, in the famed episode, "It May Look Like a Walnut" (February 6, 1963); Leonard took the gangster lead in "Big Max Calvada" (November 20, 1963), a similar character of which he would reprise in the short-lived sitcom *Big Eddie* (CBS, 1975). Meanwhile, the "Calvada" moniker doubled as the acronine/title of the production company formed by and combining the names of Reiner, Leonard, Thomas, and Van Dyke.

According to *Dick Van Dyke Show* historian David Van Dusen: "'Calvada' is broken down as follows: CA = CArl Reiner, L = Leonard, VA = VAn Dyke, and DA = DAnny Thomas. Calvada Productions, administered through the William Morris Agency, was formed distinctly and separately to handle only the affairs of *The Dick Van Dyke Show*—no other shows.

"Danny and Sheldon had previously formed Thomas Leonard Productions," continued Van Dusen, who was "not sure exactly which shows fell under this umbrella." Although he was "confident that Marterto Enterprises was Danny's company, comprised of his children's names [Mar for Marlo—Ter for Terry—and To for Tony]."

With that clarified, save for *Gomer Pyle, U.S.M.C.*, the three remaining Calvada sitcoms featured holiday segments, beginning with *Make Room for Daddy/The Danny Thomas Show*.

Of Thomas in general, TV and film historian Robert S. Ray said: "Danny's versatility with its emphasis on home and family made him a natural for the young, growing medium of television. The key to his success was this: he was boisterous but never vulgar and then, on a dime, he could turn impossibly sentimental. That old-fashioned sentimentality, at just the right moment before it got too thick, was a zinger that told you he was in charge at all times."

A jack-of-all-trades, Thomas, along with colleagues Reiner, Leonard, and Van Dyke, did it all. Beyond TV, he performed live on stage and appeared in feature films, namely *The Jazz Singer* remake of 1952. His lifelong charitable leadership of St. Jude Children's Hospital, which continues its noble mission with his daughter Marlo Thomas, has catered to and remains to care for millions of youths stricken with cancer. That alone forever seals the Thomas family's integrity and humanity, and the essence of what Christmas and the holiday season are all about.

In the Leonard-directed episode titled, simply, "Christmas," which first aired December 22, 1953, Danny Williams, Thomas's successful nightclub performer persona, may not be home for Christmas. But in the end, he surprises his wife, Margaret, played by Jean Hagen, and their children, the pubescent, wise-cracking Rusty (Rusty Hamer) and the teenage Terry (Sherry Jackson).

One year later, Leonard helmed "The New Year's Show," which debuted on December 28, 1954. Here, Danny and Margaret, against all holiday odds, attempt to spend a tranquil, intimate New Year's Eve for two. But of course, that doesn't happen.

Three years after that, Leonard directed "Christmas and the Clowns," which premiered on Christmas Eve, 1956. By this time, Margaret has passed away (Jean Hagen had left the series), and Danny faces his first Christmas as a widower. To help muster some holiday cheer for Rusty and Terry, he invites a troupe of circus clowns over for Christmas dinner.

According to PopCultureReferences.com, "Christmas and the Clowns" is "a well-written, well-performed episode."

Two Christmastimes hence, "The Saints Come Marching" on December 29, 1958, with Leonard back behind the camera. Although not technically a Christmas episode, the story is infested with the holiday spirit, with Danny taking under his wing a gifted, if somewhat rebellious, musical band of young men. After working with school authorities to direct the group on a more productive path, Danny helps to launch their career in the entertainment industry.

By the time "The Singing Sisters" debuted on December 19, 1960, Danny has married Kathy, portrayed by Marjorie Lord, who's joined the family with her daughter Linda, played by future *Lost in Space* star Angela Cartwright. In this episode, Kathy convinces Danny to meet Sister Beatrice (Jan Clayton) and Sister Margaret (Rose Hobart), two talented Catholic nuns who have composed a Christmas song. Upon learning that the sisters have been swindled out of $75 in a shady pre-publishing music contract, Danny and his manager Charley (Sid Melton) make it their job to get that money back.

On December 23, 1963, another "Christmas Story" is told. This time, Danny Thomas pulls double duty as director and as Danny Williams, who finds himself disillusioned over the holidays. Kathy and the kids have seemingly become so materialistic, which makes Danny think they have lost touch with the true meaning of Christmas. So, he seeks to set them straight.

On February 15, 1960, Sheldon Leonard is back again behind the camera with a non-Christmas episode that paves the way for *The Andy Griffith Show*: "Danny Meets Andy Griffith," in which Danny Williams is arrested by Sheriff Andy Taylor for going through an unnoticed stop sign in the rustic town of Mayberry.

The tremendous success of this episode served as the back-door pilot of *The Andy Griffith Show*, which in its first season, aired its one and only "Christmas Story" of the entire series.

"Christmas in Mayberry: Christmas Story" is directed by Bob Sweeney and written by Sheldon Leonard, Frank Tarloff, and Aaron Ruben. Here, crotchety old businessman Ben Weaver (Will Wright) wants moonshiner Sam Muggins (Sam Edwards) locked up for Christmas but, after seeing the holiday spirit in Andy's jail, he tries to be arrested himself.

Entertainment historian Bob Barnett: "Mayberry is like a second home to millions of viewers through the small screen. Andy Taylor's wisdom and the charm of Opie always leaves a mark. The 'Christmas' episode where Opie is disappointed with his gift but learns the importance of giving is a heart-warming lesson. The simplicity of the *Andy Griffith Show*, in general, mirrors the values that many baby boomers grew up with."

Elinor Donahue, meanwhile, recalled a few memories of performing, that is, singing, in the *Griffith* series "Christmas." Her main recollection of the episode is the recording of the song "Away in a Manager." By that time, she didn't enjoy singing anymore. She had performed in vaudeville and sang as a child, but as she explained, "When my voice changed . . . well, my voice changed. And I wasn't comfortable singing anymore." Even after her mother reminded her that she frequently sang the song in church at Christmas, Donahue was still anxiety-ridden in doing so on the *Griffith* episode. When "Away in a Manager" was written into the script, she didn't have a choice.

As Donahue continued to explain, she and Griffith pre-recorded "Away in a Manager" after a workday at the studio. At one point Griffith asked her, "Do you want to try it a couple times and see if we can find a key that's good for both of us." To which she replied, "Ok. But I'm very nervous."

"I know, I know," Griffith told her, "but it's gonna be alright."

And it was. They found the optimum music key for Donahue, and they performed the song. As she recalled, "We only did it the one time. And I could never, ever, ever had done it if Andy Griffith hadn't been as sensitive to my anxiety as he was. He was just lovely.

"Of course, they sweetened it in sound-editing," she noted, "and made it stronger. Later, some people thought it wasn't my voice that was used, until I would attend the various Andy Griffith reunions over the years. There, each of the cast members are supposed to perform in the talent show. And I didn't have any talent to participate and I certainly wasn't going to sing. But one year I decided that I was going to give it a shot, and sing 'Away in a Manager.' And by golly, everybody just went crazy for it. They realized it was indeed me in the episode that was doing the singing. It was wonderful."

Meanwhile, here's a few other sidenotes about the *Griffith* "Christmas" episode:

In the cell during the "Away in a Manger" sing-a-long, when the camera pans up to Ben, the initials "R.S." are noticeable. This was done by Reggie Smith, the show's prop master.

Will Wright makes his first of three appearances here as the stubborn old Ben Weaver. Previously Wright had appeared as Mr. Johnson in the aforementioned "Danny Meets Andy Griffith" episode of *The Danny Thomas Show* that led to *The Andy Griffith Show*.

During the "Away in a Manger" number, when the camera pans up to Ben, a pinup girl can be seen on the wall right next to the sink.

Bess Muggins, married to Sam, is portrayed by actress Margaret Kerry, who was the character model for Tinker Bell in Disney's 1953 animated film *Peter Pan*.

Brett White recently noted on Decider.com:

Christmas comes to Mayberry, and it's not the upbeat event that you might expect. All Sheriff Taylor and Deputy Fife want to do is clear out the holding cells for Christmas Eve so everyone can spend the night with their loved ones. But right before Andy hits the lights on the empty police department, the town scrooge demands that a moonshiner be arrested. Andy's solution: stage a big family Christmas behind bars so everyone can be together—everyone except that old scrooge. This episode ramps up *The Andy Griffith Show*'s usual sincerity to tell a tear-jerking story of one lonely old man who doesn't know how to ask for friendship.

CHAPTER 40
A SEASONAL SCI-FI/FANTASY/
HIGH-CONCEPT PALOOZA

"All men are brothers, even if they're girls."

—Samantha Stephens, "Sisters at Heart," *Bewitched*

Although the Christmas special in any format may be categorized to some extent as fantasy programming, high-concept/fantasy/sci-fi weekly TV excursions such as *The Twilight Zone*, *Lost in Space*, *The Munsters*, *Bewitched*, *My Favorite Martian*, *Mork and Mindy*, and *The Six Million Dollar Man*, among others, have easily melded into that mainstream merriment mix over the years.

For example, *The Avengers*, starring Patrick Macnee and Diana Rigg as super sleuths John Steed and Emma Peel, even had a Christmas episode. An American/British hybrid production, the offbeat adventures of *The Avengers* (not to be confused with the Marvel comic book franchise) were initially broadcast on ITV in the United Kingdom and then ABC in the United States. Such was the case with "Too Many Christmas Trees," which first aired early in 1966 in Britain and then in the States on the following August 11.

According to Kevin Olzak on IMDb.com, February 24, 2011, "Too Many Christmas Trees," which was a personal favorite of Macnee's, made an impression:

"One concession to the Americans is having the bearded one referred to as 'Santa Claus' rather than 'Father Christmas,' and it has to rank as a most unlikely holiday theme, a dark, brooding tale of terror more suited to the 1980s than the 1960s."

In the story, as Olzak explained:

Steed is suffering sleepless nights consumed by sinister images of Santa Claus, while the sympathetic Mrs. Peel tries to lighten the holiday festivities by inviting him to a Charles Dickens–themed house party at the estate of publisher Brandon Storey (Mervyn Johns, 1945's "Dead of Night").

Talent agent/author Pierre Patrick also recalled a high-concept Christmas TV series favorite episode. This time, the over-the-top characters involved are Batman and Robin, as played by Adam West and Burt Ward, who met up with Santa Claus (Andy Devine) on the 1960s *Batman* TV series, which Patrick, overall, described as a "phenomenon." *The Dark Knight* eventually and directly teamed with *Father Christmas* in a new DC Comics *Batman* miniseries book, *Santa Claus: Silent Knight*. But as Patrick explained, in the TV *Batman* episode "The Duo Is Slumming," from December 22, 1966, Bruce Wayne and Dick Grayson's alter egos connect with Kris Kringle in one of their most usual, *unusual* ways: when they vertically scaled a skyscraper. "*Batman*'s producers knew Santa had to be included on the show at some point, especially in an episode that aired at Christmastime," Patrick said.

What better place for Mr. Claus to suddenly appear than in one of those surprise big building window *Laugh-In*-like cameos that various celebrities, personalities, or public figures of the day would utilize on the show over the years? Patrick explained, "Santa popped his head out of one of those windows to wish the cape crusaders a Merry Christmas. It was perfect."

Another example of a high-concept weekly TV series that embraced a Christmas setting was *The Avengers*. In the aforementioned episode, "Too Many Christmas Trees," which originally aired on August 11, 1966 (though nowhere near Christmas), another dynamic duo, in the form of British super spies John Steed (played by Patrick Macnee) and Mrs. Emma Peel (the Emmy-nominated Diana Rigg), "styled the 1960s from the U.K. and gave us a Dickensian psychedelic Christmas," Patrick said.

In this unique adventure, "Steed is drugged and Mrs. Peel gets invited to a castle for the holidays where Dickens is king. Mrs. Peel sets out to save Steed with a devilish plan of song and dance," Patrick noted. "This was a very different episode for the series where the chemistry of the two leads was even more than usually superb and legendary."

As a big-screen sidenote nod to Rigg's and James Bond's feature film legacy, her character, Contessa Teresa "Tracy" di Vicenzo, meets and weds the debonair secret agent in 1969's *On Her Majesty's Secret Service*. In this 007 adventure, partially set near Christmas, George Lazenby temporarily replaces Sean Connery in the lead (to mixed results) while, as Patrick observed, the movie remains "the only holiday-themed film in the Bond franchise."

Two years after the premiere of *Dr. No*, the initial Connery-Bond film, a double TV dose of spooky situation comedies featuring married couples would produce Christmas episodes: *The Munsters* (CBS, 1964–1966) and *The Addams Family* (ABC, 1964–1966).

On December 24, 1965, *The Munsters* aired "Grandpa Leaves Home," in which the Dracula-esque Grandpa, as portrayed by Al Lewis, has a tiff with his Frankenstein-ish son-in-law Herman, played by Fred Gwynne. Tensions elevate to the point of Grandpa moving out of their creepy hallow digs. "But as strange as the Munsters appeared and behaved," said Patrick, "they are very much a typical wonderful, caring family and dealt with their grandfather leaving home as any family would, trying to bring him back for the holidays."

"Grandpa Leaves Home" also starred series regulars Yvonne De Carlo as Lily Munster, Herman's vampy wife, and young Butch Patrick as their wolf-bane son, Eddie. Pierre Patrick (no relation) also noted how this episode was the first to feature the Munsters' "unattractive" niece Marilyn as played by Pat Priest (who took over the role after Beverly Owen fell in love and departed the series and the entertainment industry to get married in real life).

Exactly one year after "Grandpa Leaves Home" on *The Munsters*, "Christmas with the Addam's Family" aired on December 24, 1965. That alternate smiley-scary show's eclectic regular cast included John Austin as the loveable oddball Gomez, Carolyn Jones as his sultry supernatural spouse Morticia; Lisa Loring and Ken Weatherwax as their oddball children, Wednesday and Pugsley; Blossom Rock (a.k.a. Marie Blake) as the moody brood's fraternal Grandmama; former child star Jackie Coogan (who ignited the benchmark 'Coogan's Law,' also known as the 'Coogan Act,' the California Child Actor's Bill) as feisty Uncle Fester, Felix Silla as the Tribble-hairy-like Cousin It, and Ted Cassidy, who played a dual role of sorts: the family's lanky, lurking butler Lurch and Thing, the household's pervasive and body-less "Hand-in-a-Box."

As Pierre Patrick explained, the question at hand (sorry) in "Christmas with the Addams Family," became "Is Santa real or not because Wednesday and Pugsley were told by their neighbor he wasn't.

"Even if these Munster and Addams families and their holiday episodic adventures were a little bit strange," Patrick noted, "they certainly were at least all about Christmas."

Along that same vein, Patrick referenced the sci-fi TV show *Lost in Space*, which was producer/creator Irwin Allen's fanciful take on the already-fanciful Robert Lewis Stevenson novel from 1812, titled, *Swiss Family Robinson*. In that classic tale, a band of relatives and their seabound boat are stranded somewhere on an island in the East Indies.

On *Lost in Space* (which originally aired on CBS, 1965–1968), the galactic version of the Robinson family, headed by Dr. John Robinson (Guy Williams) and his wife, Maureen (June Lockhart), leave the overpopulated Earth of 1997 in their Jupiter 2 spaceship in search of a less-crowded planet in the Alpha Centauri quadrant. But due to the mishaps of Dr. Zachary Smith (Jonathan Harris), the family, including children Will (Billy Mumy), Penny (Angela Cartwright), and Judy (Marta Kristen), along with Major Don West (Mark Goddard) and the Robot (played by Bob May and voiced by Dick Tufeld) crash-land on the planet Priplanus (where they remain for the first two seasons).

Pierre Patrick described *Lost* as "the first science fiction series to celebrate Christmas in space. Though not really." That is to say, at least in reference to the first of what became two holiday-themed episodes. In the initial *Lost* Christmas adventure, "Return from Outer Space," the Robinsons, "were not really in space at the time," Partick clarified. "Their son Will Robinson actually goes back to Vermont on Earth, to celebrate Christmas in a very old-fashioned city called Hatfield Four Corners. He has a deadline to get a bottle of carbon tetrachloride to save his family's food purifier and desperately tries to come back to his lost planet."

Upon Will's return to the Jupiter 2 with the life-saving carbon tetrachloride, his family, Dr. Smith, and Major West are in a special state of disbelief. Or as Patrick put it, "By the magic of Christmas their food was saved.

"Return from Outer Space," Patrick concluded, "is a heartwarming Christmas episode, which just also happens to be one of Billy Mumy's favorites, one that is also most lovingly remembered by fans."

In deciphering the second *Lost in Space* Christmas episode, "The Toymaker," which originally aired January 25, 1967 (one month after Christmas), Patrick called it "a Pinocchio story in reverse." In the story written by Bob Duncan and Wanda Duncan and directed by Robert Douglas, Patrick explained: "Will, Doctor Smith, and The Robot get transported to another planet where toys are being made by the Toymaker who thinks Will is a toy and not a real boy. They later try to escape through opening a door to Earth and Times Square, where Christmas is being celebrated, a place they will probably never see again."

Beyond the two *Lost* holiday episodes, Patrick noted: "Christmas would not be celebrated in space on TV again until George Lucas's *Star Wars* extraordinary musical special with guest stars like Beatrice Arthur. But while that's another story [see chapter 13], a fun connect-the-dots fact about *Lost in Space* and *Star Wars* is both productions feature incredible musical themes created by multiple Academy Award–winner John Williams."

In 2003, Patrick, who holds a significant measure of music appreciation, "had the privilege" of producing a Grammy-nominated Christmas album that was based on the Ogden Nash children's poem for all ages, "The Christmas That Almost Wasn't." The musical production benefited the National The-ater of The Deaf and was, as Patrick explained, "a story of an upside-down Christmas."

The album featured legendary actor John Lithgow, who was fresh from his Emmy-winning role as Dick Solomon on TV's *3rd Rock from the Sun*, Trina McGee (from TV's *Boy Meets World*), former teen-pop idol Leif Gar-rett, Canadian singer and TV host Rene Simard, and as the Hero, Billy Crawford, who had just completed recording the Pokémon theme song.

"Although we didn't win the Grammy," Patrick said, "we were celebrated right after the Grammy ceremony with a stamp given for Ogden Nash's unforgettable poetry, which was inscribed with his famous quote 'Candy is dandy but liquor is quicker.'"

Meanwhile, the aforementioned John Lithgow's *3rd Rock from the Sun* series presented a Christmas episode of its own: "Jolly Ol' St. Dick," which originally aired December 15, 1996. Besides Lithgow's Dick Solomon, this episode featured the show's other regular band of alien irregular family mem-bers, even though they were not technically related other than being non-humans. Those include Kristine Johnson as Sally Solomon, Stuart French as Harry Solomon, and Joseph Gordon-Levitt as Tommy Solomon. *SNL*'s Jane Curtin, who played the mother Conehead in that late-night show's famed sci-fi skits, this time played it straight as the mortal Dr. Mary Albright.

Of this *3rd Rock* venture, as journalist Brett White once decided on Decider.com: "Who better to ride the roller coaster of emotions that come along with Christmas than a family of secret aliens learning about all the holiday hoopla for the first time? The Solomons go all in on Christmas by getting mall jobs and searching for the perfect presents. It doesn't take long for these scouts to observe the dark side of the holiday. Sally gets mobbed by shoppers at her gift-wrapping station, mall elf Harry finds out his new boss is just a random dude in a red suit, and Dick learns that you can't just chop down any tree you see. This episode makes the nightmares of Christmas legitimately hilarious."

Some years before *3rd Rock from the Sun*, TV's *Mork & Mindy* alien-based sitcom (ABC, 1978–1982), starring Robin Williams and Pam Daw-ber, presented a Christmas episode. Airing on December 14, 1978, "Mork's First Christmas" was about planet-Ork-resident Mork's inability to afford

Christmas gifts the human economic way on Earth. To compensate, he creates odd, unique presents for Mindy and his closest friends.

Years before Williams and Dawber dabbled in alien sitcom land, another "relative" half-hour alien-based comedy appeared on CBS (1963–1966): *My Favorite Martian* did a Christmas episode. *Martian* starred Ray Walston decades prior to his performance beside Sean Penn on the big screen in 1982's *Fast Times at Ridgemont High* and Fred Savage in the charming 1991 TV-movie *Christmas on Division Street*. Walston's otherworldly Martian posed as Uncle Martin (get it?) to Bill *Courtship of Eddie's Father* Bixby's all-too-human Tim O'Hara, after the former's alien ship crash-lands in the latter's Earthly backyard.

In the episode "Humbug, Mrs. Brown," which originally aired February 21, 1965, Uncle Martin learns that neighbor Mrs. Lorelie Brown (Pamela Britton) is facing economic challenges due to her all-too-generous disposition. As only a good Martian friend could, Uncle Martin sends her subliminal messages to increase her financial savvy. But as only any good sci-fi/fantasy comedy situation could develop, Martin's alien wizardry proves to have an extreme effect on Mrs. Brown; she empties her bank account with a thief watching from the side.

Besides *The Courtship of Eddie's Father* (ABC, 1969–1971), Bixby went on to star in two other TV series: *The Magician* (NBC, 1973–1974) and *The Incredible Hulk* (CBS, 1977–1982). In the latter, the actor, who died of prostate cancer in 1993, shared the bill with Lou Ferrigno as the not-so-mild-mannered David Banner, who when angry or agitated, transforms into Marvel's initial live-action, if small-screen, not-so-jolly-green giant super-hero with a heart.

On December 21, 1979, four days before Christmas, the *Hulk* series aired an episode titled, "Captive Night." Here, David Banner, ever on the run from tabloid journalist Jack McGee (played by Jack Calvin), goes incognito as Bishop, who works overtime at a department store that two criminal brothers decide to break into. When the safe proves to be more challenging to crack than initially anticipated, David pretends to join their gang and get in on the action. Of course, his true green colors come into play when David transforms into the Hulk and ultimately clobbers the bad guys.

The guest stars in "Captive Night" include Mark Lenard, who played Leonard Nimoy's Vulcan father to his Mr. Spock on *Star Trek*; Anne Lockhart, the real-life daughter of *Lost in Space* star June Lockhart; and Parley Baer, who was semiregular on *The Adventures of Ozzie and Harriet* and a guest star on *Bewitched*, both sitcoms of which produced several Christmas episodes. Meanwhile, too, Ted Cassidy, from *The Addams Family*, lent his vast vocal talents to *The Incredible Hulk*, for which he served as an uncredited narrator.

Although not technically a Christmas episode, beyond its premiere shortly before the holiday, "Captive Night" features one scene in which the Hulk finds himself in the department store's toy department. So, at one point in the episode's production, it may have been intended as a Christmas episode.

Three years before *The Incredible Hulk*'s quasi-Christmas experience on CBS, another 1970s superhero TV show featured a holiday-themed episode: *The Six Million Dollar Man*, which originally aired on ABC from the fall of 1973 to the spring of 1978. Several episodes of this show also happened to be written and produced by the *Hulk*'s developing producer Kenneth Johnson.

In this series, Lee Majors, later of *Owen Marshall, Counselor at Law*, *The Men from Shiloh*, and *The Big Valley*, starred as Col. Steve Austin, an astronaut-turned-test-pilot who, after a horrific aircraft accident, is rebuilt, made "stronger, faster, better" with bionic parts: two legs, one right arm, and a left eye.

On December 12, 1976, the episode "A Bionic Christmas Carol" made it to the airwaves as yet another adaptation of Charles Dickens' *A Christmas Carol*. This *Six Million Dollar* segment features series star Austin reaching out to help a family headed by *Bewitched*'s Dick Sargent deal with the Scrooge-esque played by none other than *My Favorite Martian*'s Ray Walston.

Here, Steve forgoes his Christmas vacation to inspect a disruption at a main system supplier for the space program. A conspiracy could alter plans for an exploration of Mars. The supplier's president is the mean-spirited Horton Budge, who's extremely careful with his money. His nephew, Bob Crandall (an employee at Budge's factory), doesn't make enough money to care for his wife and family. Steve employs his powers to warm Budge's soul and bring some cheer to the Crandall family.

A few behind-the-scene notes: show executive producer Harve Bennett had always wanted to work with Ray Walston, ever since he saw the actor perform in a stage production of *Damn Yankees*.

A slight sight gag: When Steve and Bob visit a toy store to pick up some gifts for the Crandall family, *Six Million Dollar Man* dolls are viewed in the background, on the store's shelves.

Budge's factory houses a chamber called "Artificial Martian atmosphere," which is a nod to Ray Walston's character on *My Favorite Martian*.

In addition to *The Six Million Dollar Man* and *My Favorite Martian*, other sci-fi shows featured Christmas episodes, including such anthology programs as *The Twilight Zone*.

The Twilight Zone produced two holiday-themed episodes: "Night of the Meek," which aired December 24, 1960, and "Changing of the Guard," which debuted June 1, 1962.

"Night of the Meek" was written by series host and creator Rod Serling and directed by Jack Smight. Here, *Honeymooners* legend Art Carney portrays a derelict Santa Claus who is fired on Christmas Eve. After he discovers a strange bag that gives out presents, he sets out to fulfill his one wish—to see the less fortunate inherit the bounties of Christmas.

Bob Barnett: "*The Twilight Zone* was unlike anything else on TV, and 'Night of the Meek' is a unique Christmas entry in the history of episodic television. Art Carney's portrayal of a downtrodden Santa who receives a miracle on Christmas is both mysterious and touching. It leaves the viewer pondering the mysteries of the season and the idea that magic might just be real."

As documented on IMDb.com, due to an unintended extended budget, six consecutive episodes of the series were produced on videotape and then transferred to film. "Night of the Meek" was one of those episodes. Utilizing videotape for all six segments saved approximately $30,000 in total, which in the minds of many fans of the show was not enough to justify the loss of depth of visual perspective that added to *The Twilight Zone*'s visual gravitas. Fortunately, the videotape process was not utilized again after those initial six episodes.

Show producer Buck Houghton recalled making this episode in author Marc Scott Zicree's all-encompassing *Twilight Zone Companion*. "Once in a while, [Rod Serling] would have an enthusiasm. He'd say to himself or to Carol or to me or whomever, that he particularly liked somebody. There was a Christmas show that we did just because he wanted to see Art Carney play Santa Claus."

A few tidbits about "Meek": near the end of the episode, Art Carney's Corwin/Santa is sitting on the steps of the mission talking with the character listed in the credits as simply "Old Man." However, he addresses him twice as Burt, which fits like a glove because the character was played by the beloved actor Burt Mustin.

The episode's title is based upon the biblical quote from Matthew 5:5, "Blessed are the meek, for they shall inherit the earth."

A stage musical based on this episode was written by lyricist/librettist Patrick Cook and composer Frederick Freyer but has not yet been produced due to rights issues.

Sister Florence's bonnet bears the legend "Save A Soul," which is a reference to the Save A Soul mission operated by Sister Sarah and Brother Arvide in the musical *Guys and Dolls*.

Art Carney would later play the role of Santa Claus in the 1984 TV film *The Night They Saved Christmas*, which also starred *Charlie's Angels* actress Jaclyn Smith.

John Fiedler, who also appeared in the episode, would go on to perform with Art Carney on Broadway as Felix Unger and Vinnie in the original production of Neil Simon's *The Odd Couple* (the TV adaptation of which features Jack Klugman and Tony Randall, both of whom star in a Christmas episode of that show).

The department store train display seen in "Night of the Meek" is the same one shown in *The Addams Family*.

According to the production slate, the videotaping-turned-filming of the episode began on November 26, 1960, just four weeks before its premiere.

The episode has the first of four times that Val Avery plays a bartender. He subsequently did so in the following big-screen films: *The Hallelujah Trail* (1965), *Identity Crisis* (1975), and *Easy Money* (1983).

In "The Changing of the Guard," the 102nd episode of *The Twilight Zone*, Donald Pleasence portrays Professor Ellis Fowler, an elderly English literature teacher at the Rock Spring School, a boys' prep school in Vermont, who is forced into retirement after teaching for fifty-one years at the school. In perusing old yearbooks and memories of former students, Fowler believes the academic and subsequent life lessons he taught were for naught and that he accomplished nothing.

Severely despondent on Christmas Eve, Fowler prepares to kill himself alongside a statue of the famous educator Horace Mann, with its quote, "Be ashamed to die until you have won some victory for humanity." However, just as he is about to place a gun to his head, Mann is called back to his classroom by a phantom bell. There he is visited by spirits of several former students, most of whom died heroically. The boys tell Fowler just how much his wisdom and guidance inspired and enhanced their lives.

The Twilight Zone featured several actors before they became stars, including future *Bewitched* icon Elizabeth Montgomery, who starred with future film-legend Charles Bronson in the episode titled, "Two," which aired September 15, 1961.

Approximately three years later, Montgomery was cast as Samantha on *Bewitched*, which did four Christmas episodes: "A Vision of Sugar Plumbs" (from the first season with a pre–*Lost in Space* Billy Mumy as a guest star and

Cecil Kellaway as Santa), "Humbug Not to Be Spoken Here" (*A Christmas Carol* takeoff with Charles Lane as Scrooge and Don Beddoe as Santa), "Santa Comes for a Visit and Stays and Stays" (with Ronald Long as Santa from season 6), and the groundbreaking episode "Sisters at Heart" (featuring Don Marshall from *Land of the Giants*). "Vision" and "Humbug" feature Dick York as the "first Darrin," while "Santa Comes for a Visit" and "Sisters at Heart" features "second Darrin" Dick Sargent, who would later guest star on "A Bionic Christmas Carol," the holiday episode of *The Six Million Dollar Man* (which also features guest star Ray Walston from *My Favorite Martian*).

Bewitched in general protests prejudice and hails human unity, or put another way, humanity. The episode "Sisters at Heart," which originally aired on December 24, 1971, represents, more than any *Bewitched* segment, the show's core message of embracing cultural diversity.

In "Sisters at Heart," set at Christmastime, Darrin is removed from an important toy account because a bigoted client, Mr. Brockway (played by Parley Baer), mistakes a little girl named Lisa (Venetta T. Rowles, a.k.a. Venetta Rogers), who happens to be African American, for the Stephens' daughter. In reality, Tabitha (as played by Erin Murphy) is Samantha and Darrin's daughter, while the child Lisa is the daughter of Darrin's colleague, Keith Wilson (Don Marshall) and his wife, Dorothy Wilson (Janee Michelle).

Meanwhile, Tabitha and Lisa have become such good friends that they view themselves as sisters. Unfortunately, while playing in the park one day, a bully tells them they can't be sisters because they are not of the same race. Upset upon hearing this, Tabitha employs her "wishcraft" (anything she wishes comes true) and transforms her and Lisa into look-alike sisters of sorts: White polka dots appear on Lisa, and black polka dots appear on Tabitha.

Samantha acquires an antidote from Dr. Bombay (Bernard Fox) and tells Lisa and Tabitha, "You can be sisters without looking alike. . . . Sisters are girls who share something. Actually, all men are brothers . . . even if they're girls."

"When we did that," Elizabeth Montgomery said of "Sisters at Heart," I thought, "Yeah . . . this is what I want *Bewitched* to be all about."

"Sisters at Heart" was a special episode for several reasons. The story was written by students of the fifth-period English class at Thomas Jefferson High School in Los Angeles. *Bewitched* writer Barbara Avedon, who would later go on to write for such shows as *Cagney & Lacey*, had assisted the students with the story elements of the episode. "That was my favorite script of all time," said Avedon, who was, before *Bewitched*, a veteran of *The Donna Reed Show* (which like *Bewitched*, heralded female empowerment).

"I had stopped writing for *Bewitched* and everything else when Bill Asher phoned me and explained how these kids had written this great script, but that it needed a slight rewrite. So, I went down to Jefferson High," Avedon continued, "which was an inner-city school, and I was horrified. Locker doors were hanging off their hinges, and there wasn't a blade of grass in sight. And what was worse . . . these kids had been reading on a third-grade level. It was awful.

"But," as she went on to explain, "I walked into their classroom, and their teacher, Marcella Saunders, had asked them who had watched *Bewitched* the night before. And every hand in the room went up. And then she asked them why they liked it. 'Well,' said one young man, 'it's a mixed marriage. She's a witch and he's human . . . and she could have anything she wants but doesn't use her powers for selfish reasons . . . only once in a while to help her husband.' It was really a wonderful moment," Avedon said.

The distinguished writer then read the story the class had written and "was amazed."

"That script," she said, "was as good as any that I had seen from established writers. It just had to be polished up a little. So, I was honest with the kids. I said, 'I don't like to be rewritten and I don't want to rewrite you, but maybe if we work together, I think we can create something really beautiful."

As Avedon further recalled: "I told them I wouldn't make any changes that they wouldn't approve of because I loved their basic idea. The one major change I suggested was that we make it a Christmas show because it was so infested with the spirit."

After Avedon finished speaking with the class, "they all kind of just sat there stone silent for a minute. Then one of them stood up and introduced himself. Almost immediately, the other students rose one by one, and the class and I became friends."

Marcella Saunders, who continued to teach for years after the show, could not say enough good things about this unique *Bewitched* experience. "We were writing a Christmas story and were experiencing a Christmas story. Everyone on the show was so pleasant and supportive."

By the time "Sisters at Heart" went into production, Dick Sargent was into his second season playing Darrin. He credited Saunders as the main motivating force behind her students' creativity. "She was the inspiration," he said. "She was interested in innovative forms of teaching. And these kids, who might have been stuck in the ghetto for the rest of their lives, loved *Bewitched*, and with just a little approval and motivation, came alive on the set.

"One of them," Sargent continued to explain, "was the assistant director, who had the chance to scream, 'Quiet on the set!' And it was marvelous.

Doing the show gave them, at least for a brief time, a change of pace and scenery, and they just reveled in it."

The entire cast and crew of "Sisters at Heart," including Saunders and her gifted students, continued the celebration at the subsequent Emmy Awards ceremony. That night, "Sisters at Heart" won the coveted Governor's Award.

CHAPTER 41

THE FESTIVE FEMININE MYSTIQUE

"I just stopped by to take one of Santa's helpers to lunch."

— Ted Bessell's Don Hollinger, in *That Girl*'s
"Christmas and the Hard Luck Kid"

Eve Arden, Ann Sothern, Gail Storm, Marlo Thomas, and Mary Tyler Moore each represented the independent career woman in their leading-role sitcoms, all of which but Sothern's two shows featured Christmas episodes.

As high school English teacher Connie Brooks, Arden led the female brigade in *Our Miss Brooks*, which first ran on CBS radio from 1948 to 1957 and was adapted for TV, partially concurrently, from 1952 to 1957. With Arden's ace-in-the-whole double takes and comic timing, this show even made it to the movie stage in 1956 with a big-screen adaptation of the same name.

Four years prior, in the holiday TV episode "Christmas Show," from December 27, 1952, Arden's Connie is eager to hand out Christmas presents but has limited funds. To help her muddle through the season, she goes to the local department store and exchanges a few of the gifts she's already received, oblivious to the fact that the gift-giving Mr. Osgood Conklin, her principal (played by Gale Gordon), and Mr. Philip Boynton, her secret crush (Robert Rockwell), had the same idea.

From 1952 to 1955, first on CBS, then NBC, Gale Storm starred with Charles Farrell in *My Little Margie* which, like *Our Miss Brooks*, began and was broadcast concurrently on radio and produced only one holiday episode. That segment, titled "Timmy's Christmas," aired December 21, 1952.

In the fall of 1956, Storm returned to TV with *The Gale Storm Show*, a.k.a. *Oh, Susanna*, which was broadcast until 1960, first on CBS and then ABC in its final season.

Sothern hit the airwaves as the star of *Private Secretary*, a.k.a. *Susie*, which screened on CBS from 1953 to 1957. She played Susan Camille "Susie" Mac-Namara, a dedicated secretary to her debonair talent agent boss Peter Sands (Don Porter, later Sally Field's TV father on ABC's single-season *Gidget*). From October 1958 to March 1961, Sothern headlined her second sitcom, *The Ann Sothern Show*, created by the legendary writing team of Bob Schiller (who died at age ninety-eight in 2017) and Bob Weiskopf (who died at age eighty-six in 2001). They penned benchmark episodes of such female-driven hits as *I Love Lucy* (when she stomped grapes in Italy), *Maude* (when Bea Arthur's fiercely independent liberal gets slapped), *All in the Family* (when Jean Stapleton's angelic Edith Bunker battles a rapist), and more.

To compensate in historical terms for Sothern's lack of Christmas charm, *That Girl*, Marlo Thomas's groundbreaking sitcom (ABC, 1966–1971), and *The Mary Tyler Moore Show* (CBS, 1970–1977) presented somewhat connective holiday-themed episodes.

On December 21, 1967, *That Girl* screened "'Twas the Night Before Christmas, You're Under Arrest." Here, Thomas's aspiring New York actress Ann Marie has a misbegotten run-in with the law when her boyfriend, *Newsview* magazine journalist Don Hollinger, played by Ted Bessell, purchases Broadway show tickets from a scalper on the street. Upon learning that residents are being robbed when away from home, Ann and Don remove Christmas gifts from their respective apartments, but they are then mistaken for criminals and end up at the local precinct.

Seven years later, on December 9, 1974, the *Moore* sitcom, officially titled, just *Mary Tyler Moore* (without the "The" and "Show"), presented "Not a Christmas Story." Here, Moore's fictional local news associate producer Mary Richards and her Midwest WJM-TV colleagues are on their last nerve amid a November Monday snowstorm passing through Minneapolis.

While the newsroom staff works on stories about the weather, TV cooking-show host Sue Ann Nivens (Betty White), who just completed taping her Christmas special, invites everyone to her set for one of her perfectly prepared holiday dinners. With each professing previous plans, Mary, Lou (Ed Asner), Ted (Ted Baxter), and Murray (Gavin MacLeod) decline the offer. By the time the newscast begins, a massive argument ensues, with fingers pointing over an editorial issue with Murray's script. Ultimately responsible for what's reported on the air, he threatens to quit. But due to the snowstorm, everyone is office-bound until the plows clear the streets, which won't happen until after midnight. Consequently, the staff reconsiders and accepts Sue Ann's dinner invitation, despite the lack of any true Christmas spirit in the air.

However, it's a previous *Mary Tyler Moore* Christmas episode that proves the most intriguing, as it serves as an interesting "crossover" event of sorts with one episode of *That Girl* while sharing a similar sense of isolation.

On December 22, 1966, *That Girl* showcased "Christmas and the Hard Luck Kid." On December 19, 1970, *Mary Tyler Moore* produced "Christmas and the Hard Luck Kid II."

The episodes were completely unrelated other than both were written by Jim Brooks, who cut his literary teeth on *That Girl* before he went on to partner with Allan Burns to create *Mary Tyler Moore*. What's more, it was the first time that two different networks aired two different shows that featured two different episodes with essentially the same title, in two different decades. The only real similarity between the two episodes is the sense of isolation that both Ann and Mary experience in their separate situations.

That Girl's "Hard Luck" story from 1966 begins with Ann working as a department store Santa's helper, with Donald close by. While guiding the line of young children to see Santa, Ann receives an unexpected Christmas gift from a woman, whose son Ann comforted three years before on a lonely Christmas Eve. In a flashback to when Ann was in her final term teaching at a boarding school, we meet the eight-year-old Tommy Phillips (played by Christopher Shea), who was one of her students. Tommy's parents are busy actors always away working on some movie. As a result, he is frequently alone, especially during the holidays. Ensuring that doesn't happen this Christmas, Ann invites Tommy to spend the holiday with her at home. But due to liability issues, that's not possible, so Ann remains at school with Tommy. In the process, she learns Tommy is Jewish and doesn't celebrate Christmas, but Hannukah. And they both walk away from the experience with a reverent and respectful understanding of different cultures.

When this episode initially aired, Christopher Shea was a regular cast member in the short-lived Western TV series *Shane* (starring a pre–*Kung Fu* David "Caine" Carradine, which was based on Allan Ladd's iconic 1953 big-screen film of the same name). However, Shea is best known as the voice of Linus in several *Peanuts* animated specials, including *It's the Great Pumpkin, Charlie Brown* (CBS, 1966) and *A Charlie Brown Christmas* (CBS, 1965). It's in the latter of which, Shea's Linus delivers the now-famous and poignant speech about the true meaning of Christmas.

In *Mary Tyler Moore's* "Hard Luck" story, Part II, from the show's first season in 1970, Mary Richards has been working at WJM-TV only for a short time. She finds herself alone in the office on Christmas Eve. It's never easy to work on any holiday, much less Christmas Eve, and being alone doesn't much help matters.

As journalist Brett White once observed on Decider.com: "The perfect Christmas sitcom episode has to be, well, *perfect*. It has to be funny, obviously. It has to have a heightened level of heart and it has to tug at *your* heart. And to really be great, it has to stir something within you and stay with you. *The Mary Tyler Moore Show*'s "Christmas and the Hard Luck Kid II"—named so as it was co-written by the legendary James L. Brooks, who also wrote the *That Girl* episode—crosses all of those must-haves off the list. It will make you giggle and cackle [Ed Asner's Lou realizing he gave Mary a blank check for Christmas]. Your heart will swell when you see how excited [Valerie Harper's] Rhoda is to give Mary a rotisserie (and one egg), and your heart will break when Mary has to scarf down a sandwich so she can make it back to the office in time to work the Christmas Eve night shift.

"The part that will stick with you, though, is the loneliest part—the stretch where Mary's alone in the newsroom with nothing but the TV to keep her company," White continued. "This quiet moment, it's the muddling through somehow that Judy Garland sang about. It's this very relatable resignation to the reality that the hard-luck kid is now a hard-luck adult—and there's nothing you can do about it. Christmases change as we change, and some years they look like freaking out because you're all alone in a huge building and you heard the elevator doors open. But . . . as with so many [weekly TV Christmas show] episodes . . . 'Christmas and the Hard Luck Kid II' believes in the power of Christmas—a holiday that is powered by people and not dependent on specific places or gifts above a certain price point. This episode is the reason for the season."

While Mary Tyler Moore had long credited *That Girl* for "paving the way for my show," in general, Marlo Thomas was unaware that *Moore*'s "Hard Luck" episode was a sequel of sorts to *That Girl*'s "Hard Luck," if in name and slight-isolation-plot only. Though Thomas remains proud of her *Girl*'s Christmas story ultimately being a Hannukah tale. "You can do stuff like that, even back then, when you have good writers," Thomas said. "We had an entire staff of great writers, including Danny Arnold," who, before working on *That Girl*, was one of the writers and producers for the first two years of *Bewitched*. Post–*That Girl*, Arnold would go on to create and write *Barney Miller* (ABC, 1975–1982). "He was just divine," Thomas said of Arnold, who died in 1995. "I adored him. I miss him terribly. He was so good and so diligent. I am a very hard-working person, but I would always see the light on in his office at nine o'clock at night when I was leaving the studio. He put his heart and soul into everything he did, including *Barney Miller.*"

In another crossover with the *Mary Tyler Moore* series, Ted Bessell was cast as Mary's boyfriend in a few episodes. "That was just the most bizarre thing," Thomas mused. "It was like having Desi Arnaz play your husband instead of Lucy's."

Bessell, however, took playing Mary's boyfriend after playing Ann's boyfriend all in stride. "He wasn't uncomfortable about it at all," said Thomas. "He thought it was fun. It was completely different. We had a tremendous relationship, on and off camera. When my father died [in 1991], Teddy drove me around the city and let me cry and cry. We were very dear friends until the day he died [in 1996]," which Thomas recalled as "awful."

"Losing him was awful," said Thomas, who to this day remains in touch with Bessell's brother, Frank. "Teddy's birthday is March 20. So, every March 20, Frank and I talk. [Bessell's daughter, Sarah, recently had a baby girl she named Mariah Teddy.]

Whenever Thomas talks about *That Girl*, it always sounds like a Christmas story itself. She fondly refers to the show as *That Couple*, because, as she said, "That's what it was," a show about two people and their relationship. However, as Thomas went on to explain, she never wanted the show to be called *That Woman* and objected to the network's suggestion that Ann and Don get married. "*That Girl* is about a girl trying to find herself," Thomas explained. "Between being a girl at her parents' house and being a woman in her own place following her own dreams. Ann could not get married or even become a successful actress. It was about that particular time in her life when those two things could not happen. A lot of people were passionate about us continuing the show. But I thought it was wrong to do so, and was important to remain true to the character."

Shortly before Bessell died, however, there were earlier discussions with Thomas about doing a *That Girl* feature film in which Ann and Don found each other later in life, after having other relationships. "We were very excited about it," Thomas recalled. "Teddy, especially so. We talked about storylines, where Ann would be a widow and Don would be divorced. And how they just ran into each other and ignited their relationship again. When Teddy died, I realized that we should have done the movie years before."

Off-screen, Thomas lamented, she and Bessell "loved each other. We will always love each other for all eternity. We were very connected from the moment he auditioned for the show.

"We interviewed many guys to play Don Hollinger," Thomas continued to recall, including Charles Grodin, who also became a good friend later in life . . . and Bill Bixby . . . and so many more. But we couldn't find the right fit, until, all of a sudden, we interviewed Teddy and that was it. There was complete chemistry. And we were both discovered by the same man, Peter Tewksbury."

Tewksbury was a writer/director who worked on several shows, including the unsold pilot titled *Two's Company*, which featured Thomas. "ABC saw that show and almost put it on, but then didn't," Thomas recalled. However, the network was still looking for a young actress to star in a series. "And that's how I got to do *That Girl*," Thomas noted. "Peter sent me a couple of scripts and I said, 'All these scripts, the girl is the wife of somebody or the secretary of somebody or the daughter of somebody. Have you ever thought about doing a show where the girl is the somebody?' And he said, 'Would anybody watch a show like that?'"

That's when Thomas handed Tewksbury a copy of *The Feminine Mystique*, the groundbreaking book by feminist author Betty Friedan. "Read this," Thomas told him, and he did so. "I was really lucky that I had wonderful people who believed in me," Thomas said, "like Peter and others at ABC. You have to have people [in your corner] who think that you are the one for them. They screen-tested five girls for *That Girl* . . . four blondes and me. And when I got there at Universal, I thought, 'I am not going to get this.' But I did get the part, right alongside Teddy." And it was all due to Tewksbury, who Thomas said, "found Teddy and me."

In the end, the TV audience found *That Girl*, right alongside *Mary Tyler Moore*, and both shows' "Hard Luck" and "true love" stories, amid other misadventures. More than any other previous female-led show, *That Girl* and *Mary Tyler Moore* empowered and emboldened female independence; igniting and celebrating, indirectly or not, the Women's Liberation Movement.

That's much to celebrate in any season.

CHAPTER 42
BLACK AND WHITE CHRISTMAS SITUATIONS

"Santa Claus is different colors to different people. He's really the spirit of Christmas giving."

—Julia Baker as played by Diahann Carroll on *Julia*

The African American Christmas TV sitcom experience dates back to *Amos 'n' Andy*. Like *I Love Lucy*, *Our Miss Brooks*, *Ozzie and Harriett*, and other sitcoms, *Amos 'n' Andy* began in radio. Distinguished by African American characters, the show was set in Chicago and then Harlem. The TV version also enjoyed a successful, if brief and aborted, run from 1951 to 1953 with Black actors, whereas the 1928–1960 radio series was created, written, and voiced by White performers. Freeman Godsen played Amos Jones, and Charles Correll was Andrew Hogg Brown, while both actors also portrayed other characters. In the TV adaptation, African American actors took over the majority of the roles, and Caucasian characters made sparse appearances.

The TV series produced one Christmas episode, "The Christmas Story," which aired December 25, 1952. The story was simple but effective: Usually strapped for cash, Andy at Christmas is desperate to buy his goddaughter, Arbadella (also spelled Arbadalla), a talking doll. So, he convinces a department store manager to hire him as Santa on Christmas Eve. Meanwhile, Amos teaches Arbadella the true meaning of the "Lord's Prayer."

Beulah is another early radio-turned-TV sitcom that featured African American characters, this time running on CBS Radio from 1945 to 1954 and on ABC-TV from 1950 to 1953. As the first sitcom to feature an African American female lead, *Beulah* was also ABC's first hit sitcom, and the first without a laugh track. Like *Amos 'n' Andy*, it was also considered controversial for its African Americans caricatures, and it aired just one Christmas episode, "They All Served," which premiered November 25, 1952. "Harry Builds a Den," which debuted two days before Christmas, on December 23, 1952, was the show's final episode.

Decades later, trailblazing producer Norman Lear, who died in 2023 at age 101, moved Archie Bunker's African American neighbors from the Bronx to Manhattan in *The Jeffersons*, a spin-off from *All in the Family*. In *The Jeffersons*, which ran on CBS from 1975 to 1985, Sherman Helmsley plays the bigoted George Jefferson, Isabel Sanford is his significantly more diplomatic and compassionate wife Louise (a.k.a. Weezy), Marla Gibbs plays their wise-cracking housekeeper Florence Johnson, and Mike Evans is their son, Lionel.

Evans left the series and then returned, but amid the transition Damon Evans (no relation) stepped into Lionel's shoes. Before discussing the show's Christmas segments, Damon shared his thoughts on *The Jeffersons'* widespread position in TV history. "I don't think there is any way possible to comment upon *The Jeffersons* without first mentioning the maverick and trailblazer Norman Lear. Norman pathed the way for so many new ideas that became open for discussion by using the medium of television as a means to educate as well as entertain American audiences.

"There had never been a successful weekly TV show, with perhaps the prior exception of *Julia* to a certain extent, that had introduced the American public to a Black middle-class scenario. And that differed because it was a single Black mother raising a child.

"On the other hand," Evans noted, "*The Jeffersons* created this iconic character, George Jefferson, who single-handedly created this mini-cleaning empire with stores on NYC's Upper East Side. His household included a wife, a college-educated son, and a maid. This was unheard of back in the day."

As Evans continued to explain, *The Jeffersons* episode "Once a Friend," from October 1, 1977, features his cousin, actress Veronica Redd. "She played the very first Black transexual character on network television. How prescient was that? Just like *All in the Family* broke ground, so did *The Jeffersons* with its humor and topical conversation about what was happening in the world, yet, what was rarely spoken publicly."

On a more frequent basis, *The Jeffersons* introduced TV's first interracial couple: Tom and Helen Willis, the affluent neighbors to George and Louise. Tom, played by Franklin Cover, was White; Helen, played by Roxie Roker, was Black (and in real life later gave birth to future rock star Lenny Kravitz).

On December 22, 1976, *The Jeffersons* aired "The Christmas Wedding" episode. Here, Damon Evans' Lionel marries Jenny, Tom and Helen's daughter, played by Berlinda Tolbert. The nuptials, set for Christmas Eve, are ultimately delayed by George and Tom's issues with religion and where to host the proceedings.

Ultimately, an intimate ceremony takes place at the Jeffersons' apartment, overseen by an affably wise minister, who slyly weds Lionel and Jenny right before everyone's eyes, with George and Tom oblivious to it all. [As a sidenote, the minister was portrayed by Robert Sampson. A few years before this episode aired, he played the Catholic priest brother to Meredith Baxter's Bridget, who married the Jewish Bernie (Baxter's future real-life husband David Birney) in the short-lived but also quite groundbreaking "mixed-marriage" sitcom *Bridget Loves Bernie* (CBS, 1972–1973).]

One year after "The Christmas Wedding" premiered, the Jefferson family and friends celebrated Lionel and Jenny's first wedding anniversary in a second holiday episode, "084 West 124th Street, Apt 5C," which debuted December 24, 1977.

However, the thrust of "084" rests with George, who, without Louise's knowledge, has been mailing monthly cash payments to a poverty-stricken family in Harlem, where he's also recently delivered a Christmas tree and gifts. Suspecting another woman may be involved, or worse, a love child, Louise follows George the next time he sneaks out of the house. She's led to an apartment building in Harlem where George was born and raised. In his youth, he vowed to one day help a family in that building, and the Christmas mystery is solved. [As another sidenote, *Amos 'n' Andy*'s actor Alvin Childress plays a wino in one scene.]

On December 21, 1980, *The Jeffersons* presented a third Christmas episode that also involves another vow from George while showcasing his generosity of spirit and the season. In "All I Want for Christmas," George plays Santa Claus at the local Help Center orphanage, where he promises to give the children anything they want for Christmas. But when ten-year-old Billy asks for a mother and father, George finds it a challenge to keep his word. (Sidenote: Billy is played by Meeno Peluce, the older brother to Soleil Moon Frye, later of NBC's *Punky Brewster* sitcom fame).

According to Damon Evans, "Christmases are always nostalgic in anyone's memory," and all of *The Jeffersons* Christmas episodes prove their worth and stand the test of time."

"The Christmas Wedding," however, is Damon's favorite. "I vividly recall the Christmas episode in which Jenny and I were married in a small ceremony in George and Weezy's high-rise apartment. I think it caught everyone by surprise, since so many folks—myself included—expected George to throw this huge and elaborate wedding. But the time and place couldn't have been more appropriate in the end."

Pilar Carrington, a commercial talent agent and person of color, offered her insight into *The Jeffersons*: "The show was about a loving Black family who became affluent enough to 'move on up,' in a non-stereotypical way, with style, and catchphrases we use to this day. Although it was a comedy, the series was grounded in real racial mores that displayed the culturalisms of Black family dynamics, their talent and charisma, which allowed all of America to experience the intimacy of their close-knit home and life."

A few years before *The Jeffersons* on CBS, *Julia* ran on NBC from 1968 to 1971. As another groundbreaking African American sitcom that was both ahead of the time it reflected, *Julia* stars Diahann Carroll as a nurse/single parent with a son, Corey, played by Marc Copage. And like *Amos 'n' Andy*, and *Beulah*, *Julia* coincidentally produced only one Christmas-geared episode.

On December 24, 1968, "I'm Dreaming of a Black Christmas" premiered with a story having Corey question whether Santa Claus is Black or White.

Unfortunately, also like *Amos 'n' Andy*, and *Beulah*, *Julia* had its detractors. In an interview with the Television Academy, Carroll said that more than a few African Americans were "incensed" by the series. "The suffering was much too acute for us to be so trivial, they felt, as to present a middle-class woman who is dealing with the business of being a nurse in this huge, very successful [aerospace industry]."

The lack of a positive Black male presence was also a concern, which was eventually rectified when Fred Williamson joined the show as Julia's boyfriend. Up until that point, there was no then-traditionally masculine or father image for children of any ethnic backgrounds to relate to. "That was a very loud criticism," recalled Carroll, who was confounded by but also empathetic to the protests.

"We were of the opinion that what we were doing was important," she said. "And we never, never, never varied from that point of view. Even though some of the criticism, of course, was valid, we were of a mind that [*Julia*] was a different show. We were allowed to have this show. We were allowed to put this point of view on the air. We were allowed to have a comedy about a Black middle-class family."

In the end, as Marc Copage also once told the Television Academy, "Diahann was getting all kinds of pressure," a result of those who claimed the show was "not Black enough."

However, for Damon Evans, *Julia* was relatable. "I was raised by a single mother," he revealed. "Therefore, I immediately identified with Marc and his mama Julia who was a nurse. Contrary to some folks in the Black community, I never found their portrayals false. My mother was a secretary who, like Julia, was always dressed to the 'T.' I understood her concern for her son as well as the responsibility she felt in representing her small family in a dignified way to others."

As Evans went on to relay, "*Julia* may not have been your average and most visible representation of a single Black parent when her show first aired. But to say it was false is downright ignorant and ridiculous.

"Unfortunately," Evans added, "she shouldered the same blame for misrepresentation as *The Cosby Show*'s Huxtable family. And as far as I'm concerned that makes no sense whatsoever."

With star Bill Cosby's disturbing off-screen behavior notwithstanding, *The Cosby Show* unto itself was another benchmark Black sitcom. As Dr. Cliff Huxtable, Cosby played a physician married to an attorney (played by Phylicia Rashad), who resides in an affluent neighborhood with their children (played by Malcom-Jamal Warner, Tempest Bledsoe, Lisa Bonet, Keisha Knight Pulliam, Sabrina Le Beauf, and Raven-Symoné).

However, as Erin Snyder of MainstreamingChristmas.com explained: "Surprisingly, *The Cosby Show* included only a handful of Christmas episodes, none of which fit the traditional holiday archetypes. There were three we located set around Christmas, though only one was particularly focused on this fact."

Those include: "Father's Day" from season one (December 12, 1984), when Cliff finds himself the center of attention of Christmas; "Getting to Know You" from season six (December 14, 1989), which like *Julia* did decades before, debates Santa's Black or White heritage; "Clair's Place," from the show's final season (December 19, 1991), which somewhat reflects its first Christmas episode, only this time celebrating mothers at Christmas (without explicitly mentioning Mother's Day).

In discussing the dichotomy of *Julia* and *The Cosby Show*, in general, and their Christmas adventures in particular, Pilar Carrington once more offered her astute voice:

As a talent agent of color, I think it's so important to discuss the history of our business and the opportunities to tell our stories through the medium; as a student of the industry and creator of the future of the business.

Diahann Carroll was one of the first Black actresses to play the lead on her show in the 1960s, in the midst of racial turmoil, the Kennedy presidency, and Black Power movement. Her Christmas special attempted to address this racial conflict and create a notion of acceptance. Her son asking whether Santa was White or Black was tempered by her assurance that it didn't matter because he appears to people as a reflection of who they are, and in fact, Santa is the spirit of Christmas.

Bill Cosby's career as a stand-up comedian, with shows that zigzagged America, to comedy albums, made him popular in the 1970s . . . especially for saying things that were not "ready for prime time." He pivoted in the 1980s to his sitcom *The Cosby Show* with a more family-friendly theme. Standing on the shoulders of *The Jeffersons*, *The Cosby Show* presented an affluent, Black family in New York. With plenty of humor and nuance that spoke to everyone across the board, *The Cosby Show*'s Christmas episodes not only brought families together under a universal understanding of the spirit of the holidays but elevated the genre of what a sitcom could be, with dexterous writing, characters not caricatures of the Black experience.

Other Christmas TV sitcom examples of that Black experience include episodes of *Good Times*, *Family Matters*, *The Fresh Prince of Bel-Air*, and *Everybody Hates Chris*.

When it comes to *Good Times*, another Norman Lear production, as getTV.com explains on its website, in the best episodes of the show, the Evans family often faces a challenge. They may not solve every issue, but they're always in it together. This is why the series was so groundbreaking: it was the first sitcom on American television to depict a working-class Black family as a stable, supportive unit.

James, as played by John Amos, was the no-nonsense father. Florida, portrayed by Esther Rolle, was the matriarch who became like a second mother to the show's millions of viewers. Jimmie Walker's J.J. was a mentor to his younger siblings Thelma, played by BernNadette Stanis, and Michael, played by Ralph Carter. Neighbor Willona, as played by Ja'Net DuBois, was a surrogate parent when circumstances took James and Florida away from their kids.

"*Good Times* represents so many different dynamics: a father that died, a mother who may not be there at certain points, an aunt who looks after the kid, a kid who gets married and the spouse moves in," Stanis told getTV. "It was about family, faith, and struggle."

Nowhere is the importance of family on greater display than in the show's holiday episodes. With topics like teen alcoholism and shoplifting, these episodes are *Good Times* at its socially conscious best. "*Good Times* teaches us so much," Stanis explained on the site. "I think that's why it's still popular."

"Penny's Christmas" (December 21, 1977): Season five was a transitional year for *Good Times*. Amos and Rolle had left and DuBois was elevated to adult lead, but she needed a storyline. Enter Penny (Janet Jackson), an abused child Willona hopes to adopt. In this episode, Penny loses her purse to a pickpocket and resorts to shoplifting to get her new mom a present. Look for hilarious Alice Ghostley (*Bewitched*, *Designing Women*) as Penny's social worker and comedian Dap Sugar Willie in one of his most memorable appearances as Lootin' Lenny. "Have a cool Yule and a mellow new year!"

"Sometimes There's No Bottom in the Bottle" (December 10, 1974; two parts): Uncle Oscar (Albert Reed), Aunt Millie (Marguerite Ray), and Cousin Naomi (Bonnie Banfield) visit at Christmastime in this season 2 episode from 1974. Thelma discovers her teen cousin is an alcoholic, giving Stanis an opportunity to do some of her strongest scenes in the series. This is *Good Times* as a true ensemble, with each cast member getting their moment in the spotlight. Reed would return a year later as shady alderman Fred C. Davis—and Uncle Oscar was never mentioned again!

"The Traveling Christmas" (December 20, 1978): Thelma's new husband, Keith (Ben Powers), has to work on Christmas Eve, so the Evans family brings the party to him! J.J. is the emcee, Michael sings, Bookman (Johnny Brown) dances, and Keith does musical impressions. But the highpoint of the evening is an appearance by "The Pointless Sisters"—Florida, Willona, Thelma, and Penny—singing "Steam Heat." Don't ask when they choreographed and rehearsed this polished production, just enjoy the opportunity to see the talented *Good Times* cast show off their side hustles!

"A Place to Die" (December 30, 1975): James is out of town for work at New Year's and there's a new man in the Evans household: Hubert Johnson (Arnold Johnson), a neighborhood senior citizen Michael has befriended. Hubert believes his time is up, and he wants to spend his final days in the company of a loving family. Will he get his wish? Ja'Net DuBois shines in this season three episode, leading a "memorial service" for the family's still-living guest. Viewers will recognize Johnson as Fred's friend Hutch on *Sanford and Son*!

Two decades later, two Christmas episodes of *Family Matters* contributed to the Black family Christmas experience:

"Have Yourself a Merry Winslow Christmas" (December 21, 1990): The holidays are a time for togetherness—and oh wow, do the Winslows learn that in this episode. When they find out that their epically annoying neighbor Steve Urkel has been left all alone on Christmas, the family reluctantly makes space for the nerd around their tree.

"Christmas Is Where the Heart Is" (December 10, 1993): Brett White on Decider.com said: "What's worse than getting stuck on a subway train on Christmas Eve? Getting stuck in that dirty, confined space on Christmas Eve with Steve Urkel! But y'know what? If anyone can turn a bad situation into a nice one, it's this perpetually (often cluelessly) optimistic nerd next door. Urkel knows that all you need for a rad Christmas experience is a little faith and positivity. And it turns out that Christmas cheer can overcome the most grumpy people of all: commuters. 'Christmas Is Where the Heart Is' takes the stranded-at-Christmas trope that's led to a few classics and does it perfectly. Jaleel White's performance in this one is so good that it might convince you to spend an entire Christmas Eve on public transportation."

In further retrospect, Pilar Carrington assessed across the board: "*Family Matters* was another 1990s hit, depicting a middle-class Black family neither short on laughs nor love. Although some critics panned the Steve Urkel character as a shameless rehashing of the 'shuck and jive' era of seminal Black caricature, the show raked huge ratings for ABC's TGIF block every week for years. *Family Matters* showed a multigenerational gathering of all its characters, much like the finale of a Broadway show. Tying the episode, not too ironically, up with a bow."

Around the same time as "Christmas Is Where the Heart Is," *The Fresh Prince of Bel-Air* presented a Christmas episode, titled, "Christmas Show." Here, we meet Aunt Viv's sisters, including a fantastically feisty Jenifer Lewis. As Brett White, of Decider.com, once observed: "This episode is what Christmas in a big family feels like."

Pilar Carrington offered a bigger picture of *Prince* and another of its Christmas episodes:

After a spate of much more diverse storytelling, *The Fresh Prince of Bel-Air* is the ultimate comedy of turning a paradigm on its head. Will Smith's character goes from an urban environment in Philadelphia to an urbane environment in Bel Air. A comedic version you might say of *A Tale of Two Cities*. This was best exemplified by the episode "Brother You Got a Problem with My Lights?" Will Smith's character wants to decorate in a way that upsets the neighborhood, and draws criticism from their other affluent neighbors, including world champion boxer Evander Holyfield. What it shows is the juxtaposition of values celebrated in two different segments of the Black community—the middle-class clashes with the upwardly mobile class and their efforts to fit in with the surrounding White majority of those economic climes. Ultimately revealing ongoing undertones that are felt to the present.

248

Decades after *The Fresh Prince of Bel-Air*, *Everybody Hates Chris* ran on UPN/CW from 2005 to 2009. Based on the young life of comedian Chris Rock, the show was set in the early to mid-1980s. According to Carrington: "*Everybody Hates Chris* was an irreverent take of the childhood of comedian Chris Rock. Fashioned after the late 1990s *Malcom in the Middle*, the 2000s hit countered with its first-person, breaking-the-fourth-wall format, with growing up in the inner city being the punch line. Hard truths about family, not having a lot, and the acerbic, yet ingenious cruelty only kids can cook up, hit home with millions of Americans."

On December 15, 2004, the episode "Everybody Hates Christmas" made its premiere with the following story:

It's Christmas, and the water heater breaks in the Rock household. That makes it all the more difficult for Chris's financially strapped parents Rochelle (Tichina Arnold) and Julius (Terry Crews) to donate to a local charity, give their son a gift, and enjoy the holiday with the entire family. That includes Chris's younger brother, Drew (Tequan Richman), who seeks to dispel the Santa myth for younger sister Tonya (Imani Hakim). In the interim, Chris's teacher, Ms. Morello (Jacqueline Mazarella), makes several attempts to deliver the school's food drive to his home. By the end of the day, the Rocks see Ms. Morello interviewed on TV with a basket of food standing outside a front door that looks awfully similar to their house. Upon hearing a knock at the door, Rochelle rises to open it, and there indeed stands Ms. Morello, alongside a news reporter (Julie Lancaster). Ms. Morello exclaims, "Merry Christmas!" and hands over the basket of food, as Rochelle screams, "Chris!"—all of which is captured on live TV.

For Carrington, this episode "exemplified the trifecta" of what *Everybody Hates Chris* is all about:

Chris's family attempts to help the community with a charitable donation in the midst of not being able to afford their utilities. Ironically, the leader of the charity brings the family a holiday basket that gets broadcast on local news, much to Chris's chagrin. The brilliance in the arc of this show offers up a juxtaposition of the celebrity we know, with the foundation of his humor, which came from hardship. An unromantic, often flippant, and deeply heartfelt reflection on the road to the American dream, forged in the fire of childhood angst and self-discovery. Then and now, holidays are a poignant opportunity to face ourselves and our community and who we wish to be.

There are several other examples of the African American classic TV Christmas experience, but one in particular speaks to people of all colors and cultures more than any other.

On Saturday, December 13, 1969, the *CBS Children's Hour* featured an episode called "J.T.," which ran several times on the network for well over a decade. It's the story of a sensitive young boy (played by Kevin Hooks) in a Harlem ghetto who befriends a sickly, one-eyed cat. Written by Jane Wagner and directed by Robert M. Young (co-writer and photographer of the 1964 landmark independent feature *Nothing but a Man*), "J.T." ignited more than a few tears when in a climactic moment, the cat is struck by a car.

In 1969, *Los Angeles Times* critic Cecil Smith called "J.T." "an exquisite film, a shattering experience, written with great compassion and understanding." *Time* magazine described it as the "kind of drama almost never found on commercial television."

Universal acclaim for "J.T." prompted CBS to run full-page ads in major newspapers featuring a large image of newcomer Kevin Hooks with select quotes from more than a dozen positive reviews from publications ranging from Cleveland's *The Plain Dealer* to *Newsweek*. After initially announcing that they would rerun the special in six to eight weeks, the overwhelming accolades inspired CBS to screen "J.T." in prime time a mere nine days later, preempting the super successful *Gunsmoke* Western and calling upon Doris Day (star of the network's *The Doris Day Show*) to film a special introduction for the encore broadcast.

The *Washington Post* documented that "J.T.'s" prime-time rerun "outscored all its competition in a national audience survey by Arbitron [ratings company]," also noting that the special "even outdrew [Rowan & Martin's] *Laugh-In*, usually the dominant program of the week."

"J.T." would go on to be bestowed with a prestigious Peabody Award for 1969, accompanied by the following official citation:

"A program created by CBS Television especially for young people that combined highly creative and imaginative writing and superb production. A landmark in children's television programming filled with extraordinary insight and compassion. In recognition for writing and children's programming, a Peabody Award."

As Mark Quigley, manager of the U.C.L.A. Archive Research and Study Center, more recently observed on Cinema.UCLA.edu: "'J.T.' remains a unique artistic achievement in television, evergreen in its capacity to genuinely move.

"Most people have a specific movie or television program that they fondly recall from their youth as having left a particularly lasting impression," he wrote. "For a generation of television viewers in the late-1960s through the early-1980s, that program may very well be the original teledrama 'J.T.' . . . [The episode] dared to challenge preconceived notions of what children's television can be, taking viewers of all ages on a heart-wrenching journey illuminating loneliness and love via an African American youth and his bond with a sickly stray cat."

Following "J.T.," Kevin Hooks established a distinguished career as an actor in feature films, including *Sounder* (Oscar nominee for Best Picture, 1973), and on TV in a leading role on another benchmark program, *The White Shadow* (CBS, 1978–1981). Hooks has also enjoyed a prolific career as a director for such feature films as *Passenger 57*, for TV shows such as *Agents of S.H.I.E.L.D.*, and for the heralded BET miniseries *Madiba* (2017), about the life of Nelson Mandela. He's also served as an executive producer for TV's *Prison Break*, while in 2000, he received an Emmy Award as a producer of the TV-movie *The Color of Friendship*, which he also helmed.

As to why "J.T." and all African American Christmas-geared programming is significant in the history of television, Damon Evans decided: "I have always felt that television as a medium for one of the most persuasive means of properly educating the public in ways such as how to grow into a more positive and respectable citizen and human being. Too often we get caught up evaluating only the entertainment factors of what these shows have to offer. But there is so much more given to our television watchers in the twenty minutes of a half-hour show's content (sans commercials)."

Concluded Pilar Carrington: "Each of these shows created a gateway to incorporating the Black experience as a part of the American cultural narrative. With artistry, and audacity, leaving reverberations to inspire all of us to great storytelling."

CHAPTER 43
1 *ODD COUPLE*, 3 *DORIS DAYS* AND *SONS*, AND A *PARTRIDGE FAMILY* CHRISTMAS TREE

"From all of us here to all of you there we wish you happiness, peace, and much, much love. Good night. Merry Christmas."

> —Doris Day, to the TV audience at home, breaking the fourth wall at the close of "A Two-Family Christmas" episode of *The Doris Day Show*

In the history of television and Christmas television, sitcom families are not necessarily comprised of biological members. Most host more traditional members, but not always with both parents involved. *The Doris Day Show* (CBS, 1968–1973) and *The Partridge Family* (ABC, 1970–1974) each featured widowed musical matriarchs. Although it didn't happen every week, Doris Day as Doris Martin sang in what became two of three of *The Doris Day Show*'s Christmas episodes, while the Oscar-winning Shirley Jones as Shirley Partridge performed regularly on *The Partridge Family*, specifically in what became that show's singular holiday adventure.

In the case of *My Three Sons*, the non-singing widower Steve Douglas, played by Fred MacMurray, was busy raising three sons (Tim Considine, Don Grady, and Stanley Livingston, later joined by younger brother Barry Livingston, after Considine left). Steve would eventually marry again (to Beverly Garland's schoolteacher, Barbara Harper, a single parent to daughter Dodie, played by Dawn Lyn). However, before that happened, Steve's only help in raising three sons rested with William Frawley's Uncle Bud and then Uncle Charley played by William Demerest.

My Three Sons never produced a Christmas episode, nor did any of executive producer Don Fedderson's shows (*Family Affair, To Rome with*

Love, with the exception of *The Smith Family*). However, on November 25, 1977, the *Sons* stars regrouped a few years after the show was canceled for a relatively bizarre combined reunion/Thanksgiving special with the stars of *The Partridge Family*.

Other unique, non-traditional shows with their own family dynamic included *The Odd Couple* (ABC, 1970–1974), which was based on Neil Simon's Broadway hit and subsequent 1968 feature film of the same name. In Simon's original concept, the fastidious and neurotic Felix Unger and the much-less-sophisticated Oscar Madison were envisioned as a gay couple. But that scenario was not going to fly by the time those two characters reached ABC-TV, even in the liberating 1970s.

Instead, Tony Randall's Felix and Jack Klugman's Oscar played out what the show's opening narration proposed: "Can two divorced men share an apartment without driving each other crazy?" That situation's Christmas comedy was enhanced with the *Odd* first-season episode "Scrooge Gets an Oscar," which premiered December 17, 1970. Unlike the show's remaining three seasons, this year was filmed like a movie, without a studio audience (though with a fake laugh track). Like many TV shows of every genre, however, before and after it (*Bewitched*, *The Six Million Dollar Man*), *The Odd Couple* produced its own take on the Charles Dickens classic. In the *Odd* adaptation, Oscar is the humbug complainer, haunted in a dream by Felix and their poker pals.

The episode was penned by Ron Friedman, author of *I Killed Optimus Prime: Confessions of a Hollywood Screenwriter*, who scripted more than seven hundred hours of prime-time TV and even more Saturday-morning animated shows. Friedman fondly recalled his work on *The Odd Couple* as one of his treasured accomplishments, particularly "Scrooge Gets an Oscar."

In 1970, Friedman was friends with *Odd Couple* writer/producer Jerry Davis, who phoned him to write a Christmas episode after an already-submitted segment failed to thrill the cast. After watching *The Odd Couple* for the first time, Friedman got back with Davis and said, "I've got it. It's *A Christmas Carol* with Oscar as Scrooge for Felix's theater company."

To which Davis responded, "I love that."

Subsequently, Friedman went to work and completed and submitted the script by the following day. Davis phoned him and said, "Jack and Tony *love* it, and I love it, too."

After that, *The Odd Couple* team contacted Friedman whenever, as he explained, "They were in a bind and needed something right away. They called me 'Flash Friedman.'"

As Friedman went on to explain: "This was in the days before every TV show did 'A Christmas Carol' episode. . . . The story for 'Scrooge Gets an Oscar' took shape pretty quickly for me. Charles Dickens was my role model, and *A Christmas Carol* is perfect, so I just studied that.

"Maybe my favorite moment in the episode is often cut out for syndication," Friedman continued. "Oscar is playing cards and then the doorbell rings. He answers the door, and it's a singing telegram from his ex-wife. I wrote it over fifty years ago, but I still remember how that little song went: *Seasons greetings Oscar Boy, my alimony's due. If you don't pay up right away, I'll get the cops on you. And you'll spend Christmas in the clink with other bums like you!*"

"I was very happy with that," Friedman said. "I even included it on my Christmas album, *Christmas Songs for Jewish People.*"

Friedman was on set for part of the filming of "Scrooge Gets an Oscar," and as he further relayed: "Tony and Jack's favorite part came during the *Christmas Carol* dream sequence. Felix, the ghost, is trying to show Oscar that he really is magical, so he pulls out a deck of cards and starts to do a magic trick—they loved that. It was also really fun to put Jack Klugman into shorts and curls in the scene where they flashback to Oscar as a schoolboy."

After "Scrooge Gets an Oscar" aired, both Klugman and Randall phoned Friedman to say that he would be writing more episodes.

The Odd Couple was a family affair. The show was executive-produced by Garry Marshall, who would go on to create super sitcoms *Happy Days, Laverne & Shirley, Mork & Mindy,* and more. From 2015 to 2017, Marshall rebooted *The Odd Couple* with Matthew Perry as Oscar and Thomas Lennon as Felix, and it showcased its own Christmas episode ("Felix Navidad," December 12, 2016). On the *Couple* reboot, Marshall's sister, Penny Marshall, reunited with her former *Laverne & Shirley* co-star Cindy Williams for a guest appearance, decades after Penny co-starred in the original TV adaption (as Oscar's secretary, Myrna).

In that very real sense, Christmas was about family, which was thoroughly presented on *The Doris Day Show* with its trio of Christmas episodes: "A Two-Family Christmas" (December 22, 1969), "It's Christmas Time in the City" (December 21, 1970), and "Whodunnit, Doris?" (December 13, 1971). We look to talent agent Pierre Patrick, author of *The Doris Day Companion,* for a full exploration of TV's holi-*Day* escapades:

The Doris Day Show's three very different Christmas episodes, the first of which, "A Two-Family Christmas," premiered in the second season.

The first year working as a secretary in the office of *Today's World* magazine, Doris's boss, Mr. Nicholson, played by McLean Stevenson, asks her to make sure that no one on the staff abuses the festivities during the office Christmas party. Doris not only manages to keep the party under control, but eventually inspires Mr. Nicholson, Mr. Harvey, and her friend and co-worker Myrna (Rose-Marie) to spend an old-fashioned Christmas in the country with her father, Buck (played by Denver Pyle), and two children (Philip Brown and Todd Starke). By the episode's end, she sings "Holy Night" and breaks character and the fourth wall and wishes the TV audience a Merry Christmas.

The Doris Day Show's second Christmas episode, "It's Christmastime in the City," does its own version of *A Christmas Carol*. By this time, Billy De Wolfe, Professor Hinkle from *Frosty the Snowman*, and Day's good friend in real life, has joined the series as her cranky neighbor Mr. Jarvis. Come Christmas, his Scrooge-like personality is in high gear with complaints about Doris's Christmas party (which includes Mr. Nicholson, Mr. Harvey, Myrna, and neighbors Kay Ballard, Bernie Kopell, and that blond). Fortunately, Mr. Jarvis eventually finds his humanity and joins the party ultimately due to hearing Doris and her guests sing "Silver Bells" and "Silent Night."

The third and final *Doris Day Show* Christmas episode is "Whodunnit, Doris?" and features a guest spot by Charles Nelson Riley. By this time, the show's format has changed. Doris is now working as a reporter for *Today's World* and living in San Francisco, without her father and children. In a somewhat oddly premised episode, Doris attempts to solve a murder that was apparently committed by Santa Claus, save the reputation of Santa for Christmas. One very interesting note about this episode is that Kennedy William Gordy Motown's Berry Gordy's son made his first television appearance and became very famous later on as Rockwell with his No. 1 single with Michael Jackson, "It Always Feels Like Somebody's Watching Me."

In each holiday episode Doris broke the fourth wall to wish her audience a happy holiday that also included peace; we still need those good wishes.

Patrick concluded: "Doris Day in 2007 would explore Christmas one more time with a recording of 'Here Comes Santa Claus' sample with Ludacris for the album *Ludachrismas . . . The Soundtrack of Fred Claus*."

From Doris Day we continue with the screen adventures of another beloved, multitalented female performer: Shirley Jones, who starred as the widowed mother Shirley Partridge on *The Partridge Family*, a musical comedy of sorts that made a star of her real-life stepson David Cassidy as Keith. Other members of the singing TV children include Susan Dey (Laurie), Danny Bonaduce (Danny), Suzanne Crough (Tracy), Jeremy Gelbwaks, and Brian Forster, who shared the role of the youngest son, Chris. Dave Madden was in the mix as the flustered talent manager Rueben Kincaid.

A musical family companion series to *The Brady Bunch* on what in many ways was ABC's first TGIF lineup before the network even coined that phrase, *The Partridge Family* presented one Christmas episode. "Don't Bring Your Guns to Town, Santa" aired December 17, 1971, in the show's second season.

Entertainment historian Johnny Ray Miller, author of *When We're Singing: The Partridge Family and Their Music*, offered these exclusive thoughts on the show's holiday outing:

"Don't Bring Your Guns to Town, Santa" is one of the best episodes of the entire series, in the opinion of nearly everyone involved, including the cast and producers. Executive producer Bob Claver was particularly proud that they landed Dean Jagger as the featured guest star. Jagger was most famous for his role in 1954's *White Christmas* as General Waverly, and he had been a friend of Shirley Jones, having worked with her later in *Elmer Gantry*, the only movie for which Shirley Jones won an Oscar, in 1960. It was Jones's friendship with Jagger that helped secure him for this episode.

Jones loved Christmas. Coincidentally, she had just made *Silent Night, Lonely Night*, a bittersweet made-for-TV movie only a year before *The Partridge Family* debuted, and she was given an Emmy nomination for her role. It has remained one of her favorite films of her career, and this episode of *The Partridge Family* was her favorite episode of the series.

CHAPTER 44

CHRISTMAS ON *BUNKER HILL* WITH *M*A*S*H* AND DR. HARTLEY

"Gloria, I love your stuffing."

— Rob Reiner's Mike Stivic, to Sally Struthers' Gloria Stivic,
in *All in the Family*'s "Christmas Day at the Bunkers"

Television didn't get much better than Saturday nights on CBS in the 1970s. While the Christmas episodes of *The Mary Tyler Moore Show* and *The Carol Burnett Show*, both staples for that network, period, and day, are explored elsewhere in this book, the holiday segments for the three remaining benchmark shows will now be explored, those being *All in the Family*, *M*A*S*H*, and *The Bob Newhart Show*, all of which presented several Christmas episodes each.

First on the block: *All in the Family* (CBS, 1971–1979), which later transitioned into *Archie Bunker's Place* (CBS, 1979–1983). The original show starred Carroll O'Connor as the bigoted and very conservative Archie Bunker, Jean Stapleton as somewhat dimwitted but angelic wife Edith, Sally Struthers as their feisty daughter Gloria, and Rob Reiner as super-liberal Mike "Meathead" Stivic.

The Christmas list of *Family* episodes is extensive, beginning with "Christmas Day at the Bunkers," which premiered on December 18, 1971, the show's first season.

Here, the bigoted Archie Bunker (Carroll O'Connor) is a cranky Scrooge and, like only he could, derides African American neighbor Henry Jefferson (Mel Stewart) for dressing up as Santa Claus. As a result, this leads to a debate as to whether or not St. Nicholas is Black or White; a similar premise of which was explored on the *Julia* sitcom a few years before.

In "Edith's Christmas Story," from December 22, 1973, Jean Stapelton shines as Edith faces the possibility of breast cancer.

In "New Year's Wedding," airing January 5, 1976, Gloria and Mike argue about who has the upper hand in decision making. As a sidenote, this episode features guest star Billy Crystal, who Rob Reiner later directs in *When Harry Met Sally* (which concludes with a New Year's Eve sequence).

"The Draft Dodger" episode, which aired December 25, 1976, is one of the most compelling and memorable of the show's Christmas episodes. Here, Mike's high school pal, a draft dodger, butts heads with Archie, whose friend Pinky lost a son in Vietnam.

In "Edith's Crisis of Faith, Parts 1 & 2," which aired December 18 and 25, 1977, female impersonator Beverly LaSalle pays a second visit to the Bunkers and invites Edith, who's losing her faith in Christmas, and Archie to his new burlesque show at Carnegie Hall.

For "Bogus Bills," which screened on December 3, 1978, counterfeit money causes trouble with the cash register at Archie's bar.

In "The Bunkers Go West," another Christmas-geared segment that aired the following week, on December 10, 1978, Archie, Edith, and their niece Stephanie Mills (Danielle Brisebois) plan to spend Christmas with the Stivics in California. But Mike hurt his back, which prompts Edith to switch plans for her and Archie to visit the West Coast, which they do in "California, Here We Are, Parts 1 & 2" (originally starting on December 17, 1978, the final formal *All in the Family* Christmas episode).

Two years later, *Archie Bunker's Place* showcased its first Christmas segment, "The Incident," which aired on December 21, 1980. Here, a by-now-widowed and somewhat mellowed Archie and his new African American housekeeper Ellen Canby (Barbara Meek) visit the supermarket, where she is verbally assaulted. But Archie soon punches the man who assaults her, an action that shocks one of his lodge pals who just so happens to be at the supermarket.

In "Custody, Part 1," from January 4, 1981, Archie is still struggling with Edith's demise and eventually allows Stephanie to visit her rich grandmother (played by Celeste Holm). A legal battle for Stephanie's guardianship ensues, and it continues in "Custody, Part 2," which screened on January 11, 1981. In the end, the judge names Archie as Stephanie's guardian.

One year later, the show's final Christmas episode airs. In "Father Christmas," on December 19, 1982, Archie surprises his niece Billie Bunker (Denise Miller) by inviting her father, Fred (Richard McKenzie), over for the holidays.

For a time, before it became a Monday-night sensation, *M*A*S*H* (1972–1983) aired following *All in the Family* on Saturday nights. Throughout its eleven-year Emmy-winning run, the show featured several Christmas episodes.

"Dear Dad," which aired November 10, 1973, is composed of vignettes, based on Alan Alda's role of Hawkeye, who shares his war-torn Christmas stories in a letter to his father.

"Dear Sis," from December 18, 1978, presented another "letter" format, this time written by Father Mulcahy (William Christopher), who's questioning his faith.

Two years after "Dear Sis," on December 15, 1980, "Death Takes a Holiday" presented a double dose of similarly themed tales: one about a wounded soldier; the other, concerning orphans.

That same year, 1980, "A War for All Seasons" airs the following week, with a New Year's theme.

On December 28, 1981, "'Twas the Day After Christmas" aired with a story about the 4077th *M*A*S*H* unit celebrating Christmas with British officers, who discuss Boxing Day.

The Bob Newhart Show (1972–1978) added its own lengthy list of Christmas gifted episodes for each of its seasons, beginning with "His Busiest Season," which debuted on December 23, 1972. Here, Newhart's psychologist TV alter ego Dr. Bob Hartley invites his patients to a Christmas party at his apartment with his adoring wife, Emily (Suzanne Pleshette).

In "I'm Dreaming of a Slight Christmas," from December 22, 1973, Bob is stuck in his office on Christmas Eve.

For "Home Is Where the Hurt Is," screening on December 21, 1974, Bob and Emily are stuck at Christmas with a despondent Carol, his receptionist (played by Marcia Wallace).

The following year, "Bob Has to Have His Tonsils Out, So He Spends Christmas Eve in the Hospital" airs on December 20.

On December 25, 1976, Bob seeks to reunite his separated parents at Christmas in "Making Up Is the Thing to Do."

On December 24, 1977, Bob once more deals with his disgruntled patients at Christmas in "'Twas the Pie Before Christmas."

CHAPTER 45
HAPPY CHRISTMAS *DAYS* WITH
LAVERNE & SHIRLEY

"A Christmas tree's gotta have lights. Without lights, it's like a pizza without mozzarella."

— Henry Winkler's Fonzie, in *Happy Days*'
"Guess Who's Coming to Christmas"

appy Days began as an unsold fifteen-minute pilot episode of *Love, American Style*. Then two little 1950s/1960s-focused films became sleeper hits, one sleepier than the other: *American Graffiti*, directed by a pre–*Star Wars* George Lucas, was released in 1973, and *The Lords of Flatbush*, starring a pre-*Rocky* Sylvester Stallone, followed in 1974. Each film also featured a *Happy Days* cast member, while one starred a future *Laverne & Shirley* star. In addition to making household names out of Harrison Ford, Suzanne Sommers, and Mackenzie Philips, *Graffiti* also showcased Ron Howard, a.k.a. Richie Cunningham on *Happy Days*, and Cindy Williams, a.k.a. Shirley Feeney from *Laverne & Shirley*. Besides Stallone, Flatbush featured the future Fonzie—*Days'* Henry Winkler, looking very much like his alternate *Happy* character, clad in a leather jacket and with ducktail-greased hair.

Once ABC-TV took notice of the twin success of *Graffiti* and *Flatbush*, they pulled the failed pilot from the vaults and rebooted it as a weekly series.

Initially, *Happy Days* was a sweet, half-hour sitcom that was filmed like a movie. In the middle of its second season, however, director Jerry Paris (*The Dick Van Dyke Show*) suggested shooting the series before a live audience. In the process, the Fonzie character unseated Howard's Richie role, and *Happy Days* became and remained a massive hit for eleven years.

With Tom Bosley and Marion Ross as Howard's TV parents, Howard and Marion Cunningham; Erin Moran as his sister Joanie, and Anson Williams and Donny Most as his best friends Potsie and Ralph, the family sitcom dynamic of the 1950s was reborn in the 1970s. Along with that arrived several Christmas episodes, the first of which remains its best.

"Guess Who's Coming to Christmas" premiered as the eleventh episode of the show's second season. Here, Richie and the gang opt to spend Christmas with their families, that is, until Richie learns that Fonzie will be celebrating the holiday by himself. At that point, he invites the leather-clad hood with a heart to the Cunningham abode, initially much to the unrest of Howard, who wants to have an old-fashioned Christmas . . . and that includes no gang members. But as journalist Brett White decades later documented on Decider.com:

"We see a softer, vulnerable side of The Fonz as it becomes clearer to Richie that his tough guy hero is bluffing about catching a bus home for the holidays. Fonzie has nowhere to go, and Mr. Cunningham is determined to have a strict, family-only Christmas celebration. This truly touching tale highlights a great truth about the holiday: everyone is family when you welcome them into your home at Christmas."

The second *Happy* Christmas episode is titled "Richie Branches Out," which aired on December 7, 1976. Here, Richie falls for a pinup girl from a soda pop poster. So, the gang bands together to film a commercial as a way for Richie to make his move with the girl.

The *Days* third Christmas adventure is "Christmas Time," which aired on December 19, 1978. Here, a cold, snowy Wisconsin Christmas finds Howard Cunningham trying to convince his family to put up a newfangled, artificial tree, and a mysterious sailor delivers a gift from Fonzie's father, forcing The Fonz to deal with his long-suppressed feelings of abandonment. This time, Fonzie receives a gift from his estranged father on Christmas but refuses to accept or open it. Conversely, Richie and his girlfriend, Lori Beth (Lynda Goodfriend), are having issues with the presents they exchanged, while Joanie is a little rattled with her father, who this year decided to purchase an artificial Christmas tree.

On December 16, 1980, *Happy Days* took a bold step by titling its holiday episode "White Christmas." Here, on a very snowy Christmas Eve, Marion frets over Richie's absence, Fonzie and his friends are stuck in Al's restaurant, and Joanie uses the time spent snowbound with her dad in the hardware store to try to convince him to let her spend the summer in New York City with Jenny Piccalo.

Then, on December 14, 1982, *Happy Days* presented "All I Want for Christmas," which premiered in its tenth season. In this adventure, Howard dreads his quarrelsome older brother's Christmas visit and little Heather Pfister asks Santa Claus to help her mother, Ashley, make up with the parents who disinherited her for marrying against their wishes. And Fonzie steps in to save the day to make little Heather's wish come true.

A similar sense of gratitude pervaded every episode of *Laverne & Shirley*, the spin-off series from *Happy Days*, which aired on ABC from 1976 to 1983. As the title leads, Penny Marshall and Cindy Williams, respectively, were blue-collar working girls who never gave up hope. In that way, every episode of *Laverne & Shirley* was a Christmas episode, though two were formally designated as such.

"O Hear the Angels' Voices" premiered on December 21, 1976. In this adventure, Carmine (Eddie Mekka) convinces Laverne and Shirley to perform in a Christmas show. The very spirit of the episode harkens back to several such episodes of any of Lucille Ball's sitcom segments. Many critics and viewers over the years have compared Penny Marshall and Cindy Williams' performances on *Laverne & Shirley* to that of Ball and her frequent female TV sidekick Vivian Vance.

One year after "O Hear the Angels' Voices," "O Come All Ye Bums" initially aired on December 19, 1978. In this episode, Frank DeFazio, Laverne's father (played by Phil Foster), is despondent over having to cancel his annual outreach for the homeless. That is until Laverne and Shirley help him reignite the light with the help of Carmine as they seek to raise funds to feed the hungry.

CHAPTER 46

CHRISTMAS BY MOONLIGHTING,
SHE WROTE WITH A LITTLE GOLDEN
BARNABY ON THE SIDE

"If your stocking gets stolen and your tree can't be found./You may as well call us 'cause we'll be around./We have to work Christmas, so if you're in a pinch/Just give Blue Moon a jingle and ask for the Grinch."

— Allyce Beasley's Agnes DiPesto, answering the phone,
in the *Moonlighting* episode "It's a Wonderful Job"

In addition to the regularly comedic episodic core of the 1960s, 1970s, 1980s, and beyond, weekly dramas also joined the Christmas TV specials party. Those include such mystery anthology series as NBC's *Alfred Hitchcock Presents* ("Santa Claus and the Tenth Avenue Kid," December 18, 1955), the short-lived syndicated show *Deadline* ("A Story for Christmas," March 17, 1960), and the original radio and two black-and-white, and color TV editions of *Dragnet*, each of which produced the same "Christmas Story" (about the theft of the Baby Jesus from a Nativity scene at a church).

Later detective shows such as *Moonlighting* (ABC, 1985–1989) and *Murder, She Wrote* (CBS, 1984–1986) also joined the party with their own, if sometimes brazen brand of holiday cheer.

Moonlighting, for one, presented two Christmas-focused episodes in its manic, limited-annual-episodes, overbudgeted, brilliant, multi-award-winning four-year run. Former movie star Cybill Shepherd portrays a former model named Maddie Hayes who manages the Blue Moon Detective Agency (thus the show's title) with a smart-aleck detective named David Addison, played by future movie star Bruce Willis.

Whereas Shepherd, pre-*Moonlighting*, appeared in such classic films as *The Last Picture Show* (1971), *The Heartbreak Kid* (1972), and *Taxi Driver*

(1976), Willis would go on to make such mega-hit movies as 1988's *Die Hard*, which not only ignited a film franchise, but also a long-held debate as whether or not it can be classified as a Christmas movie.

However, before that ongoing deliberation began, on December 17, 1985, Willis and Shepherd charmed the small-screen audience with the *Moonlighting* adventure "'Twas the Episode Before Christmas," which was followed one year later, on December 16, 1986, by the show's second holiday episode, "It's a Wonderful Job."

In "'Twas the Episode Before Christmas," directed by Peter Werner and written by show creator Glenn Gordon Caron, a criminal named Joseph Goodman (Ralph Meyering Jr.) in the witness protection program is killed, but his wife, Mary Goodman (Leslie Wing), and their baby manage to escape. When fleeing, and without any explanation, Mary leaves her infant at the apartment doorstep of Agnes, Blue Moon's daffy but loyal and insightful secretary Agnes DiPesto (played by Allyce Beasley). At this point, Maddie and Addison go on the hunt to locate Mary, while Agnes cares for the baby.

With a character surname like *Goodman* and first names like *Joseph* and *Mary* who have a baby at Christmastime, it soon becomes crystal midnight clear how this Christmas story is an adaptation of *the* Christmas biblical story of Jesus, Mary, and Joseph.

By the end of this episode, *Moonlighting* showcased one of the beloved break-the-fourth-wall charms that became one of its trademarks. Following the sound of voices caroling, David and Maddie exit Blue Moon's glass doors and into the show's behind-the-scenes set, where the show's entire cast, crew, and staff (with families) sing "The First Noel."

Whereas "'Twas the Episode Before Christmas" tackles the meaning and sentiment of Christmas with a more serious tone, *Moonlighting*'s second holiday-themed episode, "It's a Wonderful Job," offers a satiric take on *It's a Wonderful Life*.

This time, the expanded staff of the Blue Moon Detective Agency, which now includes Curtis Armstrong as Burt Viola—a love interest for Agnes, are not the least bit pleased about having to work on Christmas Eve. Although a guilt-ridden Maddie is also not that crazy about the idea, she doesn't see any other way. That is until her guardian angel appears and gives her a new perspective, literally, with an alternate reality.

To wit, wedded love-bird detectives Jonathan and Jennifer Hart, from ABC's previous series, *Hart to Hart* (ABC, 1979–1984) acquire Blue Moon's lease. David finds wealth, love, and marriage with model Cheryl Tiegs, while Maddie has "a very bad year" and is on the verge of committing suicide. In the end, Maddie comes to peace with keeping the agency open on Christmas Eve, as she and David share a passionate kiss, wishing "all a good night."

While *A Christmas Carol* inspired "'Twas the Episode Before Christmas," "It's a Wonderful Job" also offers, if ever slightly, a nod to Scrooge within a retelling of *It's a Wonderful Life*. Although Tiegs plays herself, ABC's *Hart to Hart* stars Robert Wagner and Stefanie Powers do not appear as their Jonathan and Jennifer Hart parts, but Lionel Stander reprised his role as their assistant, Max. That's worth noting for several reasons. Pierce Brosnan, then of NBC's 1982–1987 *Remington Steele* detective series (which was created by *Moonlighting*'s Glenn Carron), switched networks to ABC and made a cameo appearance in the *Moonlighting* episode "The Straight Poop" (which aired January 6, 1987). *Steele*, which also starred Stephanie Zimbalist (daughter of Efrem Jr. from ABC's *The FBI*, 1965–1974), *Hart to Hart*, and *Moonlighting* were each inspired in their own way by the classic *Thin Man* movies featuring Nick and Nora Charles (played by William Powell and Myrna Loy).

Some further insight:

The "It's a Wonderful Job" title is also a reference to a *My Three Sons* episode ("It's a Dog's Life," from March 18, 1965), while *Moonlighting* producers, convinced that Cybill Shepherd was unhappy working on the show, created the "It's a Wonderful Job" adventure with the intention of killing off Maddie. ABC, however, vetoed that development.

Just as *The Thin Man* films were based on the 1934 novel by Dashiell Hammett, Miss Marple, another classic detective, this time created by Agatha Christie, influenced a small-screen incarnation: *Murder, She Wrote*. That show, which aired on CBS from 1984 to 1996, featured the legendary Angela Lansbury, who made a name for herself on both the big and small screens, many times, with Christmas-geared material.

Years before Lansbury was cast as mystery maven/author Jessica Fletcher on *Murder, She Wrote*, she lent her voice to the Rankin/Bass not-so-great, but earnest animated half-hour special *The First Christmas: The Story of the First Christmas Snow*. Premiering on NBC December 19, 1975, *The First Christmas* brings a more religious element to the animated special, not seen since *The Little Drummer Boy*.

In 1845, lightning causes a young shepherd named Lucas (David Kelley) to lose his sight. A cloister of nuns care for him in a nearby abbey filled with orphans. There, Sister Catherine (Iris Rainer) offers a detailed description of snow to the visually impaired Lucas, while the nuns cast him as an angel in their Christmas pageant, during which Christmas snow falls and ignites a miracle.

The special's title refers to the Christmas pageant the orphan children presented on Christmas Eve, though the title could also refer to the initial occurrence experience of snow following his regaining sight. At one point, Lucas and Sister Theresa sing "White Christmas," which would not be composed until almost a century later. The nuns' black outfits indicate they're Carmelites, the order that St. Therese de Lisieux, The Little Flower, joined.

The special also features the voices of Cyril Ritchard as Father Thomas, while Lansbury is heard throughout the story as Sister Theresa, who also narrates.

Post–*Murder, She Wrote*, and though always held to a higher standard, Lansbury starred in the startling-successful and utterly charming TV musical *Mrs. Santa Claus*.

As such, like Marlo Thomas, Lansbury has the distinguished position of having starred in a Christmas half-hour animated special, TV-movie, and episode of a hit series.

In *Mrs. Santa Claus*, set in 1910–1912, Lansbury plays the lead, here a neglected wife opposite Charles Durning's less-empathetic St. Nick. Consequently, she takes the bull by the horns, or at least the reindeer by the antlers, and heists her husband's sleigh for a Christmas adventure of her own. But when one of the reindeer is injured, she finds herself stuck in New York City where, incognito as Mrs. North (as in Pole), she becomes a fierce advocate for women's rights and child-labor reform in the toy industry. Naturally, good ol' St. Nick misses her and Mrs. North misses being Mrs. Claus, and returns home, where her chubby-hubby sees her in a different respectful light. Their love is all the more wonderfully shared when he invites her to fly with him around the world on Christmas Eve.

A few behind-the-scenes anecdotes (some from IMDb) follows.

To lift Santa's spirits, the elves bust in his office, dancing, as we hear "We Need a Little Christmas" playing in the background. That's a song first performed by Lansbury during the Broadway run of *Mame*, with music and lyrics composed by Jerry Herman, who was genius composer and lyricist for *Mrs. Santa Claus*.

Bob Mackie, costume creator of fashions and decorated wardrobe for Carol Burnett and Cher, serves in the same fashion here with Dame Angela Lansbury's appearance, hair, and garb.

A plot point in the film involves women demanding the right to vote, which is reminiscent of Barbra Streisand's bold role in *The Way We Were*. However, women gaining the right to vote finally happened after the Nineteenth Amendment was ratified approximately one decade following the events that transpire in *Mrs. Santa Claus*.

Bluescreen filming *Mrs. Santa Claus* in the red sleigh being pulled by a herd of reindeer was filmed first on an independent effects stage located in Van Nuys, California.

After the third day, the company moved to Universal Studios for filming the New York backlot street exterior scenes in the middle of July 1996.

Similarly, the Christmas episode of *Murder, She Wrote*, "A Christmas Secret" (from December 13, 1992) holds a unique place in Christmas-special history. Like *The Love Boat* and *Fantasy Island*, *Murder, She Wrote* became famous for its extensive guest-star list per episode. In "The Christmas Secret," those include Diane Baker, Amy Brenneman, Ken Swofford, Mary Tanner, and Larry Wilcox, among others. The regular cast includes Ron Masak as Sheriff Mort Metzger, William Windom as Dr. Seth Hazlitt, and Louis Herthum as Deputy Andy Broom.

The setting is Cabot Cove, hometown of Lansbury's successful mystery-writer Jessica Fletcher; where more murders take place than any other city or town in America. However, in "A Christmas Secret" (which was directed by Anthony Shaw, Lansbury's husband, and written by show producer Bruce Lansbury, Angela's brother), no actual murder takes place.

Unlike the third and final Christmas episode of *The Doris Day Show*, a family sitcom, which quite strangely involved a murder plot, the holiday episode of *Murder, She Wrote* does not.

Set at Christmastime, "A Christmas Secret" centers around the future son-in-law (played by Sean O'Bryan, engaged to Brenneman's Amy Wainwright) of a prominent Cabot Cove family (headed by Swofford) who is a suspect in a shooting. Not a murder; but a shooting.

According to *The Unofficial Murder, She Wrote Companion* by James Parrish, the highlight of this episode is as follows: "Like George Bailey of *It's a Wonderful Life*, Dr. Seth Hazlitt has lost his faith in the Christmas spirit and the goodwill of all. As this episode unfolds, the downhearted physician regains his enthusiasm for the holidays and for his fellow human beings. As always, Windom makes what could be a throwaway cliché a telling situation."

Lansbury, who died in 2022 at age ninety-six, was a cherished actress for decades; time and again she proved her age had no bounds, while her talent held a timeless appeal. As a performer, she was an elegant element of classic film and television, even more so when it comes to such programming as Christmas specials.

Murder, She Wrote remains beloved today, as it was during its original run. The same may be said for the senior-centered 1970s CBS detective series *Barnaby Jones*, starring Buddy Ebsen. Although that show never did a

Christmas-geared episode during its run, Ebsen lent his voice to an animated TV special, titled, *The Tiny Tree*.

First broadcast on NBC, Sunday, December 14, 1975, at 7:30 p.m. Eastern time, and later airing on PBS in 1977, *The Tiny Tree* was presented as part of the Bell System Family Theater, sponsored by Bell Telephone and produced by DePatie-Freleng (DFE), one of several productions for the studio. Chuck Couch, a veteran animator and writer, was the brains behind this production, although he was never a regular with DFE studios. [His only other credit with the company is as a writer on the 1968 Pink Panther short, *The Pink Package Plot*.]

Ebsen serves as narrator on the special and gives voice to Squire Badger who, in speaking with two rabbit children, tells the tale of a little disabled girl who befriends forest animals. With the additional groundbreaking character of a special-needs child in a wheel chair, *The Tiny Tree* tells a touching tale: A tree with a face that doesn't speak befriends all the animals in a forest, while forming a special bond with the little girl who visits him every day.

Composer Johnny Marks, who already achieved fame with the "Rudolph the Red-Nosed Reindeer" tune, was hired to write and compose music for *The Tiny Tree*. Eight songs were featured altogether, with popular singer Roberta Flack performing two of them: "To Love and Be Loved" and "When Autumn Comes."

Before *The Tiny Tree* and *Barnaby Jones*, for that matter, Ebsen played the black-gold-oil-rich-struck Jed Clampett on *The Beverly Hillbillies* (CBS, 1962–1971), which produced many Christmas episodes in its nine years on the air: "Home for Christmas," "No Place Like Home," "The Clampetts Get Culture," "The Christmas Present," "The Week Before Christmas," and "Christmas in Hooterville" (the latter set in the fake TV land of its sister CBS country-coms, *Petticoat Junction* and *Green Acres*).

While Ebsen was joined on *Hillbillies* by co-stars Donna Douglas as darling TV daughter Elly May, Max Baer Jr. as dimwitted on-screen nephew Jethro, and Irene Ryan as Granny, yet another geriatric persona, later contemporary audiences enjoyed the older and more sophisticated generational comedy of *The Golden Girls* (several episodes of which were directed by Terry *Mrs. Santa Claus* Hughes).

Originally airing on NBC from 1985 to 1992, *The Golden Girls*, which stars Bea Arthur as the feisty Dorothy Petrillo, Rue McClanahan as adventurous Blanch Devereaux, Betty White as the daffy Rose Nylund, and Estelle Getty as Sophia Petrillo, Dorothy's mom, produced two Christmas episodes: "'Twas the Nightmare Before Christmas" (December 20, 1986) and "Have Yourself a Very Little Christmas" (December 16, 1989).

In "'Twas the Nightmare Before Christmas," the girls all plan to visit their respective families for Christmas, but their plans are ruined when they are held hostage by a man dressed as Santa Claus at the Grief Counseling Center.

Brett White of Decider.com once observed: ""'Twas the Nightmare Before Christmas' highlights what viewers knew all along: these four *are* family, in every way that truly matters. This episode also has the funniest punch line in the entire series ('I'm surprised you were able to walk in October!')."

In "Have Yourself a Very Little Christmas," the girls volunteer at a homeless shelter on Christmas Day and learn that Stan, Dorothy's ex-husband (played by Herb Edelman), has been thrown out on the streets by his current wife.

CHAPTER 47

LIFE GOES ON IN BEVERLY HILLS AT CHRISTMAS

"Anybody who gives presents to strangers on Christmas has gotta be
pretty cool."

> —Tommy Puett's Tyler Benchfield, in the *Life
> Goes On* Christmas episode, "Smell of Fear"

Life Goes On and *Beverly Hills, 90210* were two of the most popular family shows of the 1990s; different; yet similar. One in fact, sprang from the other. As *Life Goes On* actor Tommy Puett once noted in the book *Life Story—The Book of Life Goes On*, *Beverly Hills, 90210* executive producer Aaron Spelling was inspired to create his show about the high school privileged teens after watching the mainstream high school scenes on *Life Goes On*.

Life Goes On originally aired on ABC from 1989 to 1993, and it centered around the Thatcher family of a Chicago suburb whose middle child, Corky Thatcher, just so happened to have Down syndrome. Actor Chris Burke played Corky opposite Kellie Martin as his younger sister Becca, older sister Paige, played first by Monique Lanier, later Tracey Needham, and parents Libby and Drew Thatcher, portrayed by Patti LuPone and Bill Smitrovich. Chad Lowe and Amanda Friedman (who also had Down syndrome, and who passed away in 2023) later joined the series. Lowe, in his Emmy-winning role of Jesse McKenna, portrayed Becca's boyfriend, who's initially diagnosed as HIV-positive and then contracts full-blown AIDS; Friedman played Amanda, Corky's girlfriend-turned-wife.

Beverly Hills, 90210 initially centered around twin teen siblings Brandon and Brenda Walsh, played by Jason Priestly and Shannen Doherty, and their wealthy classmates Dylan McKay (Luke Perry), Kelly Taylor (Jenny Garth), Steve Sanders (Ian Ziering), David Silver (Brian Austin Green), Donna Martin (Tori Spelling, daughter of Aaron), Andrea Zuckerman (Gabrielle Carteris), and Valerie Malone (Tiffany Thiessen). James Eckhouse and Carol Potter played Brandon and Brenda's parents, Cindy and Jim Walsh.

Both *Life Goes On* and *Beverly Hills, 90210* offered a slate of Christmas episodes.

First up, *Life Goes On.*

Season 1, Episode 11, "Pets, Guys, and Videotape" (December 10, 1989): It's Christmastime, and Libby, Paige, and Becca uncover valuable insight into the challenges faced by modern working women, while Corky observes over the film *Casablanca.*

Although this episode is set in December, it not specifically designed as a Christmas episode, but rather an episode that happens to be during the holiday season; a rarity premise for TV at the time; and something that would later transpire on sitcoms such as *Seinfeld*. Also, too, the "just so happens to be" scenario is in step with Corky's description of someone who "just so happens" to have Down syndrome. He is not defined by his disability; but rather his humanity.

Season 2, Episode 9, "A Thatcher Thanksgiving" (November 18, 1990): Corky pictures the family at the Pilgrim's first Thanksgiving, as Drew opens a new business; a restaurant, just in time for the holiday season, and meets an old classmate who's now homeless.

The Pilgrim scenes are handled within as part of the dream/fantasy sequences that the show frequently employed (as did *Father Knows Best* decades before), while they are also reminiscent of the 1967 *Bewitched* episode "Samantha's Thanksgiving to Remember." Though in that magical sitcom, Elizabeth Montgomery's Samantha and family actually go back in time to the first Thanksgiving (due to the bumbling magic of Marion Lorne's Aunt Clara).

Meanwhile, too, both *Life Goes On* and *Bewitched* deal with the issue of prejudice. Samantha is a witch out of water in a human world; both Corky, with Down syndrome, and Jesse, with AIDS, are ostracized from society on *Life Goes On.*

Season 3, Episode 11, "The Smell of Fear" (December 15, 1991): Christmas brings anxieties to the entire family. Drew's down due to lack of customers at his new restaurant; Libby's frantic because she was just named the new substitute director for the local community theater Christmas pageant; Paige feels more lost than usual; Corky still questions the existence of Santa Claus. Most of all, Becca and Jesse are dealing with his rapidly declining health.

Season 4, Episode 9, "Happy Holidays" (December 20, 1992): The holidays take on a whole new meaning for Corky, who's celebrating his first Christmas as a married man to Amanda. However, the situation turns sour as he and Amanda decide to spend Christmas with her parents, which upsets Drew and Libby. In the meantime, Paige reunites with boyfriend Michael (played by Lance Guest).

A few closing notes: Chris Burke once expressed his displeasure with having Corky getting married too soon; an anxiety that matches Corky's angst in being forced to choose a family location for Christmas. If this episode had been produced as solely dedicated to his first Christmas away from home, minus the marriage angle, it would have been more credible. But compounded with Corky getting married, it was just simply all too much story.

Moving on to *Beverly Hills, 90210*, which originally ran on Fox from 1990 to 2000:

Season 2, Episode 18, "A Walsh Family Christmas" (December 19, 1991): Steve travels to New Mexico to try to track down his birth mother but learns that she has long passed away. Brandon visits Emily Valentine in the mental hospital, and Cindy and Jim miss celebrating Christmas in Minnesota. But Brenda ultimately gives everyone a reality check by inviting a homeless Santa Claus for dinner.

Season 3, Episode 16, "It's a Totally Happening Life" (December 16, 1992): *It's a Wonderful Life* once more gets a makeover, this time with two angels narrating the story.

Season 4, Episode 15, "Somewhere in the World It's Christmas" (December 22, 1993): Dylan meets his half-sister, Erica, Donna and David break up (he wants to have sex; she doesn't), and the Walsh family tries to fly to Hawaii in this episode, which features a first-season flashback to "A Walsh Family Christmas."

Season 5, Episode 15, "Christmas Comes This Time Each Year" (December 21, 1994): Kelly deals with burns, and Andrea struggles with her crying infant. Ray is shocked when Donna's mother offers him $10,000 to go away, while both Donna and Clare have issues with an unattractive wardrobe.

Season 6, Episode 15, "Angels We Have Heard on High" (December 20, 1995): The holiday adventures of Steve and Clare, Kelly and Colin.

Season 7, Episode 13, "Gift Wrapped" (December 18, 1996): Kelly and Valerie purchase the same Christmas gift for each other.

Season 8, Episode 14, "Santa Knows" (December 17, 1997): Donna and Valerie Martin have issues, while Brandon gets a little edgy.

Season 9, Episode 10, "Marathon Man" (December 16, 1998): Donna's birthday falls on Christmas, and every year she makes a few wishes. This time, those include the Brian Setzer Orchestra and to keep Noah in her life, both of which she realizes.

Season 10, Episode 12, "Nine Yolks Whipped Lightly" (December 22, 1999): Kelly and Matt struggle with their engagement; Dylan gets in a brawl that causes issues at the community center; and Steve and Janet try to convince her parents to love their child.

CHAPTER 48

A FULL HOLIDAY HOUSE IMPROVEMENT IN THE MIDDLE WITH REBA

"Nothing says 'Merry Christmas' like a hostage situation."

—Steve Howey's Van Montgomery, on *Reba*

The dynamic of the family sitcom changed over the years from the days of *Father Knows Best/My Three Sons* in the 1950s and 1960s into *The Brady Bunch* phase of the 1970s, to the *Full House*, *Step by Step*, and *Home Improvement* period of the 1980s and early 1990s. Those decades also brought us revolutionary dramedies like *The Wonder Years*, while the early 2000s delivered a daring, likable, and very funny *Reba* to the small screen. By media osmosis, the essence of the given sitcom's Christmas episode was subsequently shadowed with a new aesthetic.

Exhibit A: *Full House*, which features leading characters played by Bob Saget, John Stamos, and Dave Coulier combining their resources and households under one roof. Originally airing on ABC from 1987 to 1995, *Full House* and *Step by Step*, which followed it on the network's TGIF/"Thank God It's Friday"–night showcase, contemporized the blended-family concept introduced by *The Brady Bunch* (which was inspired by two feature films released in 1968: *Yours, Mine and Ours* and *With Six You Get Eggroll*).

In 1988, *Full House* broadcast the episode "Our Very First Christmas Show." Brett White years later observed on Decider.com:

Sitcom families should know better than to try to travel during a major holiday. The Tanner family learned this lesson the hard way in *Full House*'s very first Christmas show. A snowstorm grounds their flight at a random airport, leaving the Tanners and a plane full of patient passengers (can you imagine being stuck anywhere with Joey Gladstone?) stuck in a baggage claim. But just as the stranded family's Christmas spirit dips dangerously low, Uncle Jesse comes through with a rousing speech that would make Jimmy Stewart proud. We know Jesse's speech impresses at least one passenger: a cranky old man that might just be Kris Kringle.

Three years after *Full House* presented "Our Very First Christmas Show," *Home Improvement* and its *Adventures-of-Ozzie-and-Harriet*-meets-*This-Old-House* mentality took the Christmas episode celebration to new contemporary heights, alongside such shows as *Roseanne* (which took the holiday story to a few lows with episodes such as "White Trash Christmas," ABC, December 14, 1993).

In the *Home Improvement* entry, "Yule Better Watch Out," broadcast on December 17, 1991, Tim Allen's TV sons Brad (Zachery Ty Bryan) and Randy (Jonathan Taylor Thomas) tell their little brother, Mark (Taran Noah Smith), that Santa Claus died six years before—just prior to Mark's birth. Tim and TV wife Jill Taylor (Patricia Richardson) of course are incensed with their two older sons' mean-Christmas-spirited antics, while Randy makes quite an impression at his school's annual Christmas pageant. Into this mix, accident-prone Tim's typical, over-the-top illuminated Christmas decorations put him in the hospital.

While certain shows don't do much for the family sitcom reputation except tarnish it, *Reba*, which originally aired on the WB-turned-CW network from 2001 to 2007, gets the genre back on track as one of the last great traditional family sitcoms in history. *The Middle* (which initially aired on ABC from 2009 to 2018) did so to a lesser extent, if hindered by its somewhat manic family of all-too-self-aware cast who delivered performances akin more to stand-up comedians instead of actors interpreting characters.

With *Reba*, however, the family sitcom was granted a more credible, new life with a country twist, if light-years away from rural adventures of *The Andy Griffith Show*, *Petticoat Junction*, *Green Acres*, and similar sitcoms of the 1960s and early 1970s. *Reba* rocks on many levels with country-music-icon Reba McEntire front and center as Reba Hart, a Houston, Texas, soccer mom who divorces her cheating (though charming) husband Brock Hart (Christopher Rich, formerly of the CBS mainstay *Murphy Brown* (1988–1998, rebooted in 2018, inclusive of a reboot; and the short-lived but brilliant *The Charmings* fantasy-com, ABC, 1987–1988).

Together, Reba and Brock produced three children: seventeen-year-old Cheyenne (JoAnna Garcia), who marries Van Montgomery (Steve Howey) after he gets her pregnant; the tranquil and ever-wise little seven-year-old Jake (Mitch Holleman); and Kyra (Scarlett Pomers, formerly of *Star Trek: Voyager* and *That's Life*). Into the mix is Brock's new wife, Barbra Jean (Melissa Peterman, who somehow manages to cross-pollinate Jim Nabors' Gomer Pyle with Georgia Engel's Georgette from *The Mary Tyler Moore Show*, and who makes "the other woman" as appealing as she's ever gonna get).

Reba—the show—does for the contemporary family comedy what *Bewitched* did for supernatural sitcoms. The characters on *Reba* interact just like real people. They actually get mad at each other, forgive one another, move on, and deal with it (just like we all do—or *should* do). Everything about the show is top of the line. You can't beat that opening theme song ("I'm A Survivor")—and the show's writing is crisp, as is the directing (one episode was even guided by former child star Moosie *Laugh-In* Drier).

The issues in Reba's family are real: unplanned teen pregnancy, childhood sweethearts divorce after years of bliss, and teen angst—each experienced, on one level or the other, by McEntire's Reba Hart—who holds the brood's brew-ha-ha together. So much so, she joins the ranks of Carol Brady, Shirley Partridge, and June Cleaver.

All of that and more is more than clear in the *Reba* Christmas episode, "Reba Cookies for Santa," which aired on CW December 12, 2002. Here, Reba is looking forward to the first Christmas for Cheyenne and Van's new baby, Elizabeth. But Van and Cheyenne want to spend the holiday elsewhere, while Jake and Kyra go with a friend. Left alone, Reba ponders: "Just when I thought divorce couldn't hurt me anymore, I lose something else. Christmas Eve used to be so special."

Fortunately, Reba quickly reevaluates and remedies her situation with a rediscovery of the true meaning of Christmas, which she finds by volunteering at the local homeless shelter.

Some years later, on November 26, 2021, the multitalented real-life Reba McEntire, who recorded three Christmas music albums in her illustrious career, starred in the Lifetime Christmas TV-movie *Reba McEntire's Christmas in Tune*. Here, she played entertainer Georgia Winter, who years after breaking up with her singing partner and husband, Joe (played by John *The Dukes of Hazzard* Schneider), agrees to reunite for a one-time-only Christmas concert.

The film was the ideal TV-special blend of reality, fantasy, and Christmas, with a dual theme of second chances and forgiveness. As McEntire told the now-defunct print edition of *Parade* magazine on November 21, 2021: "It's hard to get to that point when you forgive and give second chances. It's easier to forgive than it is to forget. Then sometimes, you're like, 'I don't remember why I'm supposed to be mad.' That's the situation in this movie. Forgive and move on is a great point to get to."

CHAPTER 49
FESTIVUS, *FRIENDS*, AND *MOTHER*

"George, Festivus is your heritage. It's part of who you are."

—Jerry Stiller's Frank Costanza, to his son, George, as played
by Jason Alexander, in the *Seinfeld* episode "The Strike"

Several sitcoms defined by mostly single, unmarried characters have celebrated the holidays through the more recent decades. *Seinfeld* (NBC,
1989–1998) gave us "Festivus," a new December tradition. *Friends*
(NBC, 1994–2004) enjoyed Christmas three times, and also showed us how
to play touch-football at Thanksgiving. *Frasier* (NBC, 1993–2004, rebooted
in 2023 on Paramount+) frolicked with a feast of Christmas episodes. *How
I Met Your Mother* (CBS, 2005–2014) brings it all home for the holidays in
several single-minded adventures.

Festivus sashayed on *Seinfeld* in "The Strike," the tenth episode of the
show-about-nothing that centers around the life of comedian Jerry Seinfeld
(playing himself) and his friends, former love interest Elaine Benes (Julia
Louis-Dreyfus), lifelong pal George Costanza (Jason Alexander), and outlandish neighbor Cosmo Kramer, played by Michael Richards, ninth and final
season, airing on December 18, 1997. The episode designates December 23
as the "made-up" holiday's date. Based on the true-life experiences of writer
Dan O'Keefe's father, *Seinfeld*'s concept of Festivus involves an aluminum pole
(one that Jerry Stiller's Frank Costanza drags through the streets), which was
an off-camera suggestion by regular cast member Michael Richards.

Meanwhile, the Human Fund nonprofit organization referenced in the
episode was writer Jeff Schaffer's idea, based on Christmas cards the *Seinfeld*
staff would receive from its Castle Rock production company. In 2005, eight

years after "The Strike" aired, the episode inspired a real-life Human Fund. That same year, O'Keefe published the book *The Real Festivus: The True Story Behind America's Favorite Made-up Holiday.*

Beyond "The Strike," *Seinfeld* was party to a new form of sitcom that would showcase episodes set in December that feature Christmas decorations, but the premise of those episodes was not necessarily holiday-themed.

For example, in "The Red Dot," which aired on December 11, 1991, in the show's third season, George gets a job at Elaine's office, which is decorated for the holidays, but the plot revolves more around his romantic entanglement with Evie, the cleaning woman (Bridget Sienna). Meanwhile, Elaine's boyfriend, a recovering alcoholic, falls off the wagon because of Jerry's carelessness. George, however, buys Elaine a marked-down cashmere sweater, which has on its bottom left side the infamous red dot (which was really a small red thread placed by the show's wardrobe designer).

Beyond the episode's Christmas-decorated set and non-Christmas theme, Jason Alexander has long-considered the scene where George reacts indifferently to having had sex on his desk with Evie to be the defining moment for his character. This is also the only time in the series where Jerry talks to someone during his act (in this case, Dick, played by David Naughton). In the end credits, "Mr. Lippman" is listed as "Mr. Breckman," as actor Richard Fancy, who played Mr. Breckman in this episode, appears later in the series in what became the recurring role of Mr. Lippman.

On into the working of *Friends*, which not only did several Christmas episodes but many Thanksgiving segments, too. The latter began with the first-season episode "The One Where Underdog Got Away," which debuted November 17, 1994.

Here, Monica's vision of a tranquil Thanksgiving is disrupted when the gang comes over and then locks themselves out of the apartment, as the Underdog float breaks free during the Macy's Thanksgiving Day Parade.

In "The One with the List" (November 16, 1995), Monica creates "Mockloate," a synthetic chocolate, into Thanksgiving recipes, while Ross struggles with the complicated issues of loving Rachel.

In "The One with the Football" (November 21, 1996), the gang plays what should have been a friendly game of football, but becomes anything but.

In "The One with Chandler in a Box" (November 20, 1997), Monica injures her eye while preparing dinner. Consequently, she meets the son of her former love, Richard, at the eye doctor, and they later share a kiss over Thanksgiving.

"The One with All the Thanksgivings" (November 19, 1998), is a clip special to previous episodes.

"The One Where Ross Got High" (November 25, 1999), involves a Gellar family reunion.

"The One Where Chandler Doesn't Like Dogs" (November 23, 2000), has two main storylines: Rachel is thrilled when her assistant/crush accepts her invitation for Thanksgiving, while Chandler deals with his fear of canines.

"The One with the Rumor" (November 22, 2001), and is most famous for the special guest appearance by Brad Pitt, then married to Jennifer Aniston, whose Rachel role bullies Pitt's character.

"The One with Rachel's Other Sister" (November 21, 2002), features another special guest star appearance, this time by Christina Applegate, who plays Rachel's self-absorbed sister.

In the final *Friends* Thanksgiving episode, "The One with the Late Thanksgiving" (November 20, 2003), Monica and Chandler are upset with everyone being late for dinner. But their mood swings more delightful upon hearing good adoption news.

The *Friends* Christmas episodes are as follows:

In "The One with the Monkey" (December 15, 1994), we meet Ross's pet monkey, as the gang meets for a New Year's Eve party.

In "The One with Phoebe's Dad" (December 14, 1995), Phoebe deals with daddy–daughter issues.

For "The One with the Holiday Armadillo" (December 14, 2000), Ross teaches his son about Hanukkah, but with a Santa twist.

What *Seinfeld* and *Friends* were for the 1990s (and a little after with specific regard to *Friends*), *How I Met Your Mother* more or less picked up the baton for the 2000s with a *Mother*-load of Christmas episodes.

"How Lily Stole Christmas" (December 11, 2006), has Lily and Marshall breaking up, making up, and breaking up.

Two years later, "Little Minnesota" (December 15, 2008), is less Christmas-geared but still festive.

Two years after that, "False Positive" (December 13, 2010), with the adult gang looking into the future (juxtaposed to the show's main premise).

In "Symphony of Illumination" (December 5, 2011), Robin learns she is unable to have children.

"The Final Page: Part 2" (December 17, 2012), is the show's last holiday episode, which is the second-part story of Barney's significant effort to propose marriage.

CHAPTER 50

FRASIER'S FAMILY CHRISTMAS

Frasier: "Merry Christmas, Seattle! Yes, this is Dr. Frasier Crane coming to you on Christmas Day. Christmas, that very magical time of the year, when each moment is as unique as a snowflake, never to be recreated."

Roz: "I'm sorry, Frasier, the news went over you. You're gonna have to do that again."

Frasier: "Merry Christmas, Seattle . . ."

—*Frasier* Christmas episode, "Miracle on Third or Fourth Street"

Seamlessly combining elements of both the family and single-minded sitcom, *Frasier* brought a full plate of Christmas parties to the TV table during its original run on NBC, from 1993 to 2003.

To many viewers, *Frasier* is considered the last, great traditional sitcom, and it proved that with its superior scripts, elegant sets, solid writing, and esteemed cast. But the show has its origins in another great sitcom that focused on the single life, if at least mostly: *Cheers*, which ran on NBC from 1982 to 1992. That legendary sitcom starring Ted Danson and Shelley Long, and later, Kirstie Alley, gave birth to *Frasier*, the neurotic psychologist, who was a frequent visitor to the show's central bar. As such, we first see Grammer's Dr. Frasier Crane in the *Cheers* episode "Christmas Cheers," which first aired on December 17, 1987.

Here, everyone is depressed. Rebecca (Alley), by this time, the bar's owner, has forced her staff to work on Christmas Eve, including the super-snippy head waitress Carla (Rhea Perlman), who's always unhappy anyway, and flighty but lovable bartender Woody (Woody Harrelson), who misses his mother. The equally lovable, if economically challenged and somewhat hefty barfly, Norm (George Wendt) has no choice but to play a part-time Santa, while Frasier is disgusted with the commercialization of Christmas. But it is Sam who is the most aghast, upon learning that Rebecca bears gifts for the entire gang. As Brett White once observed on Decider.com, what this episode "lacks in any sentiment, which we know *Cheers* excelled at, [it] more than makes up for with an overload of late 1980s holiday vibes."

Along those relatively dark lines, *Frasier*, the series, continued with and improved upon that blend of edgy humor and warmth. For eleven ensuing years on NBC, the show brought smiles and comfort on NBC, followed by a consistent, unending syndicated run, and then its subsequent release on DVD and Blu-ray, and recent reboot on Paramount+. Critically acclaimed in every aesthetic aspect, *Frasier*'s triumphant four, core-supporting cast members accented Grammer's leading role with panache, including:

David Hyde Pierce as Frasier's near-twin, equally neurotic psychologist/ brother Dr. Niles Crane, John Mahoney as Martin Crane, Frasier's former-policeman father, an old-school, salt-of-the-earth-kind-of-dedicated-soul, who was wounded on the job and forced to retire and move in with Frasier; Jane Leeves as Daphne Moon (and later, Crane), an immigrant, English Mancunian physiotherapist and live-in housekeeper hired by Frasier to help Martin with his physiotherapy, and Peri Gilpin as Roz Doyle, the free-spirited producer of Frasier's radio show.

Bebe Neuwirth as the also-neurotic psychologist Lilith, Frasier's leftover love interest from *Cheers*, makes several guest appearances in the spin-off; while little Eddie the dog rounds out the cast as Martin's beloved Jack Russel terrier (who frequently plays foil to Frasier).

The main thrust of the series is Frasier's romantic misadventures and the competitive and spirited sibling rivalry between him and Niles, while Martin stands by in guffaw and frustrated awe. But also, at the center of the show's popularity is the key connection between Niles and Daphne, who he falls for instantly upon their first meeting. Niles' obsession with Daphne and her obliviousness of this obsession is developed throughout the earlier seasons, while by the end of the series, a mutual attraction between the pair grows into true love and finally marriage.

With that kind of gradual truth in storytelling rarely seen in sitcoms of any era and so many other victorious (and Victorian!) elements, *Frasier* garnered thirty-seven Prime-time Emmy Awards, a record at the time for a scripted series, and earned the Prime-time Emmy Award for Outstanding Comedy Series for five consecutive years.

The all-important mainstream audience has also given the series high ratings. "We all agreed to play up to the audience" was how Grammer once explained the show's success. "People want to be entertained on a sophisticated level. If you do that, you'll get a great response. The results have borne out that theory."

A theory proven with more than a few Thanksgiving and Christmas episodes along the way:

In the first-season Christmas episode, "Miracle on Third or Fourth Street," which aired December 16, 1993, Frasier is frustrated: he won't be able to see his son this Christmas. Because his misery usually loves company, Frasier decides to do a special episode of his radio show to bond with depressed callers. But by the episode's end, a homeless man at a local diner lifts his Christmas spirit. A terrific script by Christopher Lloyd, directed with the usual poise of veteran James Burrows.

In "Frasier Grinch," which debuted on December 19, 1995, within the show's third season, Frasier struggles with what to buy his son, Frederick, for Christmas.

This is the first time we actually see young "Freddie" Crane, here played by Luke Tarsitano. In future episodes, and for the remainder of the show, the character will be played by Trevor Einhorn (who decades later is replaced by Jack Cutmore-Scott in the 2023 *Frasier* reboot).

In moving forward to season four, we celebrate "A Lilith Thanksgiving," which originally aired on November 26, 1996. As a prime example of the show's famed farcical episodes, this segment also happens to center around Frederick, even though his name is not in the title. On Thanksgiving, Frasier and Lilith go above and beyond sanity to secure their son's acceptance into a prestigious hall of academia, while Frederick spends the holiday with Niles and Martin, who struggle preparing dinner.

One year later, on December 16, 1997, "Perspectives on Christmas" consists of four vignettes featuring Martin, Daphne, Niles, and Roz.

Almost exactly twelve months after that, "Merry Christmas, Mrs. Moskowitz" debuts on December 17, 1998. Here, Frasier pretends to be Jewish to appease the mother of his current love interest. A nice bit, if a little over the top, features Niles dressed as Jesus for a Christmas pageant.

On November 18, 1999, "The Apparent Trap" once more features Lilith and Frederick, this time spending another neurotic Thanksgiving with the Cranes in Seattle.

In the seventh season, "The Flight Before Christmas" made its debut December 16, 1999, in a most dramatic manner. There's a relative rising sexual intensity between Niles and Daphne, as she learns of his romantic interest amid a relationship with her beau Danny (Saul Rubinek), while Frasier hosts an unforgettable Christmas party.

That episode was followed a little less than a month later with "RDWRER," a New Year's Eve adventure first broadcast on January 6, 2000. Here, Frasier, Niles, and Martin take a New Year's journey in the latter's new Winnebago (with a license plate that reads RDWRER, for "Road Warrior").

In "Mary Christmas," from the show's eighth season, specifically December 12, 2000, Frasier reconnects with the overbearing radio show host Dr. Mary (Kim Coles), with whom he finds himself hosting a Christmas pageant.

On December 10, 2002, "We Two Kings" arrives in the show's tenth year with a roar. Frasier and Niles clash on who will host Christmas, while Martin throws up his arms and decides to work that night instead (as a part-time security officer, a job he by then had recently attained).

For "High Holidays," from season 11, December 9, 2003, Niles decides to throw caution to the wind of his atypical life and gets high on weed for the holidays. Additional trouble ensues when Martin mistakenly eats Niles' intended brownie laced with pot. Cute scenes with Eddie seen speaking with Frasier's voice in a TV commercial add to the mayhem, if mostly for a confounded Martin. Although Frasier of course is not in the least pleased, as his visual presence was replaced by a dog for all the world to see.

Esteemed entertainment historian Ken Gehrig offered a closer look and detailed assessment of what he classified as his two favorite *Frasier* Christmas episodes, while incorporating commentary about a few other Christmas TV episodes and specials, and some big-screen flicks as well.

Of the many *Frasier* Christmases, I'd say my favorites are the season three, episode nine, "Frasier Grinch," and the season five, episode nine, "Perspectives on Christmas!" Some sugar, some spice, scathing wit, stressful situations, even some shouting!

In "Frasier Grinch," Frasier Crane is in search of the perfect "educational" gift for his son Frederick, while the world around him seems to be urging him to buy the "outlaw laser robo-geek!"

In "Perspectives on Christmas," four plots are recounted by Martin, Daphne Moon, Niles, and Roz Doyle, oddly told in wraparound scenes while each are getting massages. Not exactly a typical image of Christmas!

UNWRAPPING THE CHRISTMAS PRESENT

An Afterword about Today's TV Holidays

Thus concludes the fullest spectrum possible of the Christmas television landscape, if with a relatively selective list. Certainly, there is an endless list of variety shows, animated specials, TV-movies, and episodic television segments that have not been mentioned.

However, rest assured, they are just as treasured by countless more. And if this book could have been one thousand–plus pages, each would have been explored in detail.

With that said, the Christmas TV beat goes on amid the continued appreciation and rediscovery of classic pop culture contributions of every creative sector.

In December 2023, the ninety-something music sensation Brenda Lee basked in the afterglow of the No. 1 resurgence of her classic hit, "Rockin' Around the Christmas Tree."

With all new Christmas albums, Cher and Barry Manilow returned to the top of the pop music charts, the latter even with a small-screen special called *A Very Barry Christmas*.

Cher made a special guest appearance at the ninety-seventh Annual Macy's Thanksgiving Day Parade (broadcast by NBC on Thanksgiving Day), which for the first time in its history, began a half hour earlier (at 8:30 a.m.), and it also included performances by Jon Batiste, Bell Biv DeVoe, Brandy, Chicago, En Vogue; Ashley Park with the cast and *Muppets of Sesame Street*, and Pentatonix. Beyond even that, the parade began the festivities the night before on NBC, with a prime-time preview special, titled, *Countdown to the Macy's Day Parade*.

If Guy Lombardo and Dick Clark had been alive to see it all, they would have been proud and in competition to have any of those mentioned above to appear on their respective New Year's Eve TV specials. Thus, both proving, and dissipating the designated generation gap which, when it comes to talent and the holidays, ultimately does not exist.

Assuredly, one TV holiday special that represents one of the grandest ways for all generations to align, unite, and celebrate is the Kennedy Center Honors.

For decades, the Kennedy Center Honors special has traditionally aired between Christmas and New Year's Eve as a black-tie gala presented in Washington, D.C. Those honored with a lifetime achievement tribute are creative members of the arts and entertainment industries, including television.

On December 27, 2023, the Kennedy Center honorees included comedian Billy Crystal and rapper and actor Queen Latifah, opera singer Renée Fleming, music star Barry Gibb, and prolific hitmaker Dionne Warwick. Each received personalized tributes, including appearances and performances that are typically kept secret from the honorees themselves.

President Joe Biden welcomed the 2023 honorees to the White House prior to the festivities, saying the performing arts "reflect who we are as Americans and as human beings." The honorees, Biden continued, "have helped shape how we see ourselves, how we see each other, and how we see our world."

Biden then introduced that year's honorees with a set of glowing superlatives about their work. After which he and First Lady Jill Biden then proceeded to the Kennedy Center to attend the ceremony, which began with 2017 Kennedy Center honoree Gloria Estefan leading a troupe of dancers down the aisle while performing her megahit "Get on Your Feet."

Television Christmas specials may not be the same as they once were, but an example by the enthusiasm presented in programming like the Kennedy Center Honors, today's TV gives it its best shot. The medium of television is simply not what it once was, nor is the world in general. Life is about change; no radical insight there, right?

Fortunately, for those of us who love classic Christmas specials, either from their initial broadcast or with new discovery, those shows will continue to entertain generations to come.

A few new contemporary Christmas TV gems with a nostalgic bent have surfaced over the years.

Exhibit A: Lawrence Welk's "musical family" reunited in 2016 for the PBS TV special *Lawrence Welk Precious Memories*. The special included Welk legends Tom Netherton, Dick Dale, Jack Imel, Jo Ann Castle, Kathy Lennon, Janet Lennon, Mimi Lennon, Ken Delo, Bob Ralston, Joe Feeney, Norma Zimmer, Mary Lou Metzger, Guy Hovis, Ralna English, and Gail Farrell.

Exhibit B: In November and December 2019, old-fashioned favorites were celebrated through the generations performed by legendary artists in the PBS special *My Music: A Classic Christmas*, which was executive-produced by T. J. Lubinsky and produced by Jim Pierson.

The special premiered in the greater New York area on Saturday, November 30, on WNET Thirteen at 4:00 p.m. with an encore broadcast on sister station WLIW Channel 21 at 7:30 p.m. on Sunday, December 8.

Hosted by Gavin MacLeod (*The Love Boat*) and Marion Ross (*Happy Days*), *A Classic Christmas* spotlighted traditional carols ("Silent Night," "Hark! The Herald Angels Sing") as well as popular standards ("White Christmas," "Have Yourself a Merry Little Christmas"), children's tunes ("Rudolph the Red-Nosed Reindeer," "Frosty the Snowman," "I Saw Mommy Kissing Santa Claus"), and romantic selections ("The Christmas Song," "Winter Wonderland," "Merry Christmas, Darling").

Among the iconic artists featured in rare, archival footage from the 1950s through the 1970s were Bing Crosby, Perry Como, Judy Garland, Nat King Cole, The Carpenters, Andy Williams, Rosemary Clooney, Johnny Mathis, Gene Autry, Brenda Lee, Burl Ives, The Beach Boys, The Lennon Sisters, Eddy Arnold, Mahalia Jackson, The Harry Simeone Chorale, The Supremes, José Feliciano, Mitzi Gaynor, Jimmy Boyd, Mitch Miller, and, in an all-new performance, Ronnie Spector.

Exhibit C: the teaming of real-life love birds Kurt Russell and Goldie Hawn for a couple of Netflix *Christmas Chronicles* from 2018 and 2020.

According to the booklet *Santa Claus: The Story Behind the Legend*, Russell presents "a blend of his iconic Wyatt Earp and Snake Plissken characters," in portraying Santa with "real good hair." "I want to do the real guy," Russell said of the role. "He's seventeen hundred years old, the magic of that . . . and how they've commercialized him." Combining what *The Story Behind the Legend* described as "Santa's existential issues" are a couple of children who cause his sleigh to crash, leading Mr. Claus to heist a car and end up in prison. "But it's all in an effort to save the Christmas spirit."

The initial *Christmas Chronicles* received mixed reviews, but the *New York Times* noted, "The star makes the unfolding shenanigans tolerable, playing Santa as a kind of jovial emcee with sincerity, pathos, and gravitas."

With his "mostly" real whiskers and contemporary perspective, Russell's Santa just cuts to the chase. "He's up to date," the actor once observed of his role. "He's like, 'No, I don't do Ho, ho, ho. Fake news.'"

According to Marlo Thomas, she and her husband, talk show legend Phil Donahue, once discussed "how someone should do a new *Ed Sullivan Show*. I would love to know we can turn on the TV once a week and see a variety show. New comedians, singers, etc. Nobody does that anymore," (beyond American Idol-type of programming).

Entertainment historian Telly Davidson described more recent holiday specials, such as *Dolly Parton's Christmas of Many Colors: Circle of Love*. Davidson referred to Parton as "the ultimate sole example of an 'old-school' star of the past decade or so," who is "by far the best" of the genre; "a master blend" of the qualities that made classic shows special.

Davidson described the Parton specials as "charming and homespun at times decorated with beautiful scenery, knowingly campy showbiz bits and clichés, and genuinely heartfelt and fun singing and dancing."

From Davidson's perspective, Parton is "one of the only performers who can credibly carry that off today. She has the A-level talent and the Betty-White-like universal likability."

For Davidson, there are only a few contemporary performers who might still be able to "carry off" a new variety show or special today, Christmas or otherwise. "If," he clarified, "with more of a sharp edge, but while still being thoroughly enjoyable."

Some performers who Davidson said might do the trick include Tina Fey, Amy Poehler, Maya Rudolph, Justin Bieber, Kelly Clarkson, Drew Barrymore, Jennifer Hudson, J-Lo, "and maybe even Jimmy Fallon." Davidson described the latter as "an acquired taste, doing a great job," while noting, "the list is certainly a lot thinner now than it was for shows in the 1960s and 1970s heyday."

Talent agent Pierre Patrick, a baby boomer who was in a hospital until he was ten years old, put it this way: "As we look back and forward and rewatch the classic holidays specials, our holidays in real life become all the brighter. The Christmas specials gave me the Christmases that I couldn't experience. They made me happy, and I'm grateful for the joy they brought me when I needed that joy the most. And I'm grateful for the joy they continue to bring me. What could be better than that?"

ACKNOWLEDGMENTS

First and foremost, my heartfelt gratitude to the lovely Marlo Thomas, who not only graciously composed the beautiful foreword to this book but also shared insightful memories of working on several of her Christmas TV specials chronicled within these pages.

Thank you, as well, to all of those who took the time to share their memories, reflections, and insight for this book, including Peter Ackerman, Bob Barnett, Melissa Byers, Pilar Carrington, Tina Cole, Jim Colucci, Kami Cotler, Telly Davidson, Terry DiOrio, Elinor Donahue, Damon Evans, David Harper, John R. Holmes, Jerry Houser, Ken Gehrig, Craig Kausen, Randal Kleiser, David Laurell, Michael Learned, Lisa Lucas, Mary McDonough, Pat McFadden, Johnny Ray Miller, Judy Norton, Pierre Patrick, Les Perkins, Jim Pierson and MPI Video, Christopher Pufall, Robert S. Ray, Rene Reyes and Shane Rosamonda (both of Polly O. Entertainment), Eric Scott, Randy Skretvedt, David Van Deusen, Mark Villano, Jon Walmsley, Tanya Welk, Alexander Williams, and Dan Wingate.

Sincerest appreciation to my terrific publisher, John Cerullo, the remarkable Barbara Claire and Chris Chappell, and all the good people at Applause Books.

Thank you also to literary agent extraordinaire Lee Sobel, the Lee Sobel Agency, and my colleagues Greg Tanner, Esq. and genius author Nat Segaloff.

For their assistance and support in a variety of ways, thank you to my dear sister Pamela R. Mastrosimone, my brother-in-law Sam Mastrosimone, my nephew Sammy Mastrosimone, my cousin Marie Burgos, my beautiful mother and father in Heaven (a.k.a. St. Frances of Turri and St. Pompeii), and my cousin Eva Easton Leaf (also in Heaven); to the countless loving-kind family members, friends, and colleagues (of this world and the next), and to the True God of Love in Heaven.

As Christmas TV special icon Bob Hope would frequently relay over the airwaves, "Thanks for the memories." And if I may add to that the following phrase, "from the bottom of my heart."

BIBLIOGRAPHY

Books

Archer, Sarah, *Midcentury Christmas: Holiday Fads, Fancies, and Fun from 1945 to 1970*, Countryman Press, 2016.

Arnold, Jeremy, *Christmas in the Movies: 30 Classics to Celebrate After the Season*, Running Press, 2018.

Cole, Stephen, *That Book about That Girl: The Unofficial Companion*, Renaissance Books, 1999.

Dickens, Charles, *A Christmas Carol and Other Christmas Classics*, Fall River Press, 2012.

Duralde, Alonzo, *Have Yourself a Movie Little Christmas*, Limelight Edition/ Globe Pequot, 2010.

Eisner, Joel; Krinsky, David, *Television Comedy Series: An Episode Guide to 153 TV Sitcoms in Syndication*, McFarland & Co., 1984.

Graham, Jefferson, *Frasier: The Official Companion Book to the Award-Winning Paramount Television Comedy*, Pocket Books, 1996.

Green, Joey, *Hi, Bob! A Self-Help Guide to The Bob Newhart Show*, St. Martin's Press, 1996.

Hill, Thomas (editor), *Nick at Nite Classic TV Companion: The All Night, Every Nite Guide to Better Living Through Television*, Fireside Books, 1996.

Holmes, John R., "The Adventures of Ozzie Nelson," McFarland & Co., 2021.

Hyatt, Wesley, *The Carol Burnett Show Companion: So Glad We Had This Time Together*, BearManor Media, 2016.

Manago, Jim, *Love Is the Reason for It All: The Shirley Booth Story*, BearManor Media, 2008.

Miller, Johnny Ray, *When We're Singin': The Partridge Family and Their Music,* When We're Singin' LLC, 2020.

Parish, John, *The Unofficial Murder, She Wrote Casebook: The Definitive Unauthorized Companion to TV's Most Popular Whodunit,* Kensington Books, 1997.

Pilato, Herbie J, *The 12 Best Secrets of Christmas: A Treasure House of December Memories Revealed,* Archway Publishing, 2022.

Ross, Marion, with Laurell, David, *My Days Happy and Otherwise,* Kensington Books, 2018.

Tucker, David C., *Shirley Booth: A Biography and Career Record,* McFarland & Co., 2008.

Wilson, Joanna Wilson, *'Tis the Season TV: The Encyclopedia of Christmas-Themed Episodes, Specials, and Made-For-TV-Movies,* 1701 Press, 2010.

Special-Interest Magazines

Giovanelli, Janet (editor), *Santa Claus: The Story Behind the Legend,* A360 Media, 2023.

Sullivan, Robert, *LIFE: The Story of Santa,* Dotdash Meredith Premium Publishing, 2023.

Parade Magazine: A Happy Holiday Guide, November 14, 2021.

Periodicals

Airey, Jacob, "Movie Review Flashback: *Borrowed Hearts* (1997)," Studiojake Media.com, December 22, 2020.

Bechaz, Kevin, "Review: *The Gathering*" (TV 1977), CinematicRandomness.com, December 20, 2017.

Case, Mike, and Gohn, Sandi, "For 40 years, Bob Hope USO Christmas Shows Brightened the Holidays for Deployed Troops," USO.org, December 23, 2021.

Crossan, Ash, "Jon Favreau Wants to Do a 'Star Wars Holiday Special' For Disney+," ETOnline.com, September 16, 2019.

Curnyn, Sean, "Frank Sinatra's 1957 Christmas Special (with Bing Crosby)," CinchReview.com, December 23, 2015.

Daley, Katerina, "*Frasier*: Every Holiday Episode Ranked by IMDb," ScreenRant .com, December 21, 2022.

Fox, Courtney, "These *Little House on the Prairie* Christmas Episodes Showcase the Meaning of the Season," WideOpenCountry.com, October 13, 2020.

Genzlinger, Neil, "Bob Schiller, Writer on Beloved TV Comedies, Dies," *New York Times,* October 12, 2017.

Genzlinger Neil, "The Ghosts of TV Christmas Specials Past," *New York Times*, December 3, 2015.

Goldschmidt, Rick, "Catching Up with Aaron, *The Little Drummer Boy*, Teddy Eccles, *ReMind Magazine*, July 25, 2023.

Harmonson, Todd, "Thanksgiving Viewing to Fill Up On," *Orange County Register*, November 21, 2023.

Jeffrey, Joyann, "The History of the Rockefeller Center Christmas Tree Spans All the Way Back to 1931," Today.com, November 17, 2023.

Khalil, Ashraf, "Kennedy Center Honors Fetes New Inductees, Including Queen Latifah, Billy Crystal and Dionne Warwick," Associated Press, December 4, 2023.

Kile, Meredith B., "How Donny and Marie Osmond Unknowingly Spoiled 'Star Wars' in 1977 TV Special," ETOnline.com, December 8, 2023.

Lloyd, Robert, "Review: 'Sullivan's Crossing' on CW is a Pleasant Import from the Makers of 'Virgin River,'" *Los Angeles Times*, October 4, 2023.

McCormick, Colin, "All *The Simpsons* Christmas Episodes, Ranked," ScreenRant .com, December 24, 2022.

Moorehead, Monica, "Betty White's Anti-Racist Act—An Appreciation," Workers.org, January 4, 2022.

Moser, Zachary, "Why *The Little Drummer Boy* (1968) Was Taken Off TV," ScreenRant.com, September 30, 2023.

Norcross, Jonathon, "Arnold Schwarzenegger Directed This Forgotten Christmas Movie Remake," Collider.com, July 9, 2023.

Novak, Lauren, "Former Penthouse of Arthur Rankin Jr. of Rankin/Bass Productions, Up for Sale," *ReMind Magazine*, September 27, 2023.

Novak, Lauren, "The History of the Macy's Thanksgiving Day Parade," *ReMind Magazine*, November 17, 2023.

O'Connor, John J., "TV Review; George Scott in *A Christmas Carol*," *New York Times*, December 17, 1984.

Pilato, Herbie J, "Julia Set the Standard—Julia and Diahann Carroll Changed Television and Racial Perceptions," Emmys.com, June 30, 2021.

Richmond, Ray, "Saint Maybe," Variety.com, November 19, 1998.

Scott, Walter, "Walter Scott Asks . . . Reba McEntire," *Parade Magazine*, November 21, 2021.

Stoller-Lindsey, Nina, "18 Things You Didn't Know about the Rockefeller Center Christmas Tree," Thrillist.com, November 15, 2014.

UPI Archives, "*Drummer Boy* Drummed Off Detroit TV," December 13, 1991.

VanHooker, Brian, "An Oral History of *The Odd Couple*'s Classic Scrooge Parady," Cracked.com, December 23, 2022.

Villarreal, Yvonne, "A Christmas Tree Contest and a Hunt to Uncover Mel's Father: The Holidays Come to 'Virgin River,'" *Los Angeles Times*, November 19, 2023.

White, Brett, "*The Bob Newhart Show*'s Christmas Episodes Prepared Me for the Holidays Without My Family," Decider.com, December 19, 2017.

White, Brett, "The 25 Best Christmas Sitcom Episodes of All Time," Decider .com, December 7, 2020.

Zilko, Christian, "The Stoner Christmas 'Frasier' Episode Shows Why More Series Should Get Weird at the End," IndieWire.com, October 23, 2023.

Websites/Online Resources

Collider.com
Decider.com
IMDb.com
Intanibase.com
PopCulture.com
PopCultureReferences.com
ScreenRant.com
TVGuide.com
Wikipedia.com

ABOUT THE AUTHOR

As a writer, producer, actor/performer, and TV personality, **Herbie J Pilato** embraces all things nostalgic, particularly those having to do with classic television programming.

Pilato began his career in the 1980s as an NBC page at the network's facility in Burbank, California. He aspired to be an actor, with early bit roles on daytime soaps *General Hospital* and *The Bold and the Beautiful*, as well as on such nighttime fare as *Highway to Heaven* and *The Golden Girls*. For a time, he was a stand-in dancer on TV's music-variety series *Solid Gold*, and he acted and sang in clubs along the Sunset Strip.

By the early 1990s, Pilato switched gears to writing, with the publication of his first book, *The Bewitched Book*, about the classic 1960s TV series. From there, he published other classic TV literary companions and began producing and appearing on classic TV documentaries for Bravo, A&E, TLC, and the Reelz Channel, among others. Pilato also began consulting on and appearing in a number of DVD and Blu-ray packages of classic TV shows for Sony and Warner Bros.

In 2013, Pilato established the Classic TV Preservation Society (CTVPS), a formal 501(c)3 nonprofit organization that celebrates and advocates for the positive social effect of classic TV shows.

In 2019, Pilato hosted, co-created, and co-executive-produced his own TV talk show, *Then Again with Herbie J Pilato*, which began streaming on Shout! TV and Amazon Prime.

In early 2023, Pilato published *Retro Active Television: An In-Depth Perspective of Classic TV's Social Circuitry*, which explores the positive impact of classic TV. That year, the Los Angeles Book Festival named *Retro* "Book of the Year," and subsequently, Pilato, "Author of the Year." With a foreword by actor Eric Scott of *The Waltons*, *Retro Active Television* has received additional high praise, including endorsements from Marc Wade of the Television Academy and Emmys.com.

In his blurb on the back cover of *Retro*, Wade says the book "connects the dots between the medium's origins and milestones, between the past and the present . . . and how we can utilize it productively for the future."

In December of 2022, Pilato published *The 12 Best Secrets of Christmas: A Treasure House of December Memories Revealed*, a holiday memoir of his youth in Rochester during the 1960s and 1970s. Featuring a foreword by TV-icon Dean Butler of *Little House on the Prairie* and an introduction by actor/voice-over-star Jerry Houser (*The Summer of '42*), *The 12 Best Secrets of Christmas* universalizes the messages of kindness and unity for all cultures.

In the fall of 2023, Pilato published two new books: *Connery, Sean Connery: Before, During and After His Most Famous Role*, a biography of the Oscar-winning star, and a "Special Commemorative Edition" of *The Bionic Book: The Six Million Dollar Man and The Bionic Woman Reconstructed*.

The Connery biography features a foreword by actress Barbara Carrera, Connery's co-star from *Never Say Never Again*, his final film bow as James Bond 007—and which this year celebrates its fortieth anniversary and the sixtieth anniversary of *From Russia With Love*, which was Connery's favorite of his Bond films.

The new edition of *The Bionic Book* was released in tandem with the recent fiftieth anniversary of *The Six Million Dollar Man*'s debut (and features exclusive commentary from *Bionic* stars Lee Majors and Lindsay Wagner).

Additionally, Pilato recently saw the audiobook release of his *Retro Active Television* book, along with his celebrity biographies *Mary: The Mary Tyler Moore Story*, *Twitch Upon a Star: The Bewitched Life and Career of Elizabeth Montgomery*, and his Sean Connery biography.

In other recent press news, *Closer Magazine* featured Pilato's Connery biography and his commentary in their October 9, 2023, issue; *ReMind Magazine* published Pilato's *Bewitched* cover story in their October 2023 issue. In 2024, *Retro Fan Magazine* published Pilato's *Magical Memories of Elizabeth Montgomery* for their *Bewitched 60th Anniversary Celebration* cover story, followed by cover stories on *The Six Million Dollar Man*, *The Bionic Woman*, and *CHiPs*.

In the fall of 2024, University Press of Mississippi published Pilato's newest celebrity biography, *One Tough Dame: The Life and Career of Diana Rigg*.

For more information, visit HerbieJPilato.com.